T0209225

IN SEARCH OF MILLIONAIRES

(THE LIFE OF A BASEBALL GYPSY)

THE ACCOUNTS OF BOB FONTAINE JR.

TAYLOR BLAKE WARD

IN SEARCH OF MILLIONAIRES (THE LIFE OF A BASEBALL GYPSY)
THE ACCOUNTS OF BOB FONTAINE JR.

iUniverse books may be ordered through booksellers or by contacting:

iUniverse
1663 Liberty Drive
Bloomington, IN 47403
www.iuniverse.com
844-349-9409

ISBN: 978-1-6632-2287-9 (sc)
ISBN: 978-1-6632-2288-6 (hc)
ISBN: 978-1-6632-2286-2 (e)

Library of Congress Control Number: 2021918654

Print information available on the last page.

iUniverse rev. date: 10/20/2021

"For my kids." – Bob

CONTENTS

FOREWORD

by Tim Mead

He has been as good to the game as the game has been to him.

Bob Fontaine Jr. is one of those special people. His genuine love and passion for our national pastime and his craft remains legendary within the scouting community and beyond. Combined with an unmatched humility and selfless approach in all aspects of his being, Bob's impact on so many is immeasurable.

Often, great influencers are those who do so via their own consistency without a premeditated or conscious effort. The power of that influence is based on one's ability to listen, observe, evaluate, and formulate.

Bob Fontaine Jr. excelled in incorporating those characteristics throughout his amazing journey. And what a voyage it has been!

I acknowledge without hesitation a bias more for the character of the man than just his professional abilities. Having proudly served Major League Baseball and the Angels organization for four decades, I met few who could consistently demonstrate Bob's integrity, compassion, knowledge, and dedication. And we have had some truly special ones along the way such as Preston Gómez, Bob Clear, Marcel Lachemann, Bill Bavasi, Mike Scioscia, Mike Port, and Nick Kamzic, to name a few.

The genesis of my association, friendship, and respect for Bob dates to 1987 after his appointment by another mentor, Angels General Manager Mike Port, to become the organization's scouting director. That was the beginning of a friendship that continues to inspire and educate.

It was almost as if Bob's professional future was predetermined. The son of a World War II veteran and a former professional ballplayer, scout, and executive, Bob followed in his dad's footsteps. His baseball education began well before his distinguished scouting career started with the San Diego Padres in 1973.

Bob has always spoken with tremendous pride about his father. I can think of nothing more important than having the most important role model in your life succeeding with that responsibility. Bob Sr. certainly did just that. The elder Fontaine died much too young at the age of seventy, but not before experiencing the success of his son following in his footsteps and seeing his same love of family through Bob's commitment.

This wonderful book is the journey of a man who committed the majority of his life to a career and internal passion he rarely questioned. And such can be said about so many of his counterparts and contemporaries, though their status has changed drastically in recent years.

The combined effort of Bob and the talented Taylor Blake Ward is certainly a gift for Bob's family, friends, and colleagues along the way. But it is equally an homage to the scouting community and profession.

Those long drives, early morning flights, visits to ballparks in regions where you don't know a soul…those recollections and realities pertain to an endless list of individuals responsible for locating most of the talent that has comprised Major League Baseball.

For the most part, contributors like Bob are anonymous to the general baseball faithful. However, that same group is the beneficiary of the talent, commitment, and sacrifice of folks like Bob. This book is a reflection of their efforts through recollections from one of baseball's most highly respected scouts.

Bob provides a chronology not only of his experiences, but of his own personal growth along the way shaped by a spectrum of individuals. He is gracious in the credit and attention given to others, while remaining humble regarding his own contributions and status.

There are so many well-deserved words applicable to describe Bob. Perhaps sitting atop the list is trust. It was not just the trust people has in Bob that was special, but the trust he has in others that helped set him apart.

I will always remember the 1988 draft when the Angels had the eighth overall pick. Bob relied on the expertise and opinions of scouts Nick Kamzic, Bob Gardner, and scouting coordinator George Bradley in selecting left-hander Jim Abbott. Despite a standout career, the choice was not a consensus selection within the industry.

What transpired during that decision shall remain a fond memory and important lesson: a "chain of command" education. Owner Gene Autry empowered and trusted GM Mike Port, who in turn provided a similar latitude to his baseball operations personnel.

The ripple effect of that trust trickled down to Bob and his staff. Rarely can I recall a more fluid flow of decision-making.

A great photographer is set apart from the rest of us because of an ability to see things differently through a lens than we are capable of with our own eyes.

The same can be said by those who have proudly owned the title of "Scout" within a particular organization. They are blessed with the talent to evaluate a player in the present, yet also project that individual's possible future.

For years they have offered their opinions and expertise in the inexact science of scouting. It has never been a discipline where success vastly out distances failure. However, it is also a fraternity where opinions are offered without moving models, rather an investment of real-time observation and communication.

And few have done it any better than Bob Fontaine Jr.

PREFACE

AUTHOR'S NOTE

It was a brisk winter day in the mountains of Southern California when I walked into my local coffee shop on a Thursday in December 2019. There was a slight breeze that made the already heavy door more challenging to open, but as the door closed, I began searching.

There were few patrons inside the café, and to my left sat a man alone at a table for two. White hair stuck out of his San Jose Sharks cap, while his white Fu Manchu covered the top of his paper cup with coffee inside.

"Bob?" I asked the gentleman.

"Taylor," he replied with a smile.

This was the first time I met Bob Fontaine Jr.

To this point our only connection had been via text messages and a mutual friend, Tim Mead. Tim asked us to reach out to one another regarding a project Bob had worked on for nearly a decade. Tim's approval of the other was all we needed for this meeting.

As I went off briefly to order a green tea, I joked about Bob's hat from across the room. From a fanatical standpoint, the San Jose Sharks are my least favorite team in professional sports. The back-and-forth ribbing put me at ease. Bob may have poor taste in hockey teams, but he was all right in my book from the start. Hopefully, I was all right for his book.

What was meant to be a half-hour conversation carried on for multiple hours, as Bob and I are both long-winded. Sharing baseball stories of the past and finding familiarity in names we both knew at different times in our lives, Bob and I clicked as we spoke of our appreciation for scouts who spent decades bringing talent into the sport and the grind of working in baseball. The conversation created a bond that baseball brings to so many.

The conversation carried on outside the coffee shop with a quick stroll through the Lake Arrowhead Village, and with one last jab at his hat, we went our separate ways. Bob was headed home to Washington, and I was going home with plans to map out Bob's life story and accomplishments.

This meeting was never something I envisioned.

When I entered the baseball industry as a 20 year old, it didn't take me in lightly. I didn't have much of a plan for my future, but knew I loved sports. As I pondered career choices, a friend who worked as an account representative for the local minor league hockey team told me I should attend a job fair where they would be hiring in his field. Maybe that could be a way to work in sports and enjoy a career in the industry.

Going in with a smile and eagerness to see what my limited résumé could provide; it was the black pinstriped suit that proved the only reason for an interview with the High Desert Mavericks. Two weeks and a meeting later, I would join the Mavericks as a sales intern.

At the end of my first day, I was asked to go into the general manager's office. I panicked, thinking of what I did wrong and that I would be fired short of a full eight-hour shift. As I walked in and closed the door, our GM handed me a bottle of champagne and told me of the team's need for the director of broadcasting and media relations. I asked what the position entailed but said I would happily accept, while taking the bottle that I couldn't legally drink for another six months.

The following day, I went into the office with no knowledge of what I was supposed to do in my new position. Emails quickly came in from Cleveland asking for pictures of Brandon Weeden, who had recently been drafted by the Cleveland Browns and was a former pitcher for the Mavericks. This was the kind of work I suddenly craved.

I still look back on that summer with the Mavericks. The front office consisted of a former clubhouse manager serving as general manager, and seven others in their early-to-mid 20's running the day-to-day operations of a professional baseball team. The stadium was a mess. The game-time temperature averaged in the triple digits. The buses rarely had air conditioning. And I loved every single bit of it.

After the season, I went to look for jobs within the industry when Rick Randall of Scout.com reached out asking if I had interest in doing a piece on Brad Miller, a Seattle Mariners prospect. I had never written anything outside of the occasional school essay, but once again, I gladly accepted.

One month later, Scout.com asked if I was interested in covering the Los Angeles Angels and if I could be at the ballpark for an upcoming series later in the week.

"Of course! Will I need a ticket?" I replied.

What a knucklehead I was.

From that first game on May 3, 2013 to now, I went from a wide-eyed young writer to establishing a career within the sports journalism industry. I have spent the better part of nine years covering the Angels and MLB Draft for multiple publications and affiliates. My work has been published by Scout.com, *Baseball America, the Riverside Press-Enterprise,* Fox Sports, and Yahoo! Sports.

Writing was never on my mind when it came to careers. I wanted to be a professional athlete, or a race car driver, or a fireman, or a history teacher – essentially everything any young kid wants to be, but never a writer.

From my first day on the job, I learned by fire. There was no training or schooling under my belt. Learning how to be a journalist on the fly came with many trials by error, such as being called a donkey-related adjective by Mike Scioscia my first week on the job. Despite all this, I love it.

With the help of Kyle Glaser, Jeff Fletcher, Joe Haakenson, and others, things started to become easier. I found inspiration in finding the multiple storylines any one game can provide. I studied the work of others and saw that influence can be provided from those outside of baseball. Finding a style of my own, I was molded by two of the world's best storytellers: John Grisham with the gravitas in his novels, and Brad Paisley in the honesty, simplicity, and natural humor in his songs.

As a visual learner, telling a story and painting a picture for the mind to place themselves in the moment only provided more help. It you become a good storyteller, you can help people grasp what has occurred or will occur. There's a certain drama and honesty that people are drawn to, such as when your parents tell you baseball stories of yesteryear.

Being a writer was never the plan, and a meeting with Bob Fontaine Jr. was never something I envisioned.

Being paid to watch some of the game's elite players, like Albert Pujols and Mike Trout, on a nightly basis is enjoyable. I always found enjoyment in baseball. However, as the world transcends into new heights, so does the game, and covering it with such a deep perspective of the sport allows you to see the behind-the-scenes flaws of the game you thought was so simple.

I'm not a scout. I have never been a baseball scout. I still have hope that in time, I can eventually become a talent evaluator for a Major League Baseball organization, but as I get older and have seen what is occurring across the scouting world, that dream has faded.

The sacrifices that these nomads of baseball – or gypsies as we will call them in the book – have put into their line of work is remarkable. Some spend weeks and months away from their families to work a thankless job while assisting in multi-million dollar decisions that will have decade-long impacts.

Scouts often remind me of a forgotten group of historical importance. The Medjay, a group that dates back to 2700 B.C., were known as protectors of Egypt, conditional to the land and the Pharaoh. They policed certain regions of Egypt, with chiefs and captains primarily overseeing the large cities. In time, they were the driving force behind Egypt becoming a world military power. I believe scouts are the driving force behind what makes baseball so great and could be considered the protectors of the game. Outside of the players themselves, they may be the most important asset to baseball.

However, sometime around 1100 B.C., the term "Medjay" vanished from records. It has never been noted whether the title was changed, or if the group itself dissipated. If you can now remember back to when you were in grade school, or even high school or college, the Medjay were rarely, if ever, mentioned in the history books. It is now nearly a forgotten people entirely. I fear that with the current state of baseball, scouts may go the way of the Medjay.

As baseball has changed, so has scouting. I've watched organizations go from trusting scouts on players around the world to using calculations that replace the opinions of scouts. Many call these calculations and new evaluation systems analytics or advanced metrics, and there was discrepancy between Bob and I regarding these new-age methods. However, during the writing of this book, I watched teams use these calculations and information to eliminate some of the traditional scouting process.

I stand by the information these numbers provide and feel there is a middle ground to be had, where all information available is used to make the best decision possible for the future of a team or player. However, writing during a pandemic, I watched organization after organization furlough and fire groups of their own scouts because these numbers provided answers teams felt were superior to scouts' opinions.

It sickened me. All those sacrifices made by scouts for an organization, just to be told that a formula would provide better evaluations of players.

I'm not anti-analytical or anti-progressive and feel these statistics have their value, but it will never be able to replace the opinion of someone who is on the ground. Scouting has suddenly become less evaluating, and more calculating.

For someone who thrives on every battle in a baseball game, from every pitch to every at-bat, I believe baseball can trend back to a place of sanctity for those who evaluate talent, and these men and women can return to their line of work and be rewarded for their sacrifices and effort.

For the casual baseball fan or supporter, I hope this book sheds light on some more profound subjects of baseball and brings you joy and perspective on how deep the game goes.

For those with a more profound knowledge of the game, I hope it opens your eyes to how a favorite memory transpired behind the scenes, and how it came to fruition from its origins.

NOTES FOR THE READER

After finalizing each chapter, I would send the unedited manuscript to my niece. She is in her mid 20's and has some interest in baseball, but had many questions about the lingo involved with each chapter.

"What is arm extension? How did a player pitch with one hand? Why did this player go from playing for the San Diego Padres to playing for the Walla Walla Padres?"

For some reading this, these are simple terms commonly used or understood in the baseball world. For others, it is all brand new, and that is okay.

No one expects someone to know everything. I didn't expect my niece to know who Jim Abbott or Ozzie Smith was, or what above-average fastball velocity might mean, or what a tight slider could be.

Working with the assumption that readers of this book would have varying degrees of baseball knowledge, I concluded each scouting item would need a bit of depth and explanation.

As you read along, you'll see terms like arm action, extension, balance, breaking ball, cutter, and many others. There are titles such as General Manager, Scouting Director, and Crosschecker. There are many references to the Major League Baseball Draft, and the minor league affiliations of major league franchises. Bob and I did our best to give a brief explanation of each scouting and baseball term within the book.

As you learn more about the game, you will grow a new appreciation for those in it. Whether it be a player, coach, scout, executive, or owner, everyone in baseball has a unique story of how they got to where they are, and it can be fantastic to learn and hear those stories.

During the process of writing, I found that asking Bob to remember every event over the last half-century didn't always come with an answer. Heck, I don't know what I had for dinner last night. How could Bob remember the name of a coffee shop in Timbuktu four decades ago?

There was a lot of research involved in the process of writing this book, whether it was to find an exact location, signing bonus amount, college and high school statistics, backgrounds on opponents, and events that occurred prior to my lifetime. For this research, I must thank Bill Bavasi, Ann and Mike Port, Tim Mead, Bob Protexter, Joe Maddon, Kyle Glaser, Rick Randall, and the staff at Baseball-Reference for their assistance helping retell every story accurately.

No names or locations have been changed, though some have been omitted.

Unlike most books, there are no villains. No good or evil.

There are over one thousand people mentioned by name in this book. We did our best to explain who they are and give a background of each person, but creating over a thousand characters within a book can be nearly impossible. Though someone may not have a full background or character-building process written, the names mentioned were placed in this book for a reason. Bob wanted to mention the names of as many veteran scouts as possible, some of who are out of the game.

THANK YOU

Thank you to all who have assisted in the process of this book. It is a long list that includes Fabian Ardaya, Bill Bavasi, Matt Birch, Jacob Breems (USC Sports Information), Tim Brown, Adam Chodzko, Pat Eberly (Mrs. E), Jeff Fletcher, Jimmy Fontaine, Jason Hernandez, Eric Longenhagen, D.C. Lundberg, Joe Maddon, Kelly Munro, Noah Musick, Jeremy Neill, Ross Newhan, Mike and Ann Port, Bob Protexter, Rick Randall, Tim Salmon, and Virgilio Tzaj.

I hope that I do not omit anyone during this procession, but there are some in particular who deserve my sincerest gratitude.

Tim Mead. You are the leading power behind the introduction to Bob, and I believe the leading power on moving forward with this project towards its conclusion. There are few people in the industry, or anywhere, that leave such a lasting impression of humility and genuine care for others. The conversations shared in the dugout at Angel Stadium are things that I walked away from knowing that my life had been drastically enhanced, and it was very rarely ever about baseball. You are a wonderful man, Tim. I thank you greatly, my friend.

Kyle Glaser. From that first game in Adelanto to today, you have been an inspiration to my career. From the late-night calls after high school football games stressing while trying to make deadline, to the simple conversations about life, you have aided my work in a way few have or will. I cherish our friendship and am ecstatic to see what life has granted you in the years we have known each other and beyond.

Natalie Gonzalez. From reading the unedited versions of each chapter and asking the questions that needed to be asked, you have been a strong force in making this book not only entertaining for the baseball audience, but also informational for those who dabble in the sport. I'm so glad you found interest in this project. I couldn't ask for a better niece.

John and Suzanne Ward. Helping establish a love for baseball from a young age, you would take me to Angels, Dodgers, and Padres games on a regular basis. You would tell me stories of watching some of the games' legends and inform me that Graig Nettles was just as gifted a defender as Brooks Robinson, and that Duke Snider possessed as much authority at the plate as Mickey Mantle. In the summer, you would come home from work exhausted, but say, "Hey, it's Two-Dollar Tuesday at the local minor league stadium. Let's go." These are things I cherish, and I thank you for establishing that love for baseball, and always showing your deepest love for your children, myself included.

Heidi Ward. As I would sit on our living room couch, writing about Ozzie Smith and others I grew up seeing as immortals within the sport, you would prepare dinner, do laundry, clean up after the dog, and wait to vacuum until I had finished listening to any prepared audio that would assist each chapter. You helped provide a sound environment that every household desires and needs.

Like a baseball scout, much time is spent away from home while covering the game, which isn't ideal for a family. Trying to understand the process when you didn't grow up around the game or understand that every night brings a new game can bring challenges. You comprehended these challenges and allowed me to chase a dream of pursuing a career in sports. It's a *cliché*, but I can honestly say I have the best wife in the world.

Mostly, I would like to thank Bob.

As you read through this book, you'll see it is a first-person account from Bob's eyes. The stories are all direct from the source and give a liveliness that you can only gain from those who have put forth the time and effort that a scout gives.

Writing a book was something I thought of from the day I began writing about baseball. This book is single-handedly the most significant project I have worked on, and I owe it to you, Bob. From all the challenges of power outages, blizzards, kidney stones, and a pandemic, I am ecstatic to say, "We did it!"

The trust you showed in me to share *your* story led to a dream finalized, and a lifelong friendship.

Thank you.

BOB'S SIGNING LIST

Bob Fontaine Jr. has signed or supervised the signing of 114 Major League Baseball players in his 48-year career as a scout and Scouting Director.

Hall of Famers

Tony Gwynn	OF	San Diego
Randy Johnson	LHP	Montreal
Ozzie Smith	SS	San Diego

All Stars

Garret Anderson	OF	California
Jason Dickson	RHP	California
Gary Disarcina	SS	California
Damion Easley	2B	California
Jim Edmonds	OF	California
Darin Erstad	OF	California
Troy Glaus	3B	California
Ozzie Guillén	SS	San Diego
John Kruk	1B	San Diego
John Lackey	RHP	California
Troy Percival	RHP	California
Francisco Rodríguez	RHP	California
Michael Saunders	OF	Seattle
Chris Tillman	RHP	Seattle

Other Notables

Player	Team		Player	Team
Jim Abbott, LHP	California		Mark Lowe, RHP	Seattle
Kyle Abbott, LHP	California		Brandon Maurer, RHP	Seattle
Ruben Amaro, OF	California		Kevin McReynolds, OF	San Diego
Alfredo Amezaga, SS	California		Adam Moore, C	Seattle
Brian Anderson, LHP	California		Brandon Morrow, RHP	Seattle
Phillippe Aumont, RHP	Seattle		Steve Mura, RHP	San Diego
Jamie Burke, C	California		Ramón Ortiz, RHP	California
McKay Christensen, OF	California		John Orton, C	California
Jeff Clement, C	Seattle		Orlando Palmeiro, OF	California
Chad Curtis, OF	California		Eduardo Perez, 1B	California
Seth Etherton, RHP	California		Matt Perisho, LHP	California
Jorge Fabregas, C	California		J.R. Phillips, 1B	California
Josh Fields, RHP	Seattle		Robb Quinlan, 1B	California
Doug Fister, RHP	Seattle		Tim Salmon, OF	California
Tim Flannery, 2B	San Diego		Jeff Schmidt, RHP	California
Bob Geren, C	San Diego		Scott Schoeneweis, LHP	California
Rene Gonzales, SS	Montreal		Scot Shields, RHP	California
Todd Greene, C	California		Bob Shirley, LHP	San Diego

Joe Grahe, RHP	California
Aaron Guiel, OF	California
David Holdridge, RHP	California
Mike Holtz, LHP	California
Mark Holzemer, LHP	California
Rob Johnson, C	Seattle
Shawn Kelley, RHP	Seattle
Phil Leftwich, RHP	California
Bill Long, RHP	San Diego
Eric Show, RHP	San Diego
Bill Simas, RHP	California
Mark Sweeney, OF	California
Ron Tingley, C	San Diego
Matt Tuiasosopo, OF	Seattle
Chris Turner, C	California
Anthony Varvaro, RHP	Seattle
Jarrod Washburn, LHP	California
Matt Wise, RHP	California

A BASEBALL GYPSY

A baseball scout is truly a sports gypsy. You work alone the majority of the time, you are required to gather the information that you need to survive, and you are constantly on the move, city to city, town to town. Some receptions you receive are welcoming, some are cold. But scouting is a lifestyle that can be gripping and in a personal way, rewarding.

After more than 48 years in baseball as a scout, I was urged to write down the things I experienced during that time. In the beginning, I didn't think it was something I wanted to do, but after some time, I decided I wanted to document for my family and kids what I did and why I missed so many birthdays, baseball games, school meetings, conferences, and other important events. I also wanted them to appreciate what this life has given them in opportunities to travel, take Major League Baseball games for granted, meet a lot of prominent people, and most importantly, a secure upbringing. I wanted them to know why working in a glamorous profession doesn't mean that all those that work in it share the glamor, even though they are a major contributor to its success.

As time went on, I also realized that my story could be written by many others and that as the game is changing, it is important that there is more documentation of the people and profession that operate with slight change for over 125 years. The veteran scout that gives his or her life to the game is vanishing at an alarming rate as the influence of numbers, analytics, video, and models replace the human element. It is a fraternity that needs to be acknowledged, documented, and appreciated.

Baseball scouting is a thankless profession, but is filled with tons of personal satisfaction contributing to the game they love. Known as the backbone of baseball, it is more often treated like a wart on baseball. The pay is low, the travel can be lonesome, the time away from home difficult, and personal acknowledgement is almost nonexistent. Yet, once you start in this profession, it grabs a hold of you and is tough to let go.

Change is a part of almost all industries and can be good when added carefully and mixed with things that are established and successful. For most of the time baseball has been in existence, the evaluation of players has been fairly consistent with gradual change added. Since the early 2000's, there has been radical change to the profession. Teams are putting more emphasis on statistics, formulas, models, and video and less on the opinions of experienced scouts. Up until the 21st century, the experienced evaluator was sought after by teams for their knowledge, rather than their ability to travel extensively. The comparisons they could make, the lessons they had learned, as well as the mistakes they had made, and the success they had enjoyed could become a great asset to a team. In other words, you wanted them for their knowledge and not their legs.

So many baseball teams today are using so many of the same tools to make their decisions, which really just tends to lump them all together in how they select players and separates them mostly by the amount of money they are willing to spend. The competitive edge that teams in all sports talk about is decided by the people involved making the decisions. Not a number or formula doing it for them. Formulas and numbers categorize, but don't separate players who are in the same group. Human element and opinion are what separates. These support systems can contribute to a decision, but the emotion, instinct, and reference of a person is what can give you the competitive edge. Numbers don't take responsibility. People do. The more experienced personnel that a team has, with the experience to back up why a decision is made, tends to enjoy the most enduring success and get more value for the money spent on players.

In this day, numbers, formulas and OFP's (Overall Future Potential) dictate where a player is grouped for selection more than the opinion of the scout. Long-range projection of a player, as well as a younger age, can place a player over another one who is older but who has *now* ability. A big change I have seen with stats on amateur players is that they are used regardless of the quality of talent they faced. Many players face poor competition and teams in warmer areas have a big edge on teams in colder regions. You must keep in mind that players that are amateurs often do things wrong that can limit their statistical success, but with proper instruction and aptitude can improve. Stats really only have one true area of accuracy – the major leagues.

What happens with the analytical approach is that things like Fielding Independent Pitching (FIP), spin rate, walks-and-hits per nine-innings (WHIP) and walk-to-strikeout ratios become more important than delivery, arm action, size, arm extension and angle to the plate. As with hitters, strikeout percentages, on-base percentage plus slugging percentage (OPS), exit velocity, and launch angle take precedence over balance, wrists, load, bat speed, and contact in the strike zone. Ability can't be taught and should never be overlooked just because a number may say otherwise.

For many years when a team had a bad season, they would evaluate their club and decide to either stay the course because it was an off year, make slight changes, or change direction and personnel. Because players tend to have off years occasionally, you would evaluate carefully why and not be tied just to the numbers. Clubs that rely on numbers and formulas over scouting evaluations tend to spend more money covering up decisions that don't work out initially.

When the book "Moneyball" became a big item in baseball, I was asked by every club I worked for why we didn't take that approach. I would tell them that we can't be tied to a number or just a player from a certain level of play. Although there were some good items in that approach, it just limited the pool of players you would select from and gave more players to the other teams to select. Talent is talent, whether at age 18, 21, or 22, and not every kid is ready at the same time. I've met kids at 18 that are better prepared to start their career than kids that are 22. Again, it is human element and not the number. Be open-minded of all talent venues.

Impulse over instincts is another thing that experience brings to the table. The longer you are around the game, the more you rely on the references you have developed, and not the immediate thought. Oftentimes the performance of a player can override what that type of player he usually ends up being. Early in a scouting career, this is a hard thing to overcome, but gets easier the longer you scout. When scouts get older, their knowledge of situations can help not only a club from making a mistake but save them a lot of money in doing so.

Communication is an area that changed drastically. The days of communicating by a phone call or voicemail have lessened and been replaced by texts and emails. Nothing is wrong with a text or email on certain items, but you don't get a person's real feeling or emotion with those methods of communication. When you hear a person's voice you hear the emotion, or lack of it, when describing a player that oftentimes doesn't equal what you read on a report. That emotion is often what determines where a player fits on a list and the likelihood of your club trying to select him.

You often hear about the character or nucleus of a ballclub. I do believe that most good clubs do have character, and it is important. However, to develop the character of a team, it is important that you have experienced, individual-minded evaluators to do it. If you have these scouts, you have the characters to develop the character of a team.

I hope this book documents what it was like to be a part of teams that developed foundations to be good and with people that dedicated their lives to it. By illustrating what it has been like to be a scout, scouting director, minor league farm director, and a personnel director, I hope it gives insight into what thousands of others like me experienced in this game.

I spent years learning the scouting trade from people that knew much more than I did, and in many cases ever will. I experienced failure with occasional success, and through it, I learned from my failures and humility in any success that I have enjoyed. As the scouting industry is changing rapidly and the experienced, dedicated scout who has devoted his life to the game is being replaced by a new approach that doesn't contain the human element nearly as much, it is important that the effort of all veteran scouts is recognized for the accomplishments and the love they had for the game.

My story is one that many could tell, and my story is their story. I hope that you understand that the veteran baseball scout truly is, a Baseball Gypsy.

THE BEGINNING

I started my career as a baseball scout in 1973 at the age of nineteen, but in many ways, it started as soon as I could talk. I have spent my life around a ballpark as my father, Bob Fontaine Sr., had spent most of his life around one.

He enjoyed a 50-plus year career as a player, scout, scouting director, player personnel director and general manager for four different organizations: the Brooklyn Dodgers, Pittsburgh Pirates, San Diego Padres and San Francisco Giants. As far back as I can remember, I would go to games and travel with him any chance I could. It was a lifestyle that I knew that I wanted to follow early on.

I grew up in San Jose, California, where my father at the time was the West Coast Supervisor for the Pirates. He spent over 20 years with Pittsburgh and growing up, I was of course, a Pirates fan. It was the years of Roberto Clemente, Bill Mazeroski, Harvey Haddix, Bob Friend, Vern Law, Dick Stuart, Dick Groat, and my personal idol – Willie Stargell.

I remember going to see the Pirates play in San Francisco with my dad at old Seals Stadium, and later, Candlestick Park. One day during a doubleheader at Seals Stadium, I went in the clubhouse with my dad and sat at a table with him, manager Danny Murtaugh, and his coaches, while being around all the players. Even though I was only five or six years old, I still remember that time perfectly.

During those years in Northern California, there was a scout's winter league in which teams were comprised of minor league players who were home for the offseason. Unlike today when these teams are comprised of high school players, these teams had professionals you were keeping active in the winter to make sure that their weight was good, and they were in shape before heading off to spring training. If they were working on something in their development, they could do it here and not in spring training where mistakes could be exposed.

An occasional free agent or released player would get a tryout, but the overall emphasis was on the signed players within your club.

The Pirates team that my father ran was in the Winter Peninsula League that played in San Mateo, Burlingame, and South San Francisco. From about the age of five, I was the bat boy on the team, and it is amazing how much of that experience is still imprinted in my mind. That team had many players who went on the play in the major leagues, with Stargell being the most prominent.

From the moment I met Willie, he took me under his wing and spent time with me. He had just signed out of Encinal High School in Alameda and was at the beginning of his professional career. He would make sure that I sat next to him on the bench and looked after me to make sure I was okay and didn't get in the way or hurt.

"Willie Stargell"

This went on for several years until he reached the major leagues and every year after, he would send me a Christmas card asking how I was doing. The interest he showed in me even after he had become a major league star and future Hall of Famer meant so much to me. He was my idol then and is to this day.

Players would constantly come by and ask for tryouts on the scout team. Willie had tried talking my father into signing a young infielder, but my father thought the player was too small. Willie tried but to no avail, and the player signed with the Houston Colt .45s.

That player was Joe Morgan, who went on to play 22 years in the major leagues and was elected to the Baseball Hall of Fame in 1990. My father always said it was his biggest mistake. I would learn when I got into the profession how those are mistakes you never get over, but you learn from them.

It was several years before I saw Willie again at the Winter Meetings after his playing career had ended and he was a special assistant with the Atlanta Braves. When I approached him, it was as though I had just seen him recently. He said it was great that I followed in my father's footsteps and that he was happy for me.

He was not only one of the greatest players of all time, but one of the greatest people. I still feel his impact on me and the way he taught me to treat this game. Willie and my father left the largest impact on how to treat people, appreciate the privilege of being in the game, and the effort that you owe the job.

As I grew up in San Jose and went to Del Mar High School, I of course thought I could play. Being short and slow with no power didn't hinder my thoughts of being a major league player someday. The only thing I could do remotely well was throw. I am sure I inherited that from my father, who pitched in the Brooklyn Dodgers organization. I now know that I stunk and even though I didn't get drafted, I did receive an invitation to the Angels minor league spring training camp as an outfielder.

I planned on going and trying out with the Angels, but got sidetracked and joined the Federal Bureau of Investigation at 18 years old.

My short career with the FBI is one I am sure they wish they could delete. I started with the best of intentions, but soon found that they used real bullets and that wasn't my bag. I went to Washington D.C. to work in the Identification Division, go to college to get the needed courses, and then, hopefully, go to the FBI Academy to become an agent.

My career with the Bureau lasted three months. It was an interesting time and even though it was short, I experienced some historical events in the Capitol.

Arriving at the Department of Justice Building on my first day to start my journey with the FBI, I was sent to a room with many new young employees where we were to receive our assignments, receive instructions of what would take place that day, and then be sworn in by J. Edgar Hoover.

Director Hoover was ill that day and instead we were sworn in by the assistant director. After we took the oath and were sworn in as official employees of the FBI, they proceeded to ask us for items needed to complete our hiring process.

We were asked for personal identification, such as a driver's license, birth certificate and such. One of the items they wanted from the male employees was a copy of their draft card, which in those days was required by law to always be in your possession until you were 30. When I opened my wallet to get it, I realized it wasn't there but in another wallet at home.

The ironic thing is that I didn't have more than $37 to my name, and yet, I had two wallets.

I was scared to death to go up to the second-most powerful man in the FBI and tell him that my first act as an employee was to forget my draft card that was required by law for me to have. I remember the look of disbelief on his face as if to say, "Who are we hiring?"

There was a brief silence as he looked down on me and shook his head.

"Bring it tomorrow."

After hearing how tough Director Hoover was, I can only imagine what he would have done with me if he had been the one swearing me in. That was the first bullet I dodged in my illustrious three-month career with the FBI.

My assignment was to the Identification Division, where I was to learn the art of reading fingerprints, filing and learning the system where sheets on people with fingerprints were located. Before everything was computerized, it was done by hand and human inspection. I got so good at flipping through cards in a file to match up documents that I gave myself the code name, "Flipper." It was a boring job that seemed to last 16 hours a day instead of the eight we worked.

The Identification Division Building was near the Capitol Building. I would look out the window and see it in the distance. On my route home, I would walk past the White House every day to get the bus to head home. A beautiful sight and city that makes you proud when you see all the buildings and monuments, but also a city that seems to operate in its own world.

After about a month and a half, Hoover died. All FBI employees could pass by his casket in the rotunda of the Capitol Building before the general public. He was an immensely powerful man who received State treatment, and with the history involved, I went through the rotunda to pay my respects.

After Hoover's passing, L. Patrick Gray became the new director and things changed almost immediately. Before, we had to wear black suits with skinny black ties, have short haircuts, and take a profoundly serious business approach. Now, we were able to grow our hair out with a very relaxed dress code. As my hair grew long and curly and I wore wild shirts, it really ticked off the agents and lifers that worked there, but I was just adhering to the new rules. I liked L. Patrick Gray.

When I reached the three-month point, I was told I was going to be taught how to read and compare fingerprints. It was a step in the right direction, but I knew deep down that it wasn't for me.

My father mentioned I should come home and try something else. I mentioned I might like to become a scout and he said he would work with me. My career with the FBI was over and my last paycheck - after all the deductions for leaving before one year - came out to 87 cents. I still haven't cashed that check.

I moved to San Diego, California, and got a job at Robinsons Department Store where I would work to make enough money to survive while my father – who was director of player personnel for the San Diego Padres — spent time trying to teach me the trade of being a baseball scout. He spent months working with me and yelling at me as I tried to learn the trade.

For one month I was only allowed to watch major league games in San Diego, and he would quiz me after each game with questions like, "Was his arm average or above-average? What kind of runner was he? Tell me about his swing."

In the beginning, I was almost always wrong, but as time went on, I started to be right occasionally. He felt – and was absolutely right – that you better know what below-average, average and above-average abilities at the major league level look like before you try to evaluate a college or high school player.

That's the greatest thing he did for me professionally. Once you understand a Major League Baseball player and his capabilities, it's easy to bring it down the line. I tried to do that with scouts we hired to benefit the most from this ability to evaluate.

One thing my father instilled in me was to never use a stopwatch to time a runner. His reasoning was it only tells you a portion of the player's running ability. He kept hammering away at me that the first step and stride are what determines a good baseball runner. Running speed was important, but the first step was the most important and the stride would show ability to increase speed, and most importantly, a good stride usually meant a player had a better chance to maintain his speed over time.

After the intense period of trying to get all these things through to me, I was allowed to see some high school and college games. I knew right away that this is what I wanted to do, and I would continue to work in a department store or whatever it took to keep doing this.

Luckily, my opportunity came sooner than I thought, and my journey in professional baseball would begin.

MY FATHER, THE BAVASI FAMILY, AND MR. RICKEY

"My father, Bob Fontaine, 1948"

I was fortunate to grow up in a baseball family. My father was a pitcher in the Brooklyn Dodgers organization and then started scouting at the end of his playing career.

He signed for a significant bonus of $500 out of Bellarmine High School in San Jose, California, as a right-handed pitcher. Before his contract was approved, he had to return to San Jose High School to finish his senior year since he was 17 years old and wasn't yet eligible to sign.

He had a promising start in the Brooklyn farm system, playing for Santa Barbara of the California League and Olean of the PONY League in 1941 and 1942. During that 1942 season, he won 14 games and was on track to reach the majors until he had to leave for three years to join the Army Air Corps during World War II.

While he was stationed at Marana Army Air Field in Arizona, he made a name for himself playing for the team representing the base. Military bases during the war had good teams, as they had many professional players to choose from. That made the games between the different bases quite competitive, drawing big crowds. Betting on these games was common and added more intensity to the atmosphere. He would pitch in games at Hi Corbett Field and when he would win, his life on the base improved tremendously.

On weekends, he would go across the border to pitch in Nogales, Mexico. It was forbidden for members of the military to go across the border, so he would change his name to Roberto Fontaiño, and wear a mustache. He could make a lot of money in those games, so it was worth the gamble.

In one of those games pitching for Nogales, they were playing a team from Tucson. He was covering first base on a ground ball hit to the first baseman, and when he got the throw, it was a close play. The umpire signaled that the runner was out. The runner argued vehemently, but the umpire just shrugged his shoulders and said, "*No comprende.*"

After the runner headed back to his bench, the umpire turned to my dad and said in perfect English, "We took care of that guy."

After the war, he returned to playing, and in 1946, he went to spring training with the Dodgers in Daytona Beach, Florida. He was slated to start the year with the Triple-A affiliate in Montreal and trained with them that spring. From what my parents had told me, Montreal was a great place to play and live in.

The year 1946 was also when Jackie Robinson reported for his first year with the Dodgers, breaking baseball's color barrier. During the spring, my father was one of the first players to be in a picture with Jackie. My parents really liked Jackie and his wife, Rachel.

My sister, Sandy, who was just a small child, still remembers that year and meeting the Robinsons. Jackie and the players would buy her candy in the hotel lobby, and she specifically remembers Pee Wee Reese being so nice to her.

My father broke camp with the Montreal club and would tell us about that 1946 season, and what it was like with all the attention they received with Jackie Robinson making his debut in the Dodgers organization. He described the atmosphere in Jersey City, New Jersey, where the Montreal Royals opened the season that year in front of 50,000 fans, and how Robinson started with a fantastic opening game with four hits, a home run, and flawless defense.

All the pressure that sat in the air before the game started to disappear in a hurry, and Jackie went on to have a great season, leading Montreal to the International League title and to the Little World Series Championship against Louisville of the American Association.

One thing I found out after my father passed away was that he was the Opening Day pitcher for the Royals when Jackie made his debut in Montreal. Even though he didn't get the decision, Montreal won the game against the Jersey City Giants.

I will always remember my father and mother telling us how hard the challenges were on Jackie and Rachel, and how they handled things so well. He was amazed at Jackie's ability, and how he could make so many things happen in a baseball game to help his team.

When I see shows on television about Jackie's life and career, I often see pictures or film of my father sitting next to him on the bench in Montreal. It is still a thrill to see him as part of that historical time.

My father pitched between Montreal and Mobile of the Double-A Southern League in 1946, even though he spent most of the year with Montreal. The next year would be an unfortunate turn in his career, as he experiences an injury that would ultimately end his career.

"Montreal Royals Team Photo, 1946"

He started the 1947 season with Montreal and was brought up to travel with the Brooklyn club to throw batting practice, with the idea he may be activated at some point. During one of these sessions, he was throwing well when a pain went through his shoulder. He tried to work through it, but to no avail.

He had to have surgery to remove calcium deposits in his pitching shoulder, leaving large scars on his back where they went in to get the deposits. Today, these are dissolved and don't require surgery. When he recovered, his arm was never the same.

He tried to come back in 1948 with Montreal, but the arm never recovered. With his playing career now ending at the age of 24, he looked for a new avenue.

Branch Rickey, the historic general manager of the Dodgers, had taken a liking to my father and suggested to him that he thought he would make a good scout. In our house as a kid, Branch Rickey was always referred to as "Mr. Rickey," and he held a great respect that was special. Mr. Rickey offered my father a job as a scout with Brooklyn, working the Northern California territory.

During his time as a scout, my father learned the philosophy that Mr. Rickey instilled in St. Louis and Brooklyn. Mr. Rickey started the modern-day minor league system and brought player development to a new level. My father never did tell me why Mr. Rickey took such a liking to him, but I have to believe that he knew of my father's love for baseball and how much he liked to be at the ballpark.

My father settled into his new job and learned the Dodgers way of evaluating and the type of players they liked. He was in the position for a couple years when Mr. Rickey left the Dodgers to join the Pittsburgh Pirates as their new general manager. Mr. Rickey took some people with him to Pittsburgh, my father being one of them. My dad would be there for 20-plus years before moving on.

Mr. Rickey was only in Pittsburgh for five years before leaving, but he left his mark with the acquisition of Roberto Clemente and many of the players that would be part of the 1960 World Series championship team. He primarily was the one who helped my father establish his foundation as a player evaluator.

When I was a young kid, I would travel with my dad in the summer for about a month, seeing teams in the Pacific Coast League, Northwest League and Pioneer League. It was a great time traveling to so many neat towns, staying in motels, and eating out every meal, not to mention the best part: going to a game every night.

It was a lifestyle that seemed special to me even then, and baseball had already gotten into my blood.

On one of these trips, we met up with Branch Rickey Jr., Mr. Rickey's son and the Pirates farm director. He was a genuinely nice man who loved cherries. In the Northwest in the summer, there are fruit stands everywhere, and we would stop all the time to get him cherries. He traveled with us for about a week, and it was a great time.

That summer, I had my heart set on being a peanut vendor at Forbes Field in Pittsburgh. Why *that*, I will never know, but Branch Jr. thought it was great and the whole week he worked with me yelling out, "Peanuts! Get your fresh roasted peanuts here."

I kept yelling it out all summer. I am sure I drove my father crazy.

I only wish I had been older to pick Branch Jr.'s brain about baseball. He died soon after and I never saw him again. What a nice man.

I would travel with my dad like that for a few summers while he would go on the road for a month to cover those leagues for potential trades. Travel was more difficult as you didn't have many freeways, and it took longer to get around. Most scouts didn't fly, so there were many long days on the road. There were no computers or cell phones, and most correspondence was by telegram or mail, and maybe an occasional phone call. He would write up his reports on the teams he saw and send them to his front office by mail.

During these travels we would go to games in Vancouver, Portland, Tacoma, Seattle, Boise, Idaho Falls, Twin Falls, Pocatello, Lewiston, Ogden, Great Falls, and Billings.

Often, I could be a bat boy or help in the clubhouse, but just usually ran around the ballpark having a great time. Hanging around scouts and managers, staying up late every night, and sleeping in the next day was *the* life.

Sandy, who is nine years older than me, used to travel with dad when she was my age as well, helping him with tryout camps that he would hold. Open tryout camps were commonplace and would be held in many locations by clubs. She would help register players for the tryouts and keep track of all the information cards for my father. When she was done with registration, she would shag after foul balls hit and receive 25 cents for every ball she returned.

While my father worked for Pittsburgh, they had an affiliation with the Hollywood Stars of the PCL. My dad spent a lot of time with the club and Sandy took some trips with him to Hollywood, California. She would go to games and see movie stars show up. My father got to know several celebrities while being around the Stars. Sandy got to go to a filming of a Jerry Lewis film, as dad was a friend of popular director, Frank Capra. She would sit alongside my dad and Dean Martin as they chatted during games. She was at a game when Jayne Mansfield was crowned Miss Hollywood Stars. Another time my father let her run the scoreboard up in the press box. I got to do it as well in Sacramento at a Solon's game. Things were a lot more informal in those days.

Bing Crosby was a part owner of the Pirates while my father worked for them, and my dad used to get letters from him about players he heard about and thought needed to be seen. Dad used to go to Bing's Pebble Beach Golf Tournament and Clambake. Sandy and my brother-in-law, Jim, would go with him to the tournament, and told me dad would be interviewed on the radio. Like Sandy has said, "Scouts were revered more in those days."

My brother, Rick, didn't spend as much time traveling with dad as Sandy and I did because my parents split up when he was very young, but he still got to share in some of that experience. One time he was with my father at a tournament for the Joe DiMaggio League and Joe DiMaggio was there. DiMaggio and my father were friends, and Rick and my dad spent some time with him. DiMaggio signed a program for Rick. It is a great item signed on a program from the league named after him. I have been trying for 50-plus years to get it from him, but with no luck to this point.

We had some special experiences that when you look back and see how many kids never got to enjoy things like that, you realize now that we were fortunate. I have always tried to take my kids to games whenever I could and now that they are grown, I believe they have looked back and are appreciative like I was to travel to different places and to have taken for granted a baseball park.

During the 20-plus years my dad scouted for Pittsburgh, he worked for and with some of the most successful scouts and baseball men in the business. Many had come over with Mr. Rickey, and the Pirates philosophy was much like the Dodgers.

Joe Brown, the son of actor Joe E. Brown, became the general manager of Pittsburgh after Mr. Rickey departed. Towards the end of my father's time with Pittsburgh, he was the West Coast Supervisor, where he would work with Joe Bowen, Rex Bowen, Howie Haak, Bob Zuk, Jerry Gardner, Rosey Gilhousen, Al Kubski, Ron King, and Larry DiAmato.

This staff was responsible for many fine players through the years: Willie Stargell, Dick Stuart, Gene Clines, and Bob Bailey, among others. A great group of evaluators who all went on to great careers. The Pirates were a great player development organization.

For almost all of the time they worked together, there was no draft, so you had to work hard to identify the players, establish a good relationship with the player and his family, and then be able to sign them for whatever money you were given. You had to work hard and have good contacts and references, or you wouldn't be able to survive.

Without social media, publications, radio, and television coverage of high school and college baseball like today, it was a job that required a lot of time and many diverse actions. Today, it is possible for someone to not work as hard to get a good player with information so readily available to everyone possible. Much less likely then.

Information sharing was at a minimum and hiding at the ballpark as not to be seen was commonplace. I still take pride in hiding at a ballpark so that no one will know I am there.

The Pirates were known for having a lot of tryout camps and were known as a "tools club." In other words, they looked for players with God-given abilities. A player that could run, field, throw, show bat potential with power, and pitchers with good deliveries and loose arms that could be projected to throw harder and be likely to have a good breaking ball.

They had positivity when looking at a young player, and as my father would say, "If a kid shows you something once, they own it."

Great advice that is true and that I have used my whole career.

My dad never used a stopwatch, and during these times there were no radar guns. He always said a time doesn't tell the whole picture with a runner. First step, quickness to full stride, and effort to stride is what describes a runner.

I was taught not to use a watch as well, but remember when I was working in Texas, he called and asked me how fast a kid was. I had just bought a stopwatch three days before and thought I would start being like other scouts. I told him, "He's a 4.3 runner to first."

For the next ten minutes, he aired me out about how he didn't ask what the watch said. He wanted to know what kind of runner he was. So, it is safe to say I have used a watch for three days in 48 years. I learned the hard way.

A pitcher's fastball was judged by the life at the end of the pitch, and the velocity that the naked eye picks up. A hitter will tell you a lot about how a fastball affects them, and how quick it gets on him. It is the way I was taught, and I haven't used a radar gun during my years as well.

I have seen pitchers throw in the high 90 mph range get hit hard, and someone throw in the 80's be highly effective. Velocity is important, but is not the only component to a good fastball. To learn these things makes it easier to be able to project the future, both good and bad, for a pitcher or player.

The process of signing a player before the draft existed was quite interesting and very hectic. My dad would tell me that a player could sign the day after graduation. With a player that was highly sought after, scouts would attend the graduation ceremony to be in position to immediately try and sign the player. He would say there may be 10-12 scouts sitting at the graduation holding a present and waiting for their meeting with the player and his family later that day. Then, each team would go into the house and make their pitch to try and sign him.

There were many things that would go on that scouts would do to try and get an edge to sign a kid. It was extremely competitive and particularly important that the scout knew the player and his family well. A scout's list may not be too long, as he needed to get to know the players he really liked well, and this required a lot of time.

They would sign players after the top kids were signed by holding tryout camps and offering contracts to players that they didn't know as well or saw play as much. Those players usually received little, if *any*, bonus money.

There were all kinds of stories of what scouts or club officials would do to try and get the families confidence to sign a player. I don't know if it's true or not, but I was told a story that Charles Finley, the owner of the A's, showed up at the home of Blue Moon Odom to try and sign him, and when he got in the house, he had brought groceries and cooked them dinner. After dinner, he had persuaded Blue to sign with the A's, who went on to have a big career with the club.

My father told me one time he was the penultimate scout to visit with a player, and at the end of their conversation, the family said everything sounded good and that they thought they would sign with my father and the Pirates. They had to meet with one other club that evening and decide. My father knew that the last team in the house for a negotiation usually had the best chance if their bonus offer was at least the same, so my dad said, "Ok."

The only thing is that my father refused to leave. He said, "He can come in and talk with you, but I'm not leaving until you sign with me."

The player signed with my father.

There are all kinds of stories of teams buying families presents, such as cars, washing machines, appliances, and even give jobs to relatives in an effort to sign a player. You could donate to a player's church as part of the contract. *Anything* that could be an edge was tried, and it made things interesting.

My favorite story was when there was a player in Utah or Idaho that came from a deeply religious background and 8-10 scouts were waiting in the hotel lobby for their turn to meet with the player and family. One scout decided to get an edge. He bought a box of cigars and distributed them to all the scouts before they went in for their meeting. He would go up to each guy, placing a cigar in their shirt pocket, saying, "Have a cigar, and here's one for later."

Scouts are very receptive to free things, so they gladly accepted the cigars. Most would wear coats and ties in those days when negotiating and walked into the player's house with the cigar sticking out of their shirt pockets.

The family, whose religion didn't believe in tobacco or alcohol, were put off when the scouts one-by-one walked into their home with the cigar showing. It was an instant negative. The scout that bought the cigars went into the house with no cigar, said he didn't use tobacco, and then proceeded to sign the kid. I thought it was genius.

My father was with Pittsburgh until 1968 when San Diego was awarded a National League expansion team for the 1969 season. He was hired to be their first scouting director. Buzzie Bavasi was the new club president after leaving the Los Angeles Dodgers as their general manager. Buzzie, Peter Bavasi, Eddie Leishman (the new general manager), and my father became the Padres first front office.

The Bavasi family is one of the most successful and respected in baseball history and have been involved in the game for over 80 years. Buzzie and three and of his four sons: Peter, Bob, and

Bill, have all been important to the game and my career. Their knowledge and love for the game is incredible, and they are great people who understand and appreciate the game and people in it.

Buzzie was the GM of the Brooklyn Dodgers when they won the World Series in 1955, as well as other championships in Los Angeles. My father first met Buzzie in 1948, his first year as a scout, when Buzzie was GM of the Montreal Royals. That was the beginning of the Bavasi and Fontaine families working together in baseball for two generations – 72 years in total.

The Padres were owned by C. Arnholt Smith, a local banker and businessman who eventually had to sell the club in 1973 due to financial troubles. The club was run on a shoestring budget and had little extra money to compete with the big-market clubs. But with Buzzie, Peter (who had been the GM in Albuquerque in the Dodgers organization) and my father, they had a background on how to develop a farm system and get players to the majors quickly.

They developed good, albeit small, scouting staffs and minor league systems. The flow of players from the draft moved through the system and to the big-league team quickly. The philosophy was consistent throughout the organization and the influence of Mr. Rickey and the Dodgers everywhere. It was a great environment to work in for a veteran baseball person, as everyone's opinion was valued, with the process of developing players understood.

When a team like the Padres works under an extremely tight budget, it is exceedingly difficult to keep your better players when they start getting into larger salary years. The Padres didn't draw well in the early years, and there was no television money like there is today. Often, you had to trade your better players in their prime.

During the time I worked with the Padres, we had to trade veterans at times for cash considerations so we could have enough money to sign our number one pick in the draft and make an upcoming payroll. It was a tough task for the club, but it was a true baseball organization.

In 1973, the Padres were put up for sale and looked to be headed to Washington D.C., when Mr. Ray Kroc, who was the owner of McDonald's, bought the club and kept it in San Diego. Peter became general manager after Eddie left, and Mike Port joined the club as the minor league farm director.

Although Mr. Kroc had a financial empire, he didn't put a lot of money into the club initially, and the Padres continued with a limited budget. My father, along with Peter, became more involved with player personnel.

During this time, Bob Bavasi joined the club as an assistant in scouting and the minor leagues. Bob spent a few years with the Padres before going on with his wife, Margaret, to become highly successful minor league owners.

When the Padres Triple-A team in Honolulu went bankrupt during the season, Bob and I offered to run the team as the Padres were going to have to take it over. We were turned down. Still ticks me off.

I ended up working with the youngest Bavasi, Bill, later in my career for three different organizations. It is a great baseball family, and I learned a lot about baseball from not only Buzzie, but each one of them. Bill and I would go and work together for many years, and I believe our upbringing made it easy for us to work well together and maximize our strengths while trying to minimize our weaknesses.

In 1976, Peter left the Padres to run the expansion Toronto Blue Jays, and my father was elevated to player personnel director, who along with Buzzie, ran the baseball operations. When Buzzie left in 1977 to go to the California Angels and run that organization, he took along Mike Port. Mr. Kroc then made my father general manager of the Padres.

It was the start of a three-year run in that role. It turned out to be his most exciting time in baseball, as well as his most disappointing time. General managers oversaw all departments with a team during that time, including business, public relations, finance, marketing, and of course, baseball. Much different than today.

His first year as general manager the team was still under .500 and had yet to have a winning season in club history, but it was getting better. He let go of Alvin Dark as manager and hired Roger Craig to be the new manager.

Going into 1978, the club looked stronger, with more depth. This was the year Ozzie Smith would make his debut. Dave Winfield was starting to become an established star in the league, and the younger players were improving.

The 1978 season was the first the Padres finished over .500 in their history. With a long winning streak in September, the club was in the pennant race. They came up short but ended up with an 84-78 record, and the future looked promising. With the new success, my father was given some room to try and sign some free agents to help the big-league team get to the next level.

The 1979 season started with a lot of excitement and expectations but ended with a disastrous 69-93 record. With this poor season over, the pressure started to mount to get back on track in 1980. Roger Craig was let go as manager, and my father caught the baseball world by surprise when he hired Jerry Coleman as the new manager.

Jerry was the play-by-play announcer in San Diego for many years and hadn't managed before. He did, however, have an outstanding career as a shortstop for the New York Yankees for many years and knew the club probably as well as anyone.

The club started the first quarter of the season well, using the running game effectively. Then the wheels came off and the team started to struggle. What had looked so promising two years before was now headed in the wrong direction.

The All-Star Game that year was played in Los Angeles, and my father and stepmother drove up there for the usual activities of meeting with clubs to discuss potential trade deals. Getting there the day before the game, he went to the different parties and met with representatives from other clubs when he got a call from Mr. Kroc.

He was told he was being relieved of his duties.

I always thought that he should have been told before he left or after he got back from the game. I know it bothered him.

It is part of baseball and Mr. Kroc wanted to win, but my dad had developed so many players for the Padres with little money to work with and did help them to their first winning season in 1978.

After some time, my father went off to work for the San Francisco Giants, but he never got over what had happened with the Padres, as he loved working for them.

Bob Lurie, the owner of the Giants, was friends with my father, and came after him soon after the Padres relieved him of his duties. He joined the Giants at the end of the year and oversaw scouting and player development. Al Rosen was the general manager and Tom Haller was the minor league farm director. For the next ten years, the Giants would build a strong team through their system.

The drafts were very strong while my father was there, drafting and signing such players as Matt Williams, Will Clark, Robby Thompson, Jeff Brantley, Terry Mulholland, Trevor Wilson, Charlie Hayes, Mike Remlinger, among many others.

It all came together in 1989 when the Giants went to the World Series against Oakland. It was also the Earthquake World Series that was delayed due to the devastating 6.9 magnitude earthquake before Game 3.

This was a homegrown team that he was immensely proud of.

After the World Series, he started to limit his activities as his health began to decline. He worked a few more years before deciding to retire.

My father passed away in 1994 after spending over 50 years in professional baseball. He loved the game so much and always had a smile on his face when he was at the ballpark. He enjoyed all the people in the game and was the best evaluator of talent I have been around. He started not just my career but helped many other young men into the game to become scouts, coaches, and executives. He loved to share his knowledge and always stressed how lucky we were to be in the game, and to never forget it.

THE VETERAN SCOUT (A SCOUTING FOUNDATION)

The veteran, experienced baseball scout is a disappearing commodity in the game today. The former player, manager, and coach that dedicated his life and loyalty to baseball and became a scout is vanishing. These are the people that gave teams the competitive edge.

The wealth of knowledge through first-hand experience is leaving for a more socialized form of evaluating players. The better your experienced staff, the more likely you would enjoy success for a longer period of time. Not to mention, you could save *a lot* of money over what is spent today.

I have survived in this game for almost 50 years, and it was the knowledge passed down to me from so many veteran scouts that allowed me to enjoy enough success to stick around.

Statistics have been around forever, and everyone has access to them, but they don't all have access to the mind of an experienced evaluator. A number or statistic cannot measure heart, desire, toughness, and instincts. Only veteran observation can do that. It only makes sense if you have a game based on human element that you would have the human input as much as possible.

Anytime you are dealing with evaluating a player, the human element automatically becomes involved. There are so many intangible items that need to happen for a player to be successful that do not show up in numbers. The certain things that need to happen fundamentally with throwing, running, hitting and strength for the player or pitcher to improve.

Many times, I found myself liking a player who didn't grade out as well as another player because of these intangibles. Constant adjustments are needed to be successful and things that often don't show up in a statistic are necessary for that success.

A gut feeling or instinct is a strong inkling that cannot be taught, explained, or given a number to. It is a hunch you get about a player or pitcher that numbers often do not support. It takes years, and you will know when you get it. The excitement you feel and the recollection you have on a player lasts like you had always just seen him the day before.

Every time I went against my gut on a player, I was almost always wrong. When I changed my mind and got burned, I would always be so mad at myself. If you haven't learned and experienced being a scout, this is tough to explain.

There was a movie Clint Eastwood acted in called *Trouble with the Curve.* As the movie went on, it illustrated a veteran scout who was losing his eyesight but could hear the difference of a good pitch or the sound of contact off the bat. It is absolutely true and if you are in the game long enough you will hear it, purely on instinct.

The ball sounds different, whether it's the noise coming off the bat or hitting the catcher's mitt. You don't hear it often because only a select few can make that sound, but it is there, and no number can describe it.

It is a different world with all the analytical items, but to be your best and help a club the most, you should understand how the opposing view thinks and why. There is no shortcut to being good, and the ones that take the time to understand all aspects of evaluating usually enjoy the most success. This is why the education of being around veteran scouts and learning from their experiences helped me understand things and expedite my confidence in making a decision.

I would constantly ask questions, trying to ask pitching questions for those that had the most success with pitching and hitting questions of those who had the most success with hitting. By asking these questions and learning about the opposing scouts in my area, I learned their strengths and weaknesses. This helped me know who to talk with.

In today's scouting world, you see very few newcomers asking questions. I think today the younger scouts are afraid to admit they don't know something. Because of that, they don't ask questions and rely more on numbers than on something that might separate the numbers. I enjoy helping young scouts and discussing items to look at, but only get approached by very few.

I have mentioned many times how other scouts helped me, and I heard a lot of different ideas and philosophies. Some made sense to me, and some did not. It is like developing as a player. They take a little input from many coaches to become who they will be. There is no one exact way, but talking baseball keeps the mind active and receptive to things that may make you better and more successful.

There have been so many that have helped me, with my father being the most influential person in my scouting career, but I am illustrating what kind of things I learned from him and three others: Bob Zuk, Jesse Flores Sr., and Eddie Matthews. Things that I have learned and used my entire career.

My father taught me the importance of feet and first step quickness, strong hands, quick wrists, and the effort required to play. He said if the feet move, then the player can stay with the speed of the game and get into position for every other part of the body to perform at its maximum ability. Whether you are playing defense, throwing, hitting, or running, it starts with the feet.

Everything starts and finishes with the feet and hands. As you move up the ladder, the game gets faster. The average fan can't always see it. They just see a game at the speed of the game at that level, but the feet are what allow you to move to the next level and eventually, if your feet don't hit a block, you can get to the big leagues. Guys in the big leagues make it look easy, because their feet allow them to be in position to do everything.

Quick wrists allow you to have a quick swing and have a quick finish to the ball when you throw, while quick hands assist in your fielding. Strong hands allow you to finish everything to your ability and give strength in a swing, finishing with the hands. Same thing with throwing. It is hard to have a good arm without strong hands to finish it off.

My dad stressed the delivery and arm action of a pitcher with the less effort the better. Balance to let the body and arm work together and the quickness and freedom of the arm with proper angle and extension of the arm in back and out front. A loose wrist and a quick arm can generate power to a pitch, whether a fastball or breaking ball.

The delivery is the balance of the body going back and forward, with the arm action being the length of the arm in back and out front. There must be ease to it with little restriction. The easier the body works with balance, the easier the arm works with freedom and less effort with proper extension.

Extension in the back is where you allow the arm to gain arm speed, and the extension out front is how far you get out front before you release the ball. This is what generates power, similar to hitters. The angle to the plate is where you can come from to keep the hand behind and on top of the ball.

Ease over effort is key.

With a hitter, the important things are balance and the initial load of the hands with the bat. Obviously, you like bat speed and you like extension out front.

Extension occurs when the contact is made, and the bat extends out to drive the ball. If you cut it off, you're going to cut off the ability to drive the ball. Extension determines how hard you hit the ball and how quickly.

You must understand with young hitters, they tend to swing at bad pitches and swing and miss often. My rationale with that is amateur hitters only play two games a week and they don't want to walk, so you have to really judge that good swing when they put it all together. Oftentimes, they get fooled and are out front or wait too long to start the bat, but that doesn't mean they don't have the ability to do it right. It may take a lot of swings before a player does it right.

He felt that if those basic things were seen, and there wasn't much effort to do these things, that the player had room to get better and just as important, a better chance of retaining the ability for a longer period of time.

Projection is an important part of evaluating as long as you know why you are projecting. Too often, age is the only reason. Ability is ability *is ability* and doesn't know age. It is why some kids are ready to start their professional career at 18 years old, and others at 21 or 22. Often, a player doesn't reach full potential until many years later.

My father would stress to me that if a player showed you an average or above-average tool, he owned it, and don't give up because that player doesn't show it all the time.

This is especially true with young pitchers who will only show their top velocity, or a quick-biting breaking ball on a few occasions over the course of a season. In many cases, due to lack of strength or consistency of the proper mechanics, a player or pitcher can be very inconsistent. The natural instinct of an evaluator is that you want to see a player's best all the time, but it's all the more reason why you have to stay with what you saw only a few times. Most kids cannot repeat the peak level of success just yet.

Too often, a scout that wants to see a player repeat his best on a regular basis becomes what is known as a "performance scout." If you scout this way, it makes it difficult to project a player for the future, because you have to assume the player will one day do on a regular basis what you only saw briefly. The best scouts I was ever around were able to be confident on a short look at a player who only flashed what he may become in the future. To me, this is the fun part of scouting where you can use your imagination, knowledge, comparisons, and instincts to make a decision.

Every scout is like a player. You need an experienced teacher to share their knowledge and experiences with you to help develop your talents to become successful. Those that ask questions of the veteran scout and listen, learn.

Bob Zuk was a scout for many years with many different clubs and was as good a power-hitting scout that probably has ever worked, and the best I've ever been around. He signed so many good power hitters – including Willie Stargell, Reggie Jackson, and Gary Carter, among others – that his players totaled 2,444 career home runs. He worked with my father in Pittsburgh, and when I began my scouting career, he spent a lot of time helping me understand hitting and power.

Bob worked mostly by himself and was a character. He always seemed to be involved in some kind of controversy and did things his own way.

Bob went through a period with the Baltimore Orioles where he didn't turn in an expense voucher for two years. At the end of the second year, Baltimore was sold, but it couldn't complete the sale until Bob's expenses were closed. For about a month, he would call me two or three times a day asking, "Remember when we saw 'so and so' play a year and a half ago? Where was that at and what day was it?"

It was funny watching him try to reassemble two years of gasoline and hotel receipts with help from his friends. He finally got them completed, but I think every club he worked for afterward made him turn in expense reports every two weeks. He owned a photography business, so I'm sure his cash flow could handle it, but still, *two years?*

Expenses aside, Bob was always on top of what a young hitter could do. He taught me what to look for when evaluating power. We had some workouts together, and the things he would have players try and do became valuable tools for me.

He would tell a player in batting practice to try and see how far they can pull a ball foul. This showed not only strength in the wrists and overall strength, but extension that could get the last bit of power from the swing. To see the strength to hit a ball that hard foul on purpose, you could project what a player could do when they hit the ball in play.

He believed that a pop up was a big indicator of power. The higher a player hits a pop up, the more power he will possess. To hit a pop fly high in the air when you haven't made solid contact shows strong wrists and raw strength. I have used this my whole career and strongly believe in it.

Bob also believed strongly in watching everything a player does, even when he isn't playing. If you watched how a player reacted to success and adversity, as well as how his teammates felt about him, you could learn a lot about his makeup. If the player handled things with a somewhat even temperament and was a good teammate, it could be a key factor in deciding the players makeup.

Two things that illustrate this: I saw an extremely talented player who was selected high in the first round and while I was watching him play, I noticed that nobody wanted to sit next to him on the bench and no one talked to him. That player never made it to the majors, and although I cannot say without a doubt it was bad makeup, I would think it had something to do with it.

The second player was one I would ultimately sign: Bob Geren. I was in San Diego watching Geren play in the annual Lions Tournament high school championship game. Geren had a good game and could throw the ball well while piecing together good at-bats. He came up to hit in the last inning with the game tied and launched a home run to left field that he hit well, helping his team win the game.

Zuk was there with me and as we were walking out, he asked, "What did you see there at the end?"

"He had a good swing on the ball he hit and did what he should do with that pitch," I replied.

That's when the lesson started.

"Of course, but did you see how his teammates reacted when it was *him* that hit the home run?" Bob asked. "They were genuinely happy it was him that did it."

It turned out to be the right observation and one that I would have missed. Geren played almost 10 years in the minor leagues before he reached the majors and had a nice five-year career. He loved to play, and his perseverance was unbelievable.

Zuk picked up so many things you don't hear scouts talk about, and I am truly fortunate that he shared those things with me.

Outside of my father, when it came to pitching the one scout that shared with me the most important thing was Jesse Flores Sr. He worked many years for the Minnesota Twins and was one of the most successful scouts in their history. He pitched many years in the majors and was a member of the Philadelphia A's when Connie Mack managed them in the 1940's.

Of Jesse's many signings that reached the majors, Bert Blyleven was the one that interested me the most. I had heard that as a kid in high school, Bert had a below-average fastball. I asked Jesse how he could draft him in a high round when he only threw in the mid 80's.

"*Shorty*," Jesse replied, as he always called me "Shorty" even though he wasn't much taller than I am, "He could really spin a curveball, and that will not only lead to an outstanding curve, but much better velocity on his fastball in the future. You have to have a quick, loose, and strong wrist, which Blyleven showed throwing his curve, and that is the top intangible to project the fastball getting better."

True to those words, Blyleven threw in the mid 90's and had probably as good a curveball as anyone, leading to a 22-year Hall of Fame career.

If you have a strong wrist, strong fingers, and strong hands, you have the potential to spin a baseball, and as a young player matures physically and gets stronger, you can project the velocity to gain because of the wrist and hand.

Jesse wouldn't talk pitching often, but when he did, I tried to pick up every word he said. He was one of the nicest men in the scouting profession and certainly one of the best evaluators of pitchers I have ever been around. His sons, Jesse Jr., and Steve, have scouted as well, and had their share of big league players.

Eddie Mathews, the Hall of Fame third baseman for the Atlanta Braves, scouted for them for a few years after he was done playing and coaching. I got to know Eddie during his scouting years, and he was genuinely nice to me even when I started asking all my questions.

Much of the time, the great players know it was easy for them, and because of that they don't analyze as much. He was a great power hitter who taught me that as tough as things can be, keep it simple.

I was at a Pacific Coast League game in Phoenix with Eddie, and the San Francisco Giants had a first baseman, Rich Murray, who had great power, but had trouble hitting a breaking ball or off-speed pitch. I asked Eddie, "What do you do with someone like this?"

He looked at me as if he wanted to say, "Are you kidding me? It's so obvious." But he didn't, and he then proceeded to tell me his thoughts.

"A hitter needs to be ready and prepared for *his* pitch that *he* can hit, and not be worried or preoccupied with the one he can't hit that's a strike. Until you get to two strikes, you are focused on your pitch in your zone. When you have two strikes, you must be ready for any pitch close. During four at-bats in a game, a hitter should get at least one or two pitches that he can handle, and if he is ready, he can have a good day. If you swing at pitches that you can't hit just because they are strikes, you may never get your pitch, and if you do, you won't be prepared to hit it. If a pitcher can throw three strikes on pitches you can't hit in an at-bat, there's not much you can do. Being ready to handle your strength is what a hitter needs to prepare for."

It made so much sense and taught me to have patience with power hitters who swing and miss and strike out. Time and good instruction will allow them to understand the strike zone better and develop needed pitch recognition.

You should never penalize a young power hitter on his swings and misses out of the strike zone, as long as they are hitting the pitch they should. Time can correct this.

I really liked Eddie, and the teaching from a Hall of Fame hitter to keep it so simple was immensely helpful to my understanding of young power hitters.

The development of a baseball scout is like the development of anyone in any field. It is like going to school, and then college. If you are open-minded, ask questions, and appreciate the fact that you don't know much, you can develop and develop at a much quicker pace.

Too often, a person gets a position of authority without much experience in that field, and they think they know more than the people that they lead. I always felt that if you surround yourself with as many people that had as much ability and experience as I did, preferably more, they would not only make themselves successful, but myself as well.

SAN DIEGO PADRES

"Ozzie Smith and Tony Gwynn during 1979 exhibition game between San Diego Padres and San Diego State University"

SAN DIEGO PADRES
(1973 – 1974)

I started my scouting career in 1973, covering San Diego County for the San Diego Padres. My father was scouting director and turned me over to Marty Keough, who would be my supervisor.

Marty covered Southern California and four states, along with Cliff Ditto, who would become one of my closest friends. Marty was outstanding, allowing me to do things that he knew wouldn't work but things I could learn from.

It was my probation period to see if I had enough of a feel to become a full-time scout in the future. To cover my expenses and continue scouting, I had to work a full-time job at Robinsons department store, as I only received an occasional 10 cents-a-mile for reimbursement.

As tough as it was financially to get by, I worked hard that year, working every day that I could and rarely taking any time off. I did research and conversed with players and coaches constantly. This experience taught me the importance of the scout in the field and their relationships with coaches and people in the youth baseball community. I learned the value of the true experienced area scout that unfortunately is fading quickly today.

In some ways, that was as enjoyable a time I had in baseball. To watch games and spend time talking with players, coaches, and parents about a future in baseball was exciting. The scouts in the area; Dave Garcia, Pete Coscarart, Ray Boone, Al Zarilla, Bob O'Regan, Joe Henderson, and others were great in helping me get started. Getting the opportunity to project what you thought a player could be in five years was not only challenging, but something I enjoyed tremendously. Not many jobs let you look into a crystal ball and guess what you think will happen in the future.

The Major League Baseball Draft was implemented only eight years prior to the start of my scouting career. Amateur players, whether from college or high school baseball, would be selected by teams in order of the team's previous year's record, beginning each round with the worst record and ending with the best. This is a yearly summer event held by Major League Baseball following the amateur season in spring, where hundreds of kids around the nation are selected and then attempted to be signed by the selecting club.

I didn't get anyone in the 1973 draft, but at the end of the summer I was told I could try and sign a high school pitcher that I had turned a scouting report in on. His name was David Munoz, a big right-handed pitcher from Monte Vista High School in Chula Vista, California. I was given permission to sign him to a 1974 minor league contract with an Incentive Bonus Plan (money earned if a player proceeds to different levels of the organization) but no cash bonus. I had no idea at the time, but it was about as tough a negotiation as I could have. I know now that it was another test from my father.

David had a good arm and had gotten attention from clubs in the spring but wasn't selected in the draft. When I visited him and his family to start the negotiation, the father kept showing me business cards from scouts that had talked with them. I made the offer, and I thought the dad was either going to faint or kick me out of the house.

This is when I stressed that we sell opportunity instead of money. It was something I would learn quickly with the Padres and something we would do regularly. The Padres didn't give much in bonus money because we didn't have a lot of money to give. You may have a small radio contract, but there weren't multimillion-dollar television contracts to fund everything like today.

In the early-and-mid 1970's, we were reporting around 7,500 tickets sold nightly, but were drawing around 3,000 a night inside San Diego Stadium. We were able to operate within what we made and when you're only drawing 3,000 nightly, you're not making a whole lot.

What we didn't have in money, we had in opportunities for quick advancement through the organization. It was something we preached to players regularly and it was about as good as any opportunity inside baseball.

We approached quick advancement number one. In the 70's, there were players getting to the big leagues in 20 minutes. Not just Dave Winfield and Dave Roberts, who went right to the big leagues, but a lot of other players that got up quickly. Their time in the minor leagues was minimal, if at all. The opportunity wasn't stretching the truth, but instead, was the hard truth. We had an opportunity that other teams didn't, and for that reason, it was our number one selling point in negotiations.

I kept telling David and his family about the opportunity for quick advancement and the opportunity of signing with the hometown team, plus the Incentive Bonus Plan if realized could be worth up to $7,500. After a while, the dad relaxed as he knew David wanted to sign, and later that night I had signed my first player to a professional baseball contract.

After I left the house, I went to the ballpark where the Padres were playing at home that night. When I got into the stadium, I looked up to the press box where I spotted my father and lifted the contract and gestured that I had signed him. My father started smiling and laughing, as I realized he didn't think I would be able to do it.

-

In February of 1974, my father asked if I would like to move to the Midwest. I asked why.

"To start your full-time scouting career."

My reply was obvious. Yes.

He told me to go see Peter Bavasi the next day to speak with him. Peter was the general manager, and in those days, there were only three or four people in the baseball part of the front office, all who wore many hats and did many jobs.

I went to the office at San Diego Stadium the next day to see Peter. Even as tough as he could be at times, I really liked Peter. He had a great sense of humor and wasn't afraid of doing things a little different than other clubs. I was certainly different at the time, as there weren't many scouts under the age of 30, and I was under 20.

Peter explained the contract I was going to sign and the area that I would be covering that consisted of Central Canada, the Dakotas,

Western Illinois, Iowa, Kansas, Minnesota, Missouri, Mississippi, and Nebraska. It was a large territory in size, but few in players.

Travel was difficult as so many trips were on state and country roads, and not on the interstates. With constant bad weather in the spring, it often took a greater amount of time to get to places than you would expect. Rain was just one of the obstacles that you would face. There was sleet, hail, snow, floods, tornados, cold weather, and wind, making for interesting trips in the spring to Iowa, Minnesota, the Dakotas, and Nebraska. Most days were an adventure.

"You will be the Midwest Scouting Supervisor," Peter told me.

"That's great. Who do I supervise?"

"No one," he said as he looked at me like I didn't seem to get it. "We give titles here, not money."

After giving me the title, he proceeded to tell me that my salary would be $8,500 a year. I understood. I knew it wasn't much money, but at that time of my life it seemed like a fortune. In fact, I had more money in my wallet that first year than I did for many years after when I started to assemble responsibilities and have kids.

After finishing our conversation about responsibilities, titles, and the contract, Peter looked at me and asked, "By the way, how old are you?"

"19."

"19?" Peter asked with surprise and a little higher tone.

I figured after this response I better tell everyone I was 21. For the next three years, I was 21. It turned out for the better as I believe it would have been tougher if people thought I was under 21.

One of the toughest things I had to deal with was drinking after games with scouts. If we drank at the hotel, I was fine, but if it was at a restaurant or bar I had to always know where I was because the drinking age differed by state. When scouts would say, "Let's go have a few belts," I had to know right away if I was in a state that I could drink. If I wasn't, I would say, "I have a lot of paperwork to do so I better pass."

No one ever found out, but many years later when I would tell people, guys that knew me then said that it made sense because they knew I didn't like paperwork.

Believe it or not, having a drink or a beer with the veteran scouts helped expedite my development and reference base as a scout. My father told me to be respectful of the veterans and keep my mouth shut unless I had, or was asked, a question. It's about as good advice as you could get, as the veteran scouts accepted me and went out of their way to help me. A lot was due to my father being a friend of theirs, but I do believe they knew my sincere appreciation for how they treated and helped me.

The sessions around a bottle of scotch (affectionately known as "a cannon") were an unbelievable education. The scouts in these days were mostly former players and coaches who were in their late 30's to mid-70's. They loved to tell stories of their playing and coaching days and to argue with each other. They would never talk about the player we had all just seen, but rather they would talk about players they had seen in the past that reminded them of the kid we just saw. It was allowing me to have a comparison, both good and bad, about a player that I just saw that I would have never had otherwise. The meetings in those hotel rooms were not just educational, but some of the best memories I have of some of the greatest true baseball people I have been around.

When I left to go to my territory, I owned a 1963 Volkswagen Bug. Not a great scout's car to handle 60,000 miles a year or working in the humid Midwest and South with no air conditioning. The scouts in my territory use to rib me and say they were going to buy me a block of ice to put on the front seat and if I left the windows down, the breeze off the ice would cool me off. The only good thing was that it got great miles per gallon and at 10 cents a mile, I felt rich.

In those days, we operated on the 10/10/10 plan for expense reimbursement. $10 a day meal money, $10 a night hotel, and 10 cents a mile driven. It was a strict policy, but it was manageable as Motel 6 was $6 a night and 8 Days Inn was $8.88 a night. Expenses were a way that most scouts would supplement their income because pay for scouts was low and I know clubs realized that.

After signing my first scouting contract, some scouts at the ballpark that I saw right after told me they wanted to give me some tips. I thought they were going to give me some scouting advice, but instead, I was told, "Your driveway is 10 miles long" and "This hot dog from the concession stand is really a steak." I always appreciated learning from them.

Today, scouts stay at first-rate hotels, receive good meal money, and have well-routed driving plans, pending the IRS allowed amount per mile or a good rental car allowance. Not to mention the ability to fly more instead of driving.

Scouting expenses were a major source of conversation with scouts, and with that came stories of some bizarre things. As we stayed in a lot of old motels in many cities, several motels would supply handwritten receipts. Some guys would give a clerk money for a pad of blank receipts and then would be able to take a phantom trip because they would have hotel receipts. They would put down mileage and meals which required no receipt and then add the handwritten hotel receipt. It takes some guts to do it, but when you think of someone with a family and kids and a very small salary with no background of having big salaries as a player, you begin to understand it, even if you couldn't do it yourself.

There's a story of a scout that turned in some of these hotel receipts and the person approving the expenses in the office thought there was something familiar about the hotel being used. The hotel had burned down a few years prior and was never rebuilt. That scout was asked to leave his position of employment. It is a legendary tale that I have been told is true.

My first assignment in my new territory was to help our scout, Donny Williams, in Texas. Donny played and coached for many years and was a great mentor to me. He introduced me to many people and was patient with my evaluations and took the time to discuss them. I saw some of his better players as well as looked at some kids he had heard about but had not seen. It is common for scouts from cold weather states to start in Texas or Florida until their territories start playing. It helped me a lot before I headed to my own territory.

The first stop in my region was a high school tournament in Meridian, Mississippi. To say this was a culture shock to a young person coming from California would be an understatement.

I got into town late the night before and stayed at an older Holiday Inn. I finally fell asleep late that night and was abruptly woken up when someone started banging on my door around 3 a.m. Whoever it was tried hard to get in, and I shouted, "If you don't get out of here, I will blow you away!"

I didn't have a gun.

I think my voice wasn't who they were looking for and they left. Needless to say, I didn't sleep well the rest of the night.

When I arrived at the ballpark for the first game, I got a chance to meet a lot of scouts who would become good friends for many years.

Lenny Yochim of the Pirates became an awfully close friend and probably helped me as much as anyone when I got started. He pitched for the Pirates and scouted for them for a long time. He lived in New Orleans and had a great love for the game and patience with people like me. Although we didn't look at players quite the same way, listening to him made me think about things I wouldn't have otherwise. Scouting is opinions and different ideas, and I learned from people like Lenny that the more different things you hear, the better you can become.

This was also the first time I met Buck O'Neil, Piper Davis, and Ed Scott, who were great players in the Negro Leagues and were now scouts. They were great to me and Buck became a longtime friend. Buck is probably the nicest and most positive man I ever met. After I would talk with him, I always felt good about being a part of baseball and how much fun this is and how lucky we are to be a part of it.

While in Meridian, I ate at a famous restaurant called Weidmann's, which had great food and a jar of peanut butter and crackers at each table. I love peanut butter and crackers, so this place was great for me. The place had been there since 1870, and loving history like I do, it was cool.

Things were different in the South than where I came from. Segregation was unlawful but still visible at the school level where there were many private academies that were white students only. You didn't see many Black players other than at a public school or a Historically Black College and University. You would drive past Ku Klux Klan meetings. It was certainly eye-opening for me and allowed me to appreciate how far we have come as a society, but obviously still have a long way to go.

My first year I covered a lot of ground driving all over the Midwest. I settled in Lawrence, Kansas, which is the home of Kansas University, a great college town and a nice place to live and work. I had the opportunity to learn from great scouts like Jay Hankins, Carl Kentling, Chuck Koney, Nick Kamzic, Art Stewart, and many others. With short schedules and bad weather, it was a great area to learn as a scout since you weren't allowed as many opportunities to see players as in other parts of the country.

Something that shocked me coming from California was the commuter airline service. I once made a reservation to take a commuter flight from Lawrence to Kansas City International Airport. I was used to airlines like PSA, Air California, American, etc. for commuter service. When I arrived for the first time at the Lawrence airport it was just a small-town airport with a little building where you checked in. It was then that I found out that I was the only passenger on the flight, and when we went to get in the aircraft it was a one engine plane. The pilot told me to go ahead and sit in the co-pilot's seat. It wasn't until we were in the air that it hit me that if something happens to the pilot, I'm flying this thing! Happily, we made it safely, but it was the end of my co-pilot days as I drove to the Kansas City airport from then on.

The best player in my area that first year was Rick Sutcliffe, a right-handed pitcher out of Independence, Missouri. He was selected by the Los Angeles Dodgers in the first round, 21st overall. He had a live arm and clean delivery, not like the one he had when he made it to the majors with the wrist wrap in the back and the slower, deliberate delivery. Obviously, it worked well for him as he had an outstanding 18-year major league career, but I often thought he may have tried to pitch too much like Don Sutton, the Hall of Famer who pitched with a similar motion. Either way, it worked, but he did have a smooth delivery as a kid and was projectable.

The overall quality of play, especially at the high school level, was not particularly good. This could be expected, as they had so much less time during the year to play that it made it hard for them once they did get on the field. Athletes are just as good in the Midwest as anywhere, but when you're limited in the amount of time you can play, it delays your development as a player.

The thing that I learned with that year and territory that has helped me every year since is to make every look you have at a player count. Assume that you will never see the player again, even if you know you will, because many times it will be your only look due to weather and shortness of schedule. It taught me to watch everything a player does, from playing catch to running to his position, to swinging the bat in the on-deck circle. It keeps you active while evaluating the player and not become lazy and miss things. I still look at a player the same way today. It makes every look you have at a player important because it may be all you get.

This region was probably the best area for projecting what you think a player may become because you see so little, and you must really think through what you recommend. I always felt that if you weren't afraid to make a mistake that in areas like this you could have success, as so many don't want to take the risk.

I got one player in the 1974 draft out of Southeast Missouri State by the name of Galen McSpadden. He had a solid fastball and one of the best *true* forkballs I have seen. His fastball would set up hitters and he could put them away with that forkball (a pitch that breaks with downward sink opposite of a curveball with more velocity). Being a left-handed pitcher, he had value as a starter or reliever. He ended up playing as high as Triple-A with our Hawaii affiliate in the Pacific Coast League, and I do believe if he pitched today with 30 clubs instead of 24, he would have pitched in the majors.

After I was informed that I got him in the sixth round of the draft, I was told to meet with him and his family as soon as possible to try and sign him. From Lawrence to his home in Cape Girardeau, Missouri was 390 miles and I drove all night so I could meet with Galen and his family in the afternoon.

About 10 miles outside of Cape Girardeau, I was pulled over for driving 10 miles over the limit. The officer asked where I was going, and I told him that I was meeting with McSpadden to try and sign him.

"That's great!" the officer said. "Galen is my cousin."

Turned out to not be so great as he still brought me to the local courthouse to pay the fine for the speeding violation. All I had were travelers checks and I had to write them out and wait for approval before I could leave. I was finally told to go, and I hurried to not to miss my meeting. I thought this was a bad omen.

The meeting went well, as Galen was a college senior, and the negotiation was smooth and quick. He signed and was on his way to Walla Walla, Washington, where our Rookie League team was located. He started off well and had a good minor league career, being a prospect for most of it. He went on after his playing days to be a successful coach and athletic director at Seward County Junior College.

Thirty-three years later, I tried to sign his son.

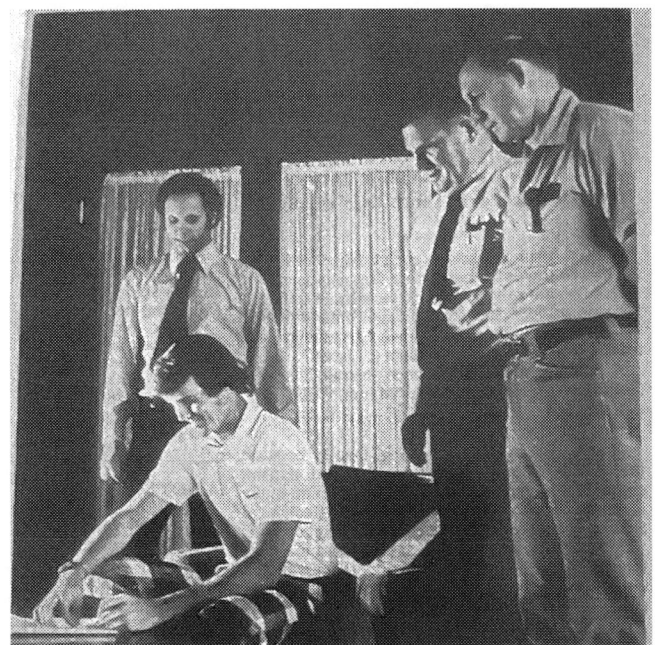

"Galen McSpadden signing professional contract, 1974"

The summer of my first year was very educational in my scouting career. I learned that the summer months were especially important when watching a player in cold weather areas. It is the time of year when they are playing regularly in conditions favorable for the game. The looks you get in the summer are important when you see a player the next spring in bad conditions, because you have a point of reference to assist you.

With American Legion games being played in Minnesota in the summer, it was apparent to me how you need to evaluate in places like this. I had seen Paul Molitor in the spring, and he was a cruder athletic kid who could run. Everything else was below average at the time. However, it was freezing conditions when I saw him play and not the condition to be at your best or for that matter, improve on your game. When I saw him in the summer, he not only ran better, but showed a good arm and the makings of a good swing. His feet worked well and showed good actions at shortstop. I realized right away that I had made a big mistake.

Molitor was drafted by St. Louis and didn't sign in favor of going to the University of Minnesota. The rest is history as he went on to play 21 years in the majors and was elected to the Hall of Fame in 2004.

I learned an important lesson about how to evaluate young kids in different environments that I have used my whole career.

One of my first summer assignments in 1974 was the Central Illinois League. The CIL at the time was one of the premier college summer leagues in the country. Many players passed through on their way to the majors. It was a great league to cover and being that I didn't have Illinois as a territory in the spring, I got to meet many new scouts. The caliber of play was better than I had seen in the spring and was another good learning venue for me.

As mentioned, I had to be aware at all times of what the drinking age was in the state I was present. In coverage like this, there is more time to socialize as you aren't traveling and moving around as frequently as in the spring before the draft.

One night in Bloomington, Illinois, I attended a game, but I was staying about 45 miles away in Pekin, as I was going to a game in Quincy the next day. After the game, a group of scouts were going out and said to me, "Come on kid. We are going to get a pop."

I was happy to be invited along and because I was of age in Illinois, I thought I would go for a beer, then drive to Pekin.

When I got to the bar they were already at a table and flagged me over. As I was getting ready to order a beer I was told, "Try this. It's good stuff."

It was my introduction to a Beefeater Martini, Straight Up. Went down easy, and we were having a great time and conversation when after six or eight martinis, I knew it was time to go. I staggered out and I'm sure those guys had a good laugh as I weaved my way to my car.

It's funny how sometimes you can remember things even when you are not totally with it and this was the case. I got to the car and laid down for a while before deciding to head back to my hotel. I got on I-55 and was heading for the I-74 turnoff to Pekin when after a while I realized that somehow, I missed it.

After about 25 miles or so, I stopped at a truck stop, went inside to the restroom, got real sick for a while, and then went to the coffee shop and drank what seemed like five gallons of coffee. After a couple hours I headed back towards the turnoff to Pekin. I was hurting so bad and couldn't see well and started driving with my head out of the window so I could see the white lines.

I have no idea how I made it back to the hotel and the next morning I woke up and it felt like a train went through my head.

I made my way to the game in Quincy that day and hurting as I was, I think the veterans were impressed that I made it. After the game they again said, "Hey kid, we are going out for a few more belts tonight. You want to go?"

As bad a shape as I was in, I wanted to show them I could handle the assignment and went. However, it was beer, and I haven't had a Beefeater Martini again since that day.

Later in the summer I made my first visit to the National Baseball Congress Tournament in Wichita, Kansas. The tournament lasts three weeks, has 60-plus teams, and plays about 20 hours a day. This was the premier college baseball event of the summer with teams from all over the country whether it be Northern California, Iowa, or Alaska. This was before the emergence of the Cape Cod League and USA National Teams as they are today.

I spent the first two weeks covering all the games from early morning until 3 a.m. some nights. Most of the best teams showed up the last week, so when they arrived all of our veteran crosscheckers came in. I got to see a lot of good prospects and learn a lot from the many veteran scouts that were there. By far the most grueling event I have covered.

This is where I got the opportunity to see Danny Goodwin, who was the first overall player selected in the draft twice, once out of high school and once out of college. I saw many other players that were drafted high and who ended up having good major league careers. Another great learning opportunity.

I stayed at an old hotel across the street where most of the scouts stayed called the Broadview Hotel. It was so old it had elevator operators and fence doors that had to be opened by the operator every time you got on and off. They had tiny rooms that were cheap, and the Dodgers used to have a suite upstairs where scouts could go after games and have a few drinks – sometimes more than a few – and talk baseball.

Kansas was a dry state in those days and to get a drink you had to belong to private clubs, which I was. It felt like what it must have been like during Prohibition. I belonged to a club that was located under a Pancake House and another one that was in an unmarked building that you had to knock on the door and a small slide in the door would open where you had to show your membership card for inspection before you could enter. It was hysterical.

In August 1974, the Major League Scouting Bureau came into existence. Sixteen of the 24 major league teams had decided to become a part of it. Clubs were to reduce their own staffs to around five scouts or less and then rely on information that would be produced by a staff of 60-plus scouts in the Scouting Bureau that were impartial. Each club would pay a yearly amount to receive this information and then use their remaining staff to look at the players they felt were of interest to them. The purpose was to trim costs to clubs, even though it would prove to clubs that they started to give up some of their competitive edge.

Scouts at the NBC Tournament were worried that their club would be one of the 16 to join the Bureau. It started after the first week of the tournament when teams started to notify scouts that they were being let go in preference of joining the Bureau. It seemed like five to 10 scouts a day were getting the dreaded call that they weren't being retained.

Most were told to go ahead and finish their work there, which made for a very somber atmosphere. The only place most of the scouts let go could look for a job was with the Scouting Bureau, and a lot of scouts were forced out of the game. It was a sad time for the scouting industry.

Luckily for me and the members of seven other teams, we didn't join the Bureau and I still had a job. I could have been done before I had barely started if the Padres had joined.

Unlike today where scout's salaries have gotten better and baseball activities are year-round, we would be encouraged to get jobs in the offseason. This would supplement our incomes and there was little baseball being played unless you were in a warm weather area.

I started my second career in sales selling women's shoes at Penny's and carpet, sewing machines, vacuum cleaners, refrigerators, and washers and dryers at Montgomery Ward. I was able to fake my way through for the three months I worked and make some extra money. It made me appreciate my job in baseball even more. I know then what I know now about selling things: nothing.

In December I was told that the next season I would be moved to another territory. Donny was going to be added to the Padres coaching staff and I would be responsible for covering his old territory of Arkansas, Louisiana, Mississippi, Oklahoma, and Texas. It would be a new and difficult challenge, but I was looking forward to it.

SAN DIEGO PADRES (1975 – 1976)

After a long, cold, snowy winter in Kansas, I was looking forward to the move south to my new territory. I decided to live in Austin as it was a central location of Texas, at least on a map. The only problem I would discover was that there weren't many players there and didn't allow for much opportunity to get home. It snowed about a week after I arrived. I just couldn't escape the snow in 1975.

I was looking forward to the challenge of a productive region like I now had. The opportunity to work against so many successful scouts and hopefully learn from them was exciting. Even though I had only scouted for two years, I felt I was starting to understand enough to ask questions that made sense and maybe get some players in the draft that could get to the majors. I got to know and learn from legendary scouts such as Lenny Yochim, Tony Robello, Billy Capps, Al LaMacchia, Jim Hughes, Mel Didier, Lou Morton, Red Murff, Boyd Bartley, Red Gaskill, Joe Campise and many others.

One of my biggest moments as a scout came this year when I was in Tulsa, Oklahoma and had the opportunity to meet Tom

Greenwade, the scout who signed Mickey Mantle. Tom was toward the end of his career. He was wearing a coat and tie at the game like so many in his generation had done. Tom was a nice man who was an elite evaluator. Mickey Mantle was the most intimidating player I have seen on a field. His ability was tremendous, but he had a presence on the field like none other I have seen. To meet the man that signed him made me want even more to try and excel at this business.

The start of the season kicked off by attending a pair of conventions in January. One was in Waco, Texas at the High School Coaches Convention. The scouts would meet and socialize as well as get information from the coaches. After the winter off, it was a good start to beginning the season.

The second event was in Baton Rouge, Louisiana at the Belmont Hotel, put on by Tony Johns of the Dodgers. There was a clinic and meetings with a dinner. Between the two events, you saw a lot of coaches and scouts who worked over a five-state area.

Most clubs employed only one scout for the entire state of Texas, with usually one or two other states. In San Diego, we were a small staff of about 12 scouts, so big territories were normal. I had five states and coverage in Mexico. Today, most clubs have one or maybe two scouts in Texas alone, as staff sizes are typically in the mid-twenties range. Without the Scouting Bureau supplying information on schedules, reports, and other information, everything fell on you. Surprisingly, it wasn't that tough if you organized well and did your prep work in the offseason.

I learned early on to try and communicate with coaches in the offseason to get schedules and establish informational avenues. It is amazing when you personally contact someone how much information they will pass on to you, not only on their players, but on opposing players as well. It is a practice that I have used for all the years I scouted for the draft.

I opened the season in Austin at the University of Texas. They had just opened their new field, Disch-Falk Field and it was a beautiful ballpark, especially by college standards. The new field had artificial turf and held around 10,000 people, which they could fill on many occasions. Texas would get many players in my area from high school to attend if they didn't sign for pro ball. As time went on and other programs and their facilities improved, things started to even out. The two years I worked in Texas, the Longhorns had notable players such as Rich Wortham, Jim Gideo, and Keith Moreland. Texas was a national power that had produced and continued to produce several fine major league pitchers.

I watched the first series of the season in Austin, and then went on to begin my travels.

It was nothing for a scout to travel 40,000-60,000 miles a year, as the area was so spread out and there were so many players to see. I had upgraded my car to a new Ford Mustang (which had air conditioning).

Texas itself was among tops in the country for professional baseball prospects. It seemed as the season started that I was driving a couple hundred miles a day. Most of the time in the evenings and early mornings were spent checking on games, weather, and pitching rotations, as we had no publications, internet, cell phones, or social media to assist with obtaining information. You would usually work with a couple of other scouts to share this information, so you could obtain more in a shorter period. Besides, this wasn't giving away any secrets, but just trying to find out who was playing. Scouts today have it made with obtaining information, and don't know how easy it is.

Weather was a big issue during the spring, and I can't tell you how many times I drove 300-400 miles only to get rained out at the last minute, not to mention tornados, snow, and floods. Without a weather channel, a lot of wasted trips were made, and the more contacts you had throughout the area the better off you were. One thing that holds true is that weather effects everyone and no one gets an edge because it can't be controlled. It does get back to making sure that you make every look at a player count.

Although a lot of time is spent in the major cities like Houston, Dallas, and New Orleans, many nights are spent in small towns and staying in tiny motels. The good thing is that scouts all stayed in the same hotel, so we could all get a better rate. When you checked in, all you had to do was ask the clerk, "Who's here?" and they would tell you. The scouts there would then get together in the evening with the cannon of scotch and talk ball.

Often after a game, I would be told, "Kid, come by the room for a couple of pops, then we are all going out for a nice dinner."

Most of those nights would start out with a couple of drinks, and then a couple more, and then a lot more, with dinner ending at Denny's with a Spanish omelet covered in chili.

"Just a few more," I was constantly told.

It wasn't usually just a few more.

I wouldn't have changed anything though, as what I learned at these sessions was invaluable in becoming a better scout. Scouts today stay at different places and don't associate like this and have no way of knowing what they have missed.

The motels we stayed in didn't always have phones, so there were many times when I would ask the front desk for a wakeup call at a certain time. The next morning, I would get a knock on the door at the requested time with someone saying, "Get up."

Nothing like being a big shot in professional baseball and the things we take for granted.

Without cell phones, you relied on your wife as your way of getting messages. People would call your house, give your wife a message, and she would then give you the message to return the calls. If she knew where you were staying that night, she would call the front desk clerk, and they would leave a message at the hotel.

The first thing I checked when I returned to any hotel was to see if that red light on the phone was flashing and how many messages I had. Some days it would take hours to do your phone work.

If you weren't married, you had a message service. I had one for a couple of years and could check at any hour to see if I had any messages. It made me feel like a hot shot. I wasn't too sophisticated.

Even though we didn't get much meal money, scouts had a great network of eateries that didn't cost much. Catfish kitchens, all-you-can-eat steakhouses, hole in the wall diners, and coffee shops, as well as the best truck stops in the region.

One night in New Orleans, I went to dinner with George Bradley with the Phillies and Steve Vrablik with the White Sox. George said we should go to a nice place. We landed at Elmwood Plantation, which was an old plantation with a beautiful house that served as a restaurant. Located near the river, it was an eloquent place, and I was having a great meal, even drinking wine (which I don't do). When the bill came, I nearly fainted. My cut was $75, which was the equivalent of over seven days' meal money. It was something you must do, but for the next seven days I was eating 18 cent hamburgers.

I loved New Orleans and wanted to work out of there. All the restaurants, bars, and jazz clubs around town were amazing. I learned to go where the natives go instead of the French Quarter, which helped stretch the dollar. I was naturally a stupid kid. Mardi Gras was cool though.

Ron Maestri, the coach at the University of New Orleans, became a good friend of mine and said he could probably get me into a dorm room. I was still the age of a college junior, so it was possible. Unfortunately, it didn't work out, as the club said I had to live in Texas. Probably for the best as I may have gotten into trouble there, potentially hindering my work habits.

Something I noticed right away was there were so many more talented players than I had in my previous territory. Even players that I didn't have interest in usually had more ability than what I was used to seeing. The colleges were strong and the high school players were excellent athletes. Texas especially used to let football and basketball players play baseball regularly. The high school pitcher in Texas was often a big, strong kid who threw hard with athleticism and potential to get better.

Junior college programs were strong because of the January Draft, which allowed all junior college players who were eligible to sign before the start of their season. After the season began, the club that drafted a player couldn't sign them until their season concluded and up to one week before the June Draft, which was known as the closed period. It made things more interesting than today, as the January Draft only lasted until 1985.

My first major league player came from the January Draft the very next year.

Working in the South was the first opportunity I had to observe Historically Black Colleges and Universities such as Grambling

State, Jackson State, Prairie View, Southern, and Alcorn State. Most of these schools were in small communities but were on the national stage with athletics, especially football. Two of the programs stand out to this day as being the most hospitable to me: Grambling State and Alcorn State.

The first time I attended a game at Grambling State in Louisiana, the coach was Ralph Waldo Emerson Jones, who was also the president of the school. He would make sure the scouts had the seat they wanted behind home plate and would introduce you to his players and invite you to watch the football team work out after the game. The Grambling State football teams were like the Green Bay Packers of college football and had several players go to the NFL. I enjoyed going to Grambling State.

In 1976, I signed a pitcher from Grambling State, Bobby Jo Dupree. Bobby was the cousin of Billy Jo Dupree, tight end for the Dallas Cowboys. Bobby had a fine arm and was a prospect until he hurt his arm in 1978.

Alcorn State is in the countryside of Mississippi and made for a fairly good drive. I took our crosschecker, Rich Schlenker, there to see Southern University play a doubleheader. Southern had Danny Goodwin, who was going to be the first overall pick in the draft. People went out of their way to make sure we had everything we needed and even offered to share their lunch between games. Considering this was in the 1970's, I probably expected a different response, but am glad I went as I had been told by some people not to go. It's really a shame that some people were the way they were then, and some are today.

My first year, the highest pick I got was a left-handed pitcher from Sam Rayburn High School in the 11th round. His name was Ronald Driver.

After I was notified, I called him and set up a meeting where he lived in Pasadena, Texas, just south of Houston. I left Austin and headed there. It rained all day and when I got to my hotel in Houston, most of the roads on the South Side were closed due to flooding. It had rained seven inches in seven hours, and it took me over five hours to go the 30 miles or so to Pasadena. I zig-zagged through the streets of Pasadena, trying to get to his house. I saw boats going down streets and cars flooded under overpasses, but finally did make it to his home.

Ronald was a strong left-handed pitcher who had potential, and I was excited to get him in the draft until I learned what I could offer him. Remember, San Diego passed out nickels like manhole covers at the time, so I shouldn't have been surprised when I was told I could only give $1,000 and the Incentive Bonus with no college money, though I was surprised, and still am. My father, who was the scouting director, was the best evaluator I had ever been around, but he sure could be cheap with money.

I had a nice meeting with Ron and his family, and everything was going well. They liked that opportunity was present and that we advanced players quickly. What they didn't like was the money. They wanted $5,000.

I called my father and he said go to $2,000 if you must. I countered, and they came back with $3,000.

"Let's take a break and I will get back with you," I told them.

I drove down to the corner gas station, got on the pay phone, and reported the progress. I was feeling good about it and was sure it would be done, but then I got the dreaded news.

"No," my father told me.

I was demoralized and went back to tell the Driver's. They said $3,000 was their bottom line and the negotiation ended. He signed with Milwaukee two years later.

As tough as it was to lose the player, I realized right then that I better learn to become a good negotiator if I want to sign players. It was tough when you heard what other clubs would give players, but I worked hard at it, and think I got pretty good and probably signed a lot of players I wouldn't have if I hadn't taken that approach.

During the summer, I got my first opportunity to do professional coverage of other organizations. I was given half of the Texas League to report on, as well as some teams in the Mexican League. I can say without a doubt that some of my greatest mistakes were made during this coverage, and they were beauties.

One of the teams I was to cover was Pittsburgh's affiliate in Shreveport, which had a big first baseman by the name of Mitchell Page. A strong kid with good power, but a long swing that would swing and miss often. I turned him down and of course he was in the big leagues two years later with Oakland, finishing second to Eddie Murray for American League Rookie of the Year.

It was a real lesson that power hitters will swing and miss but can change a game with one swing. I never forgot.

The second player I missed on was a medium-sized, right-handed pitcher with Midland, an affiliate of the Cubs. The guy had a marginal fastball at best, with an ordinary slider, but threw a funky looking pitch that acted like a forkball. It was a good pitch and I put in my report: "Fair stuff from a medium-sized right-handed pitcher who has a funky off-speed pitch that might get him to Triple-A."

Well, the pitcher saw Triple-A, but from an airplane, flying over Wichita (the Cubs Triple-A affiliate at the time) on his way to Chicago.

The pitcher was Bruce Sutter, and that funky pitch was a split-finger fastball. He not only went on to six All-Star appearances, a Cy Young Award in 1979, and lead the National League five times in saves; but was inducted into the Baseball Hall of Fame in 2006. When I make mistakes, I don't mess around.

As 1976 approached, I started feeling more comfortable about the job. I was still feeling my way through learning about the evaluation process and knew I still didn't know much, but as far as setting up territories and getting contacts in place, I was much better.

I moved to Houston in the offseason to be in a more productive place and found a great apartment next to a pool with all utilities paid that cost $135 per month. I used to keep the air conditioning on when I was on the road for weeks so it would be cool during the heat and humidity when I got home. Can't imagine doing that today.

I developed two great friendships when I moved to Houston: Joe Campise with Atlanta and Benny Galante with the Mets. We lived in the same complex and spent a lot of time together. They showed me the good restaurants in the area, and most importantly, the clubs on Westheimer Boulevard.

I also started my great friendship with Ron Maestri, the baseball coach at the University of New Orleans. Not only a quality coach, but a quality individual. In the January draft one year, I got a pick from Ron's team. Randal "Randy" Miller, a catcher who we would later turn into a relief pitcher, was one of Ron's top players. I told him that I thought we would follow him during the season and try to sign him. After the draft was over, I got a call from the office and was told to sign him because we needed him at our Reno affiliate in the California League. I couldn't believe it, and I was feeling horrible calling Ron to tell him.

When I got a hold of Ron, he was obviously disappointed and asked, "Can't they wait until the end of the season?"

I told him no, and he said okay and that he would set up a meeting room for me to meet with Randy, telling me he was pretty certain that he was going to sign.

When I got to New Orleans, I met Randy and he agreed to a modest bonus (at least we were starting to get modest instead of cheap). All Ron asked was if we could get a picture of Randy signing the contract with Ron and I looking on. He said it would help him with recruiting and make a great day for the kid. Ron always cared about what was best for his players and was a real class act.

On a separate occasion while driving to New Orleans to see Ohio State play a doubleheader, it rained all night and the field was soaked, but Ron really wanted to get the games in because they had come all the way from Ohio. When I got to the field, Ron, his dad, assistant coach, and myself started raking the field by hand, working on the field to try and get it playable. We scraped all the water off the infield that we could, and then put gasoline on the field to light it on fire and get rid of the water. This practice was done often then but is no longer done today with all the new things they have to dry fields.

I often wonder when the smoke came up from the gasoline burning on the field what people in the area must have thought. Probably thought a plane crashed or a building caught fire. Regardless, it worked, and we finally got the field dry enough for the double-header after hours of work.

Before the season started in 1976, I drafted a player in the January draft: Bob Shirley, a left-handed pitcher from Oklahoma. He was drafted the year before in the fifth round by San Francisco and didn't sign so he was eligible for the January draft. I liked his toughness on the mound and the way he challenged hitters. He had a solid-average to above-average fastball, with a late-breaking curveball that was tough on left-handed hitters. We got him in the first round, which in the January draft, there were usually only four or five rounds.

When I met Shirley, we had a difference of opinion on the money, which by now I was used to. He wanted a little more than I had to offer and wouldn't budge. Not being the accomplished negotiator yet, I employed the help of our scout in the Midwest, Al Heist. Al was a former major league outfielder who was exceptionally good in the house talking with people, and he helped to get the deal done. I felt good about this signing and Shirley turned out to have a solid 11-year career and became the first major league player I signed.

After attending the conventions and clinics to start the 1976 scouting season, I was ready to roll for what I hoped would be a big year. As history will tell, it was going to be a good one when it was over.

I started with covering the colleges and it looked to be a strong year. I really liked a pitcher at Tulane University who displayed a plus fastball and had the best short, hard curveball I had seen to that point (and still the best to this day). There were pitchers with better true curves, but his was between a curve and a slider, which today is referred to as a "slurve." It had the break angle of a curve with the power of a slider.

His name was Steve Mura, and I was really hoping to get him in the draft.

Mura was number one on my list and I knew that our club was looking for college pitching. However, we ended up taking Bob Owchinko, a left-handed pitcher from Eastern Michigan, in the first round, fifth overall.

The player that went highest in the draft from my region that year was a shortstop from Brenham High School in Texas by the name of Mark Kuecker. He wasn't a big kid but had good talent across the board. The Giants ended up taking him in the first round, 11th overall.

I didn't think Kuecker was going to be a fit for us, but I needed to have a crosschecker come in and see him.

Donny Williams came to Houston and I picked him up at the airport for the 90-minute drive to Brenham to see a scheduled afternoon game. I had made the scouting sin of not calling for confirmation of the game when someone is coming from out of town to see a player for you. When Donny and I got to the field, not only were there no players getting ready for the game; there was a carnival with rides set up on the field, with a merry-go-round set up at shortstop.

I had nothing to say. I couldn't make any alibis for the carnival on the field.

Donny was calm and sympathetic, but it was my father screaming at me that I was most worried about.

I had gotten to know the coach at Brenham, Terry Logan, and asked if there was any way we could work Kuecker out, being that Donny was there. Terry said sure, and we got to see Kuecker hit in the cage and field ground balls. The day was salvaged.

Another lesson is that you need to know and create working relationships, and not just rely on information from others than the direct source. Donny was satisfied and being Kuecker probably didn't fit for us, everything worked out well.

Scouts would do whatever they could to try and keep other scouts from knowing what they were doing and who they liked. When scouts from the Northern states would come South early in the year, the scouts in Texas would try to lead them on wild goose chases all over so as to miss players they should see.

One time, three or four guys started talking about, "The big guy pitching tomorrow in the Panhandle."

That was 400 miles away.

Of course, it was made up, and this one poor scout took the bait, hook, line, and sinker. He drove to the Panhandle and when I saw him a few days later, he told me, "There wasn't a big guy pitching in the Panhandle."

I just acted surprised, but inside, I must admit I was laughing.

Around that same time in the early spring on a trip to Oklahoma City, I almost got into big trouble at a motel. I checked in and thought my room was #114. When I got to the door, it was slightly open, and I just thought the maid hadn't closed it all the way earlier in the day. When I got in the room, I decided to rest a few minutes before unloading the car. I went in the room, turned on the television, used the bathroom, and laid down on the bed for a few minutes. After a while, I noticed in the corner there were clothes hanging up and a suitcase. I quickly got up, looked at my key, and saw that my room was actually #214.

I moved as fast as I could, straightened up the bed, turned off the TV, and made a beeline out of there. It could have been a disaster if the people had returned while I was there.

It seemed like there were stories constantly from scouts about their adventures in the type of motels we stayed at. It was like when we were at the hotel, the group would be close and share a lot of laughs, but the next day when they were at games, they would do whatever was needed to get an edge on a player and deceive the competition.

A veteran scout once told me that some scouts would hide after a game to see if anyone would talk with a player. They would figure they had interest in the player and would then go and get info on said player. He told me what he used to do to throw guys off track was after a game when he knew they were there; he would go up to a player who he didn't have interest in and speak to him and get info as the other scouts watched. He said as he was leaving, he would hide behind the stands and watch them go up to the kid. It seems like a mean trick, especially to the kid, but in actuality, it probably made the kid's day to get the attention he may not have gotten otherwise and took opposing scouts off the trail of what was actually the interest level of my friend.

Most scouts had networks of bird dog scouts all over their territories. I was once with Campise, who was scouting for Cincinnati, tell me when we were in a little town in North Texas that he thought he had a bird dog there. He had inherited the area and Cincinnati was known for having many contacts and bird dogs. They had so many that it was tough to remember them all. There were many clubs like that, as there was no available information in publications or on the internet, TV, or radio like there is today.

The most bird dogs I had at one time was four or five. If you had someone that really tried to get you information and not someone that used the association to show off in front of people, you were lucky. The best was either coaches, umpires, or former players looking to get into scouting. As helpful as a good one could be, someone that abused it could cause problems and embarrassment. You would always worry that they would say something out of line, or something they had no authority to say.

One of the best ways to obtain information in your area at the time was through newspapers. In my five-state area, I would subscribe to about 10 papers from cities in the five-state region. I could keep up on the colleges and high schools, and follow which players were getting the most attention. The only problem was when you would return from a two-week trip, there would be a huge stack of newspapers waiting. We did what we had to do.

Later in the spring I was going to attend a tournament in San Antonio and since I never had trouble getting a room there before, I didn't make a reservation. I drove a couple hundred miles and when I arrived, I couldn't find a room anywhere, as something was going on in town. The games started early in the morning, so I wasn't going to drive home.

I decided to see if I could sleep inside The Alamo and I figured being it was a church, I could spend the night. I checked every entrance, but it was locked shut. It was probably lucky I didn't get stopped and asked what I was doing. When that failed, I just spent one of the many nights to come throughout the years sleeping in my car.

It seemed that hotels back then had things happen more often than at any other time. Often when I checked in late at night, I would be given a room that was already occupied. This wasn't a good thing as many people carried guns. I was told once while putting in my room key that the man behind the door was going to shoot me if I didn't leave. I left.

This was when I learned to always open the door for the first time from the side and not directly in front of the door.

I had rooms that were dirty with rats running around, blood spots, and mud coming up in the bathtub. Things really have improved, and scouts started staying in nicer places.

One night when I was in Salinas, California, I was in a motel that had a bar outside the parking lot from my room. When I heard gunshots, I moved the dresser in front of the door. My only line of defense was a stapler and some pencils.

When the draft arrived in 1976, I thought I had a chance to get Mura. He was seen and was liked by my father and Schlenker, as well as other scouts who had seen him against their schools. When I got the call that I got him in the second round, I was thrilled. I couldn't wait to get him signed and into pro ball.

Being he was a high pick, Schlenker went with me into the house to negotiate the contract. It took a couple of visits, but we got it done and Mura was on his way.

I didn't know how good of a year this would be for me at the time, getting both Shirley and Mura, as they would both make it to the majors quickly. Shirley arrived the next year in 1977, and Mura arrived in 1978. A year or so later, I saw Shirley pitch a good game against the Dodgers at Dodger Stadium, where he even hit some balls hard during his at-bats. After the game, I went down to the clubhouse to congratulate him and said, "I didn't know you could swing a bat."

"Maybe you would have given me more money," He replied with a smile.

They never forget.

During the summer of 1976, I was sitting in Perko's Coffee Shop in the morning, having a cup of coffee and getting ready to read the paper and look at the sports page. When I got to the sports section, I noticed right away that there was an article about how the Padres owner, Mr. Ray Kroc, fired all the scouts after the club lost a close, one-run game.

I almost fell out of my chair and when I got my act together, I returned home and called the office. I was told not to worry, and that we were all rehired a few hours after it happened. Nothing like the stability of being a baseball scout.

Later that summer I was starting my first professional coverage into the Mexican League. I was given a few names to look at and was going to travel to Tampico to pick up my first game. Tampico was known throughout the league as the stadium with train tracks through the outfield and at times, they would have to stop play to let the trains go by.

I was looking forward to seeing that, but what I was really looking to was seeing Mexican League legend, Héctor Espino.

He was towards the end of his career, but he was the Babe Ruth of Mexico, and the most feared home run hitter to play there, batting .355 with 453 home runs over his 24-year career. Tampico was going to be in Reynosa, right next to the Texas border, so I was told to go there instead. I was disappointed I wouldn't see the Tampico ballpark, but at least I was going to see Espino.

Covering games in Reynosa was good in that you could stay in McAllen, Texas, and drive to the border to take a cab to the ballpark and back. After a while, I decided I would drive over and stay in a motel in Reynosa and have some extra time. That lasted one night.

Although the motel and restaurant were fine, there was Spanish music pumped into my room for 24 hours and made it impossible to sleep. I never could find where it was coming from, so back to McAllen I went. I heard mariachi music in my head for days.

I ended up spending quite a bit of time in Reynosa that summer, and got to know their manager, Jorge Fitch, and his coaches well. They were helpful in assisting me with the Mexican League. They had a pitcher on their club that had pitched in the majors, and I stayed on top of his progress during the summer.

When Tampico came to town, I finally got to see Espino. You could tell he was toward the end of his career, but he still maintained the presence and stature of a star player. When he hit a ball in either batting practice or a game, it was like watching someone hit a golf ball. The ball shot off his bat with such hard contact that it was different than the other players. I can only imagine how he was in his prime.

When the Mexico City Reds came through, I was told to concentrate on Enrique Romo, their right-handed ace. When he was to pitch, he was going up against Mike Nagy, the former Boston Red Sox pitcher, who was the ace of the Reynosa staff.

The attendance at games in Reynosa were fair, at best, but these games against Mexico City packed them in. It turned out to be a great matchup but ended up one of the most bizarre nights I've had in baseball.

I got to the ballpark early and watched a well-pitched game by both pitchers. I normally leave early to catch a taxi back to the border, but this evening, I got into the game and stayed until the end.

When I got outside the stadium, people swarmed to get taxis and I knew if I didn't get one quick, I could get stuck.

"*Taxi aquí señor*," yelled a man.

I reacted fast, jumped into the car, and after a few seconds realized it was not a great move.

The car filled up with people and I was in the middle of the front seat. Everyone started looking at me, speaking faster than my high school Spanish would allow me to follow. On top of this, I saw that the only distinction this car had that it was a taxi was that "Taxi" was written in lipstick on the windshield.

I didn't know Reynosa well, but as we sped off, I knew we were going in the opposite direction of the border. First stop was in a dark residential area that didn't have streetlights. The car came to a complete stop in the middle of the road, and the driver turned off the motor. Everyone again looked at me and then two people got out of the car and I thought I was done.

The pair paid the driver and he got back in the car, put the money in his ashtray, and off we went. We proceeded to drop off a couple of more people and I started feeling a little better as we headed back in the direction of the border.

Once all the patrons had arrived at their destination, we turned into an area I didn't know and stopped at a corner where the driver motioned over to a guy to come to the car. They started talking and looking at me, and finally the man walked over to my window.

His eyes were bloodshot, and he was cutting a piece of fruit with what looked like a machete.

"*Adónde vas?*" he asked in an irritating tone.

"Border," I said.

"*Adónde vas?*" he replied again, but in a louder voice.

All I could think of was a restaurant downtown, and said, "*La Cucaracha.*"

He turned and went back to the driver to say something. They stared at me and *suddenly*, off we went.

When we got to an area I recognized, I said, "*Aquí!*" and threw him more than enough pesos and began heading toward the border crossing.

Looking back, I'm sure they weren't used to having someone like me in that situation, but it was extremely uncomfortable to say the least.

I continued to go to Mexico many times, but I never got into a taxi again unless it had a real sign and markings, and not just "Taxi" written in lipstick.

After the game and adventure, I got back to the hotel and strongly recommended that we try to acquire Romo. He repeated his delivery and threw from many different angles with excellent command of his pitches. He showed a plus fastball, curveball, slider, and an outstanding screwball. He kept hitters off stride all night and struck out a lot of hitters with the screwball. I was hoping we could get him, but Seattle beat us to it, and he had many successful years there.

-

Earlier that year during the draft, I got a low pick in the 25th round by the name of Johnny Jones of Lampasas High School in Texas. He didn't play baseball but was an outstanding football player and sprinter who was going as a member of the United States Olympic Team to the 1976 Olympics in Montreal.

The Padres liked to draft athletes from other sports to hopefully get one to sign one day and encourage kids in other sports to play baseball. It was decided we should go after Johnny.

This kid was a great athlete, and I was excited about the prospect of him playing baseball. I was told he had played baseball up until about junior high school. Before we could draft him, I had to get needed information. This would be difficult. I tried calling the school and sending letters but got no response. I had to resort to undercover work.

I drove into Lampasas around 2 a.m. and looked for any open business. Lampasas is a small town, so my choices were limited. I found a 24-hour service station and went to get gas. Attendants used to pump gas and when the guy came to the car I asked if he knew who Johnny Jones was.

"Sure," he said.

"Do you know where he lives?" I asked.

"Sure."

When I asked if he could tell me, he just stared. Sixty dollars later, I had the address and phone number, which is what I had hoped for.

I still needed his birthdate, and I couldn't think of anyone I could bribe to get it, so the next day I called the high school and somehow talked them into giving me his birthdate.

"Who are you and what do you need it for?" they asked after I had already received it.

I told them I was a scout for the San Diego Padres, and they hung up the phone. Mission accomplished.

After the draft was over, I called and set up an appointment with Johnny, his mother, and grandparents. They were a little confused why a baseball team would want to talk with them, but I reassured them it was something that would be of interest to them.

The day I was to meet with the Jones', I arrived in town a little early and went to a coffee shop to buy a paper and cup of coffee. When I turned to the sports page there was a headline that read: *"Some Nut From San Diego Here To See Johnny Jones."*

The article said that the "Nut" was going to try and sign Johnny to a baseball contract. I, *of course,* was that "Nut." People in Lampasas wanted him to play football after the Olympics for the University of Texas. I wanted to try and change those plans.

When I got to his grandparents' home, his mother and grandparents were there, but no Johnny. We had a nice conversation, but after about an hour, Johnny still wasn't there. His mother was getting upset and said, "Excuse me, I will be back in a few minutes."

In the meantime, I started talking with Johnny's grandfather about what offer we were going to extend. He thought it was a good thing and something to be considered.

After a short time, his mother returned and said Johnny would be there in a few minutes. Apparently, some coaches had hidden close by, hoping I would leave town without seeing him. I'm sure that even though Texas was comfortable they had him attending, they didn't want any distractions.

After explaining why we drafted Johnny, I said it could be a great career choice after the Olympics. We would give him a $6,000 bonus, a college scholarship, and the Incentive Bonus. I told them when he got back from Montréal (where the 1976 Summer Olympics were being held) we could have him go to our Double-A affiliate in Amarillo, Texas. I suggested he could go through a workout and we could talk more about a career in baseball and the offer we extended.

He was a great kid, and this was a wonderful family. We agreed to speak when he returned from the Olympics.

During that summer at the NBC Tournament in La Grange, Texas watching some follows for the next year, there was a big crowd. During one of the games a guy yelled out over where all the scouts were sitting, "Are one of you a scout from San Diego?"

"I am" I replied, *of course.*

"Stay away from Johnny Jones!" the man shouted. "He is going to be a Longhorn!"

That kind of ticked me off, so I shouted back, "Oh yeah. He is going to be a Walla Walla Padre!"

That didn't go over too well, and my friends told me to shut up or I might cause a riot. I behaved but it still ticked me off. I found out later that my friends there were really worried. People take things like sports too seriously sometimes.

When Johnny went to Montréal, he was entered in the 100 meters and the men's relay team. He finished sixth overall in the 100 meters and won a gold medal with the relay team. He became an instant American hero to achieve this at such a young age. He came back to a hero's welcome in Texas.

I tried continuously to get ahold of him and his mother but wasn't having any luck. About the time I was going to give up, I called one more time and finally got in contact with his mom.

She said they decided against going to the workout in Amarillo but appreciated the interest. I thanked her and said I understood. They were genuinely nice people and even though I am sure the University of Texas was keeping close tabs on him; they made the right choice. He had a great college career at Texas and was the number two overall pick in the 1980 NFL draft by the New York Jets.

It still gave me incentive to keep trying to get some great athletes from other sports into baseball.

At the conclusion of the 1976 season, I was asked to move to Northern California and take over that region and the areas of Northern Nevada and the Northwest. It had been covered by Schlenker, who now was becoming the full-time National Crosschecker when my father was elevated to Player Personnel Director and who would spend less time seeing players for the draft. I jumped at this, as I grew up in San Jose, California, and could move and operate from home. It was to be my fourth area in five years.

SAN DIEGO PADRES – SOUTHERN CALIFORNIA

When I left Texas, I headed to my original home of Northern California for my new territory, which also included Northern Nevada and the Northwest. I started setting up the territory for 1977 and completed work in late 1976 for the January draft.

After setting up shop, I was asked to move to Southern California before my suitcase had been unpacked.

Marty Keough had left to join the Los Angeles Dodgers to be a crosschecker. That created an opening late in the year for the Southern California territory. Don Lee, who worked for Boston in Northern California, became available and was hired to cover the region, basically saying, "You move, kid."

It turned out to be a good move. Don was a good baseball man, and it gave me a chance to work in a very productive area with a great scout, Cliff Ditto.

The area that Cliff and I shared was from Fresno south to the Mexican border, Arizona, New Mexico, Southern Nevada, and the El Paso corner of Texas. Clubs today have about four scouts cover that territory. We both covered this entire area and concentrated on the players we decided would fit best for us. We weren't concerned with who liked who best, but that we both liked the player and got the needed work done to supply the proper recommendation to the club.

Cliff was a wonderful man and became one of my closest friends. He was the brother-in-law of famed Dodgers outfielder Duke Snider, worked as a high school counselor in the spring, and managed our Rookie ball club in the summer.

Our friendship blossomed from these days, and he helped lead to some of the most important decisions of my career. We had probably the greatest working relationship there was. We were a team and worked as a team, rarely running into problems. It's likely why we had such success in our years together.

As a counselor at a local high school in Downey, California, Cliff spent the early part of spring in the Los Angeles area. I would screen out the outlying areas, as well as Los Angeles. Cliff and I would spend the last parts of spring where needed. It was a great setup, and we didn't let egos get in the way of doing the proper job.

In the summer when school was over, Cliff would manage our Northwest League team in Walla Walla. It served as our Rookie-level club, and Cliff was one of the best at it. Cliff, Marty, Tom Kotchman, and Pat Daugherty are the best I have seen coach at those levels, as they were not only great teachers, but had the patience needed for players starting their careers. The foundation of the first year for a player is so important, and these four were terrific at getting players ready to move on to the next level.

In 1977, there was a new item added to our operation: the scouting combine with the Toronto Blue Jays. With us and Toronto not participating in the Scouting Bureau, it was decided we would share our reports with each other to give us more coverage than we would normally have. With Peter Bavasi as president in Toronto, and Pat Gillick the scouting director, this seemed like a good fit to try something like this due to their friendship with my father. Nobody voiced any opposition, as we were glad that we weren't a member of the Scouting Bureau and scouts losing jobs. It lasted a few years, and even though it was tough at times, there were things that we did get from this association.

We had many talented scouts with the Padres such as Cliff, Ken Bracey, Rich Schlenker, Jack Bloomfield, Mark Just, Gus Lombardo, Bob Miller, and others. Joining forces with Toronto (who was an expansion team in 1977) who had scouts like Bobby Mattick, Bob Zuk, Al LaMacchia, Bob Engle, Wayne Morgan, and others gave us an enormous amount of experience, success, and knowledge to draw from. After our first meeting together to start the season, I realized right away that I would have a great opportunity to learn much from this group.

A problem that would develop with such talented people on both staffs was that competitive nature would take over, and reports would be written in a way so that the opposite staff would be informed of a player, but not know the extent of the scout's interest. I know this firsthand because I did it. I wanted to be a team player, but I didn't want the other club to know how much I liked a player with the possibility of losing him to Toronto.

With this combine, we would hold workouts together. We would try and work out as many kids as we had on our list as possible before the draft, so that Gillick and my father – as well as all the crosscheckers – could see players in person. It was a pain for us that worked a territory, arranging the facilities and calling all the players to set up where they would work out. The rules at the time required each player get a permission slip from the principal of their school. Most clubs didn't do it, but we were told it had to be done. The other rule stated that only five players could be on the field at one time. It made for long days.

The longer the combine lasted, the more each side tried to deke the other out on who they really had the most interest in. After three years, the combine broke up, but it got us to the point where the Scouting Bureau didn't affect us any longer, as more and more teams who were involved with the Bureau began hiring more scouts. Obviously, you learn quickly that the competitive edge comes from the quality of evaluators you have, and not the shared information you receive.

When I first got to Southern California, I immediately learned two things that most scouts from other clubs weren't required to do. First, because we covered the San Diego region and it was the backyard for our club, you better not miss on anyone. Second, the Padres shared the winter Scout's League team with the White Sox, and Cliff and I were expected to run it along with Gary Johnson, Joe Ingles, and Bill Lentine of Chicago.

Our team was made up of players from our organization and only added an occasional college and high school player. For the next 11 years with the Padres and Montréal Expos, Cliff and I operated this team. It allowed us to keep tabs on the players, make sure they were getting into shape, and allowed them to work on things before they left for spring training. We had a good schedule, as we played other scout teams on weekends and colleges during the week. This helped us see how several college players performed against professionals.

After a few years, we hired legendary high school coach John Herbold from Lakewood High School. We made Lakewood our home base.

John probably had more players from his high school team sign professional contracts and receive scholarships than anyone else at that time. He had a reputation of yelling, but his players were fundamentally strong and he developed throwing mechanics and arm strength better than any high school coach I have seen.

John went to Stanford and was the backup catcher before graduating high in his class. He always wanted to be a baseball coach. He told me once that he would get a letter from the Alumni Association that asked for donations and would have a chart stating if you make a certain amount, you should donate a specific amount. John would tell me that he would write them back saying, "According to your chart, you should owe me money."

John had a great sense of humor and was a quality baseball man.

We had quite a few good players play on our scout team over the years, including Tony Gwynn, Ozzie Smith, Tim Flannery, Eric Show, Ron Tingley, Floyd Chiffer, Bob Geren, and others.

Many players that played in the majors played on this team for years, or for a short time, and it really helped to stay on top of your players before they left for camp. Teams don't do this anymore, deciding instead to have teams comprised of high school players. I know that there is some advantage to getting to know the prep players better, but I always believed you better take care of the players in your system first.

Southern California was a tough area to learn to navigate. The freeways are overwhelming, and the traffic is horrendous – nothing like it is today, though. I always referred to freeways and highways by number, but soon found out that in Southern California they are referred to by name. Scouts would say, "Take the Santa Ana to the Hollywood, to the San Bernardino, to the Pomona."

The biggest problem was if you went the other direction, it would have been taking the Long Beach to the Newport, to the Santa Monica, to the San Diego. I finally got it, but it took some time.

If you planned your schedule right, you could see a college game at 1 p.m., a high school game at 3 p.m., the second half of another high school game at 4:30 p.m., and a college or high school night game at 7 p.m. You learned to plan, and with only two scouts, it was particularly important. Today with the traffic so bad, it would be almost impossible to accomplish and why most clubs have three or four scouts in Southern California alone.

Seeing quickly that scouts would run in packs, going to most of the same games together, you learned who operated in groups and who tended to work alone. You always worried about those who worked alone, and as time went on, I paid close attention to those that did. Sometimes you learned their habits, where they might try to hide, or what it meant when you saw them at certain parks at certain times of the year.

I learned how important it was to not only know the players, but to know the competition that is trying to get those players as well. I took a lot of time researching what players scouts had signed and their tendencies. Particularly: player positions, high school or college, and basically anything that would allow me to know what players they may have interest in. It allowed me to learn what teams were most active in the area, and what type of players they tended to select. This would prove to be a big asset over the years.

My first year in Southern California, I was around so many successful scouts that I kept my mouth shut and only asked questions when appropriate. This worked wonders, as many of these veterans taught me so much and escalated my development.

However, even if they liked you, it didn't mean they wouldn't have fun at your expense.

One afternoon at a game, a couple of scouts told me there was a night game that I should see at Santa Ana Memorial Park. I thought it was great that they were helping me out. I got directions at a gas station and headed to the game.

When I got to the area where I was supposed to go, there were two large stone pillars on the sides of the road with a sign that said, "Santa Ana Memorial Park." It was dark, but I thought it was a big city park with a baseball field at the back end. As I started driving, the location was extremely dark with tall trees. I started looking around, noticing many tall headstones and monuments. That was when I realized my scout *buddies* had sent me to a cemetery.

I got the heck out of there.

Beyond the cemetery were lights in the distance. I found my way to where the lights were and found the ballpark's actual location. When I arrived, the game was in the middle of the first inning.

As I sat down, the group of scouts were laughing and asked, "Any trouble finding the place?"

"No," I said, taking the ribbing in jest.

I felt like an idiot.

Another item you quickly notice in Southern California is the attitude of a lot of coaches have towards scouts. Unlike the other territories I had where most coaches went out of their way to help, they weren't quite as helpful. I think part of it was that they saw scouts so much more, and it only took one scout to give a coach a bad time that would affect everyone. It was different.

Of course, there were coaches like Herbold, Augie Garrido, John Scolinos, Jack Smitheran, Wally Kincaid, Dave Snow, George Horton, and Mike Weathers, that were not only great coaches, but immensely helpful to assisting scouts and their players.

The gasoline crisis in the late 1970's also added to the challenges of the region. The Iran Hostage Crisis caused a disruption in oil imports, which caused a gas shortage. You could only buy gas on the day of the last number on your license plate, whether it was odd or even. I believe Sunday was an open day for purchase. I was able to acquire "C" stamp, which was helpful because it was given to people whose livelihood was dependent on driving, and you could buy gas any day of the week. If you were lucky to find a station with gas, the lines were long and terrible.

I would wake up at 4 a.m., drive my car to a station that opened at 8 a.m., and leave my car in line. I would return to my apartment, sleep until about 7:30 a.m., then go back to the car and get gas. This went on for quite a while, especially in Southern California even though you would never know it by traffic. It was a real break when I would go to Central California, Arizona, Nevada, or the other areas we had, as they didn't have these lines. It is hard to believe today that it happened and can only imagine the turmoil it would cause now.

In 1977, I got my first opportunity to see players play numerous times, due to the amount of talent in the Southern California area. There is never really a bad year in California for talent. Just some years better than others. When you can see three to five games a day, it allows for many more looks than you would get in most areas of the country. When I would go outside the area to other states, my training in the Midwest and Southwest would come in handy, and I felt it gave me an advantage over most of the opposition.

The fields are usually better, mostly because of the weather. The players, although they may not be better athletes, are more refined and polished and can easily fool you. When a kid can play most of the year and be outside, he can expedite his ability. That is why when players sign a contract from cold weather areas, if often takes them a couple of years to catch up with players from Sunbelt regions. But ability is ability, and when they get the time, they will often catch up with the warm weather player, and if ability is better, pass them.

During the time I worked in this area, players could play baseball *and* play football, basketball, and other sports. Today, kids are directed at an early age to play and concentrate on one sport all year. It is a change that I believe really hurts a young kid's overall development. When you play other sports, you learn and develop skills that can make you a better player. It also keeps the player fresh, so as not to get stale in the one sport, and eventually lose interest playing.

My first year in this area would become one of the best that I would enjoy as an area scout. It was a year that the draft would produce three Hall of Famers and many All-Stars. Paul Molitor, Tim Raines, Harold Baines, Chili Davis, Danny Ainge, Terry Francona, and many others were selected in 1977. Cliff and I would get a future Hall of Famer in this draft, in the fourth round; while six of the Padres first 10 selections were from our region, and 10 of the first 20.

We signed most of the players, including the first-round selection, Brian Greer, an outfielder from Sonora High School in La Habra, California. Brian was an excellent athlete who possessed the five tools you look for in a player. He was a strong kid who could run and throw above average as well as play an excellent center field.

He had a quick swing that would show hard contact and above-average power.

It took some time to get him signed, as we didn't spend the big bucks. The subject came up of adding a McDonald's franchise to the deal. It didn't happen, but we did offer a contract which would get him to the majors quickly.

When Brian attended his first spring training with the major league club in Yuma, Arizona, he was 18 years old and made a big impression. He opened the season in the Northwest League, and although he struggled with contact, he did show power. He ended up having some problems playing under the lights.

Brian finished the season with the major league club in September as part of his agreement and got an at-bat. He struggled the next few years making contact, though he showed good power potential and played exceptional defense in center field. He got the majors again in 1979, mostly due to his ability as a defender who would come in late in games, and enjoyed the first winning season in club history. He was one of the most talented high school players I ever saw and had he been able to make enough contact, I believe he would have been a solid major leaguer.

I learned that you can't second-guess yourself when you take a player with this type of talent. Even though he only played a few games in the majors, I would take him all over again.

In the 10th round, we selected a catcher out of Ramona High School in Riverside, California, by the name of Ron Tingley. Ron was an outfielder who we selected as a catcher, who had a lean build and did things with ease. He took to catching quickly and had soft reception with a loose arm that generated above-average throws with accuracy to second base. He was a line-drive hitter, who didn't hit a lot in his career, but played nine years in the majors as a backup catcher. Ron loved to play and would play on our Scout's League team in the winter for many years before he reached the majors. He possessed a great approach to the game.

The third player that reached the Majors was a career draftee for us, Osborne Earl Smith, better known as "Ozzie." He was the club's fourth-round selection from Cal Poly San Luis Obispo. Ozzie was the finest defensive player I have ever seen as an amateur (and as a pro). He was selected in the seventh round of the 1976 draft by the Tigers but did not sign and returned to Cal Poly. The question with Ozzie was the bat. A contact-oriented switch-hitter, he didn't have a lot of power. The feeling was if he didn't hit enough, he would be a utility infielder for many years, but because he was a switch-hitter there was a chance he would hit. It's the main reason he slipped to us in the fourth round.

Needless to say, he did hit and more. He was elected to the Baseball Hall of Fame in 2002.

During this draft, we selected Eric Mustad, a right-handed pitcher from Cal State Fullerton, in the 15th round. Eric didn't pitch in the majors, but his negotiation became a first for me. He had an agent, and I had never negotiated with an agent before, as very few draftees, *if any*, had one. In fact, most major league players were just starting to get them.

I met with Eric and his agent at the agent's house. I was a little nervous in that we were only going to offer a $500 bonus or the Incentive Bonus (another gigantic San Diego offer). I arrived and right away knew something didn't look quite right.

As I looked around, I saw swords everywhere on the walls.

"Who do you represent?" I asked the agent.

"Bullfighters."

Right then I thought he might pretend I'm a bull when he hears our offer, and we all know what they do to the bulls.

This agent turned out to be one of the best I ever dealt with. Eric was a great kid, and this gentleman was just trying to get the best for him. When I made the offer, the agent looked at Eric and said, "Eric, unless you really need the $500, I would take the Incentive Bonus Plan and try to make the $7,500 it could be worth."

Eric agreed, and signed for the Incentive. He ended up making $2,500 out of the possible $7,500 when he made it to Triple-A. I wish all agents or representatives I had to deal with through the years were like this one.

The summer coverage in this region was easier than what I had experienced in the other territories. You could see so many amateur summer teams in American Legion, Connie Mack, Thoroughbred, Babe Ruth, and other organized leagues. There were summer college teams in a collegiate league, as well as summer powers out of Santa Maria and Eureka. There would be big tournaments during the Fourth of July weekend, and regional tournaments as teams tried to qualify for their league's final national tournament.

Long Beach had the Connie Mack League play at the legendary Blair Field, originally built in 1924, all summer. Long Beach has been a hub for quality baseball players, and between the Moore League in the spring that had many of the top high school programs in Southern California, and the Connie Mack League in the summer, you would see several talented young players. You could go there almost any day and see a doubleheader. It was an incredibly competitive league that showcased many of the top amateur players for future years.

I always looked forward to the Connie Mack World Series in Farmington, New Mexico. It is as well-run an event as I have been to for amateur baseball. The town gets into it and supports it to where it is a premier tournament. Not only were the teams of quality, but provided the players exceptional experience as well. They treated the scouts as well as we could be treated anywhere, and it was a fun time. It was not uncommon for a game to draw 6,000-8,000 people, and when the home team played, it was filled to capacity.

These types of tournaments have been replaced in many ways by showcase baseball, which is basically a tryout for a player. Even though they are still playing these tournaments, most of the best players perform at showcases. You can't blame the kid for going to the showcase, as he can be seen by so many scouts and club officials, along with so many other talented players. However, the competitive environment is so important to see how a player performs to his ability when you are on a team trying to win, and that competitiveness is important in an overall evaluation. Unfortunately, there are less and less competitive events to watch a young player.

The year 1978 turned out to be a solid one for us, as we signed four players that reached the majors. It was a solid draft throughout the country with players like Bob Horner, Lloyd Moseby, Hubie Brooks, Kirk Gibson, Dave Stieb, and of course, Cal Ripken Jr. It was also the year I saw the best young high school pitcher that I have seen, Mike Morgan from Valley High School in Las Vegas.

Morgan had one of the liveliest, quickest arms I have seen. The ball came out of his hand free and easy. The delivery needed some work, but the power to his fastball and the spin to his curveball were potentially overpowering.

The first time I saw him play, I immediately thought, "Wow, we have to have him."

Our staff that came in to see him liked him as well and I really felt good about our chances and with the clubs in front of us, I thought we had a strong shot. The one club I wasn't worried about was Oakland, as they didn't usually like kids that were looking for a large bonus. Morgan had even told certain clubs that he wouldn't have interest in signing with them. Oakland didn't have many scouts and I really didn't see them as a threat. Wrong again.

Oakland selected Morgan the pick ahead of us in the first round, and Tim Conroy, a high school pitcher, in the second.

I still didn't think they would sign him, but the next thing you know he is signed, and they started both Morgan and Conroy in the majors. Morgan pitched 22 years in the majors, and although he didn't become the 20-game winner I thought he would be, how can you not be impressed with a Major League career that lasted that long? I still wish he would have been a Padre.

We selected nine players this year from my territory, with four of those kids reaching the majors.

Tim Flannery, who we got in the sixth round; and Eric Show, who we got in the 18th, had the longest careers. Flannery was a hard-nosed second baseman who was a solid line drive hitter and made good contact to all fields. He wasn't a particularly good runner, but played a solid second base, learning to play hitters and really turn the double play. He had an 11-year career, both as a regular and utility player. He was an extremely popular player in San

Diego because of his aggressive play. After his playing years were over, he coached many years before leaving and spending time as a successful musician.

Eric became a top-of-the-rotation pitcher for the Padres and pitched in the majors for 11 years. He won over 100 games and is probably most identified with giving up Pete Rose's' record 4,192[nd] hit. He had a quick delivery with a compact arm that got on hitters quickly. He showed a solid fastball with a quick, late breaking slider that was his out pitch. He was tough on hitters and got the most out of his ability.

When I met Eric to try and sign him, it was different than any other player I had tried to sign previously. I went to his apartment where he was holding a guitar, as he liked to play music and was his real interest. I found out right away that he wasn't much of a baseball fan as when I started talking about our team (which was 90 miles away) he knew almost nothing about us. When I brought up Dave Winfield's name as one of our top young players, he responded with, "I think I've heard of him."

Eric loved to play the game but didn't show much interest in it other than that. Had he not died young, I'm not so sure he would have watched too many games in his retirement years. One thing is that he always remembered Cliff and I when telling people about how he got started.

Cliff and I got to see Eric when UC Riverside played at Chapman for a night game. We thought we had this kid pretty much to ourselves, as he was inconsistent, but were somewhat worried about the Mets. When we saw their scout at the game, we decided we would stand on each side of him and try to distract him if Eric started throwing well. There were no radar guns yet, making it much easier to distract guys during the game. Eric threw some nasty sliders that night, but we talked so much that we accomplished our goal of keeping the scout from realizing how well Eric was throwing.

"L-R: Cliff Ditto, Eric Show, Me; Eric being honored at banquet in Santa Maria"

One of the big accomplishments you have as a scout is when you can learn to talk and keep other scouts distracted, yet not miss what is going on in the game yourself. It takes time, as for many years I couldn't do it, and *I* would be the one distracted. It is a great tool though once you can master it.

Is it another reason why I learned to scout from the side – anywhere from first or third base to the foul poles – and not behind home plate. I wanted to get away from all the talking and concentrate solely on what I was doing. I would be sociable before the game, but when it started, I would move down the lines. In time, I learned this is by far the best place to evaluate a game.

From the side angle, the field is in front of you, so you can see every aspect of the game. When you sit behind home plate, the game is coming directly at you or going away from you. The side look lets you see true carry of throws, foot work, balance of players in the field, hitting approach, swing load, swing start to finish and bat speed, pitching deliveries start to finish, velocity, finish of a breaking ball, angle to plate, and many other things. That's hard to see when something is coming right at you or moving away from you.

During the summer, the Padres hosted the All-Star Game. I hadn't been to one before, so I was looking forward to going. All-Star and World Series games always had a lot of pre-game and post-game parties in big tents and in large rooms of the stadium, and Mr. Ray Kroc went out of his way to make this one a first-class event.

The night before the game there was a big party at SeaWorld, with a food and drink spread like I had never seen. There was entertainment while the orcas and dolphins put on a show, with a big fireworks display ending the night.

At the ballpark the next day, there was once again a massive food spread you wouldn't believe in the Stadium Club. I don't think I've ever seen so many giant Gulf shrimp as I saw that night. Funny the things you remember.

About halfway through the party prior to the game, there came some commotion from the front door. As I looked over, there was Gerald Ford. Celebrities loved to come to baseball games, and here was the President of the United States from the year prior. He was swamped by people, but I maneuvered over with my wife to make sure we introduced ourselves and had our picture taken. Just as nice in person as he seemed on television.

"1978 All-Star Game, L-R: President Gerald Ford, Terri (Jim, Joey, and Josanna's mother), Me"

I met another president later in 2000 when returning from the general manager meetings in Amelia Island, Florida. I was in the Delta Crown Room with Duane Shaffer and our wives. While waiting for our connecting flight, Jimmy Carter suddenly walked in with a few secret service men. They went to the side room so I thought we wouldn't see him again. Suddenly, he walked out headed towards the bathroom.

Reacting to opportunity, I told Duane I'm going for the autograph.

"I'm going too," Duane replied.

Outside the bathroom stood a secret service member.

"Can I ask the President for his autograph?" I asked.

"Sure."

As soon as Mr. Carter opened the door, we hit him like a tsunami.

"Mr. President, will you sign this?"

All I had was my ticket jacket, and Mr. Carter proceeded to sign it and whatever Duane had with him. He didn't say anything and didn't look happy in doing so. The secret service member was much nicer than Mr. Carter. I figured I didn't vote for him, so no big deal. I had another Presidential autograph.

The 1979 draft was unique in that there were three future NFL quarterbacks of stature selected, with two Hall of Famers. John Elway, Dan Marino, and Jay Schroeder were selected, and although Schroeder signed after being taken third overall by Toronto, he made his name in football like Elway and Marino.

This really illustrates that good athletes can do almost anything if they want. It also shows that they used to let players play different sports, which most do not do today.

Don Mattingly and Tim Wallach also came from this draft and had long, productive careers. Watching Mattingly prepare for a game was a real clinic in how to get ready to play. A real professional player.

It was also the year I would get another first-round pick: Bob Geren, a catcher from Claremont High School in San Diego.

Bob was a big, strong kid who played the game hard and with a lot of enthusiasm. He had a good arm and power. His swing was a little long, but with bat speed and hard contact. He caught well but couldn't run, which you don't expect much from a catcher.

Bob really wanted to sign, and I negotiated with him and his parents. The negotiations were quick and smooth, and he received what both sides figured on and then left to start his career after signing for $52,000. The night he signed his contract, his parents had a big party for him with his family and friends all present. It was a fun night, and how you want to see a kid have a sendoff to start his pro career.

I used to tell every player I ever signed that the most important contract they would ever sign is the first one. It all starts there. Whether it is for $5,000,000 or $500, it is the contract that allows you the opportunity to have a great career and make a lot of money. When you think about how few get the opportunity to sign a contract, it should make you feel honored no matter what the money amount, as hundreds of thousands of players are eligible and would love to have the opportunity.

I also got the second-round selection in 1979: Derek Tatsuno, a left-handed pitcher out of the University of Hawaii. Derek had a dynamic arm that had a quick arm action and a fastball that jumped on a hitter. He wasn't very tall, but he created enough of an angle that he was equally tough on right-handed and left-handed hitters. He was the first college pitcher to reach 20 wins in a season.

Hawaii came to play Cal State Fullerton that year, and both teams were national powers. The Titans had Wallach at third base, making for a great matchup. Tatsuno showed how tough he could be against professional hitters and was extremely aggressive and confident with his approach to the game.

After Tatsuno was selected, I called him to tell him that I had gotten him in the draft and would be handling the negotiation. He was a nice kid who told me about his home in Hawaii and we discussed when to meet to start negotiating.

After setting a day and time, I got my ticket, hotel reservation, and was really looking forward to my first trip to Hawaii. A couple of days before I was to leave, Derek called me and said, "I have an agent, can you talk with him?"

"Of course," I replied. "Have him be there."

"Well..." I heard after some silence. "He is in Los Angeles. Can you meet him there?

"Yes," I said with a quiet sigh so Derek couldn't hear.

I was destroyed, as instead of the beaches in Hawaii, I was going to the smoggy skies of downtown Los Angeles. What else could I say? Beautiful.

I went to the office of the agent and right away it didn't seem like this was going to go smooth. We were offering a great deal, not just from the Padres, but from anyone. We were going to pay a solid bonus, start him in Triple-A Hawaii of the Pacific Coast League, and get him into position to get to the majors in a hurry. It didn't faze him at all.

Apparently, they had a desire to go to Japan to play and make big money. The problem for Derek was that if he was drafted in the United States, he couldn't play in the Japanese League because was the agreement between Major League Baseball and the Japanese majors.

After a long negotiation and our front office attempting to get him signed, he went to play for what I understand was an industrial league team in Japan. He did that for a while, but teams kept drafting him in the United States and he never did play in the Japanese majors. He came back to the United States and played in the minors for a few years, but never made it to the majors. This one was a real disappointment for me, as I think if he had signed with us, he would have been in the big leagues in a hurry. Such a good arm.

As 1980 approached, I had no idea that it would be such an eventful year, both good and bad. It was a good draft year with top players such as Daryl Strawberry, Darnell Coles, and Doug Drabek. We were still involved with Toronto in the combine for what would be the last year, as it was becoming obvious both clubs were trying to slant reports their way. We did have a workout in San Diego that year, which had three first-round draft picks and the fifth player taken in the second round.

The workout took place at Hoover High School in San Diego and had Coles, Cecil Espy, Eric Erickson, and Billy Beane. It was an interesting workout because all possessed a lot of ability. Coles was the fastest of the group that could all run well. They could all throw and had good bat speed with power potential. Erickson was primarily a pitcher, even though he played a position in high school and pitched professionally. In this workout he wasn't fazed by the others at all and competed against them aggressively. He tried to rise to the competition and in his mind, he wanted to show everyone he was as good.

It was a competitive workout and Coles came out of it looking like he was ahead of the others. Although Espy and Beane got the majors, Coles had the best career. Erickson, however, never pitched in the majors. When you get quality players together, you learn a lot about the makeup and competitive nature of the individual. To realize the full potential of a player, they need these intangibles.

I did get to know Beane as I worked him out on a couple of occasions, and we have been friends since. Billy is an innovative baseball man who isn't afraid to change when it is required, and he understands the player probably better than most general managers. He went on to a lengthy executive career after his playing days.

We got six players out of the area in the draft, with only two reaching the majors: George Hinshaw, an outfielder out of La Verne University who we drafted in the 11th round; and Mike Couchee, a right-handed pitcher out of USC who we took in the 19th round.

George was a strong athlete who could generate power out of his bat. I learned a lot from George's swing, as he had a quick bat but was often late making contact and would hit a lot to the opposite side. He got a late start loading his hands for his swing and this caused a quick swing to be late making contact. I asked questions and found out if it could be fixed, and George made the adjustment to start his bat on time and give him pull power. He did make it to San Diego for a couple of short stints before playing in Japan. Learning something like this stays with you in the future so you don't penalize a hitter for something that can he helped.

Couchee had been drafted a couple of times before and was now a senior with the Trojans. He was from Los Gatos, California, which was right next to where I grew up in San Jose, and our high schools were in the same league together. I went up to sign him and was looking forward to getting him started. Mike has a great family and I got to know his father through the years while he was a player with the Padres and when we both worked with the Angels.

When we started the meeting in their house and talked about the organization, I felt comfortable this would get done. Mike had been drafted before and I am sure turned down much more money than we offered, but he knew as a senior in college there wouldn't be a lot of money. I offered the lucrative San Diego bonus (actually, this one was bigger than most as I think it was $1,000) and asked if he would rather have the cash bonus or the Incentive Bonus. He thought for a minute and said the cash bonus.

With the agreement in place, I proceeded to prepare the contract. Scouts used to write up the contracts in the house after an agreement was made.

I couldn't find a pen, so I told Mike, "I have a pencil I will write the contract with."

Mike jumped up and said, "Oh no! I will get you a pen. I don't want you erasing it when you leave."

Mike and I still laugh about that to this day.

He made it the majors, as he had a nasty slider that could be tough on a hitter, and after his playing days had a long career as a highly successful pitching coach.

As I was getting ready to start my summer coverage of professional leagues, a major change hit our organization that would affect my direction in baseball for the next 40 years.

My father, who had been the team's general manager since 1978, was dismissed from his duties by Mr. Ray Kroc while attending the All-Star Game in Los Angeles. It was done before the game, and not after he had returned. It was an obvious shock and tough to see happen, as he had been in San Diego since the Padres were formed as an expansion team in 1969. When he returned home, we spent a lot of time talking about the future.

We spent the next couple of weeks looking at options. He had a few offers immediately and was trying to figure out which direction would be best. For me, I knew it would be tough to stay. I was finishing only my eighth year as a scout, so my options were clearly more limited.

After a couple of weeks, I was asked to come down to the Padres offices at Jack Murphy Stadium. Jack McKeon, who was my father's assistant, was now the interim general manager. I figured they would probably ask me to leave.

When I arrived to meet with Jack and the club president, Ballard Smith, I figured it would be my last day with the team even though I wanted to see if they would let me finish out my contract. It was a little uncomfortable, which is understandable after what happened with my father.

To my surprise, they said they wanted me to stay.

I was told they knew it may be hard at times, but that they still wanted me to stay and take time before deciding. I said I would, and that it was important to me to finish my assignments for the summer, and that I would come back and talk with them at the end of August. Deep down, I believed I was done at the end of August.

I had a number of Triple-A teams to cover in the Midwest and East and was looking forward to getting away to think about what I was going to do after I was done with the Padres in a month.

My father decided to take a position with the San Francisco Giants as player personnel director and to oversee their scouting and minor league operations. I was starting to talk with a few teams that had contacted me about possibly working for them in 1981. Around the middle of August, I had agreed with the Houston Astros, and was looking forward to a new chapter.

Lynwood Stallings, who was Houston's scouting director, contacted me and offered a good position covering a large portion of California. Lynwood was a well-respected baseball man who did a great job helping build the Astros farm system. I had known Walt Matthews, one of their top scouts, for some years, and I was excited to be a part of their staff and learn from these men. The

Astros were on their way to the playoffs in 1980, and this looked like a team headed for good things.

As the summer went on, I worked relaxed, as I knew where my future was. I think I did a good job in my work as I was totally focused.

I went to War Memorial Stadium to see Buffalo play and Dave Dravecky – who we ended up trading for – pitch. It was an old stadium that housed both the Buffalo Bills of the NFL and the Double-A Buffalo Bisons of the Eastern League. It was an extremely odd-looking stadium, especially for baseball, but had so much history. I kept thinking of O.J. Simpson, Jack Kemp, Billy Joe, Lou Saban, and others and what it must have been like in the heyday.

It would also be home of the New York Knights in the movie, "*The Natural,*" before it was torn down. You would enter through the tunnel that Robert Redford and Robert Duvall spoke in during a scene in the movie when they were leaving the park after Redford hit the cover off the ball in his first game. I love history and it is fun to go to places like this.

Dravecky had a solid Major League career with the Padres and Giants before losing his left arm to cancer. His arm broke during a game after he threw a pitch and after a long rehabilitation, he returned only to have it break again and ultimately be amputated. He became a motivational speaker and writer who inspired many people. I sat next to him on a plane one time, and we talked about the Padres and baseball and his wonderful efforts to help people. What an example and good person.

When I returned home at the end of August after my work was done, I set up an appointment to meet with Ballard Smith and Jack McKeon again. I was all set to go in and tell them I appreciate their invitation to stay, but that I thought under the circumstances it was best that I moved on.

I got to the ballpark, sat, and talked a little about the summer, and then settled into business. I started by saying I really thought about what they said to me the month before, but that it was probably for the best that I should leave. They said they understood but give it a couple more days and come back in and tell us what it would take to keep me. I couldn't believe they still wanted me to stay.

When I got home, I called my father and told what happened and asked, "How do I get out of this graciously?"

We talked for a while and he finally said, "Tell them that you will stay if you can become the scouting director and make $25,000. That should end it one way or another."

"If I say that they won't stop laughing for a week," I replied.

After working up the nerve I went back to the stadium a couple of days later and told Ballard and Jack that I wanted to be scouting director and make $25,000, or that it would be best that I leave.

After we all had a good laugh, I said goodbye and thanked them, feeling that I did indeed get out graciously.

Two days later, I received a call from Jack.

"You've got the job. We want to offer you the scouting director's position."

I was in shock.

"Thank you, but can I have a day?"

"Sure."

I immediately called my father and he started laughing.

I'm sure it hurt him to think I would still be there, but he said to me, "If you don't take it, it won't help me get my job back. You should do it."

He knew the experience I would get from it would be beneficial for my whole career. I called Jack back.

"Thanks. I accept."

I called Lynwood in Houston right after to tell him. I think his reaction, as well as everyone else's, was shock more than anything else. He was happy for me and wished me luck. Needing luck was an understatement.

The staff in San Diego had to be more shocked than anyone, but as time would show, there couldn't have been a more loyal, dedicated group towards helping a young person in charge than this staff. I was 27, and the youngest on the staff with only nine years of field experience. Today on some staffs, I would be the veteran mentor of a staff.

After letting the shock subside for a few days, I started to get my thoughts together. I put ideas on paper and communicated with each scout individually to let them know how much I needed their help. It wasn't lip service. It was the truth and I really believe that they all accepted and appreciated it.

I went to the stadium, got situated in my office, and started a job that I would soon find that I enjoyed as much as anyone could. To be working with a group of scouts I respected and oversee selecting players for the future of your club was as exciting and as much fun as I had hoped.

The first day I was in the office, Mr. Kroc came in and congratulated me and wished me luck. He had recently had a stroke and moved around the office on a scooter. You could hear him come down the hall, so you always had a little warning that he may be headed your way. He had owned the club for the last eight years and there was never a dull moment.

People in the office knew that Mr. Kroc didn't like a messy desk, and my desk led the way at being a mess. The staff placed a tall file cabinet next to my desk that would shield its view from the hall. Mr. Kroc would never see it. In 22 years of front office experience, my administrative organization never really improved.

Not long after I got the job, I was in a meeting room by myself going over maps and lists when I heard Mr. Kroc beep the horn on his scooter, come in the room, and ride right up to me. The stroke had caused his eye to drift, so I wasn't sure where he was looking but I assumed he was looking at me.

"How are we going to get people in the park?" he growled.

This was the least of my expertise.

"Why don't we give away a car?" I replied.

He looked at me with a look as if to say, "What the hell kind of answer is that?" but instead just stared at me and rode off.

The start of my career as a scouting director was officially underway. I can only imagine what people thought. Good thing I didn't really care that much.

SAN DIEGO PADRES – SCOUTING DIRECTOR

One of the first things I did when taking after becoming Scouting Director was redesign the territories and change the crosscheck system. I knew it would be important to have a lot of opinions for me to feel comfortable making selections. I had thought about this often but didn't know I would ever be able to institute it.

One thing I had going for me was that we had a group of successful, experienced scouts, and a few young, new scouts to groom and incorporate into our staff.

We had such veteran and new scouts as; Ken Bracey, Cliff Ditto, Al Heist, Bob Miller, Denny Galehouse, Jim Marshall, Jim Zerilla, Brad Sloan, Gary Sutherland, and Jack Hays.

With a starting point like this, and the fact that I knew and had already worked with them, I experienced much less drama than if someone else from outside the organization would have received the job.

We had a meeting in Mesa, Arizona before the season to go over changes I had put in place and to talk about players going into the year. I guess I kept referring and apologizing for the fact I was 27 years old and the youngest in the room. I didn't realize it, but Cliff pulled me aside and told me to knock it off.

"Quit talking about your age," he said. "We all know how old you are. We know you are in charge and we all want to do a good job, so talk about what we are going to do and let's get started."

It's why I looked up to Cliff so much. He had so much common sense and could read situations so well. He was right and from that point I felt like I started to take charge.

As the initial meeting went on and I informed the guys of how I wanted to design our structure, they seemed to buy into it. I broke the country into three regions, with a coordinator who oversaw and crosschecked the scouts in each region. We were to have a National Crosschecker and National Pitching Crosschecker. This type of system would allow more opinions on players and have a specialized approach to pitching, which is extremely important the deeper you get into the draft. These types of structures are relatively standard today, but in 1981 most clubs had the scouting director and a few crosscheckers do the comparison work.

I believe in this type of scouting system, as it helps to get an even amount of looks at players from every part of the country and get the depth of looks needed to have a strong draft. I always tried when possible to get an odd number of looks at a player so that it would eliminate biases and allow me to not have to break any ties in opinion. It wasn't always possible, but it does help the process quite a bit.

Before I got the job, it had already been decided that we would no longer be involved in a combine with Toronto. With my father no longer with the club, it made sense to part because he had such a close relationship with Pat Gillick and Peter Bavasi. I sure would have liked to see it continue, but I think the scouts on both sides were ready to move on. Without that combine, many scouts from both sides may not have stayed working as scouts if the two teams would have gone into the Scouting Bureau.

With the domestic staff in place and a structure and plan, I turned to our international coverage. I had only one of my 19 years as a scouting director come with a substantial amount of money to work with on the international side, having truly little most years. This was one of the years where I had little money.

We had one scout in Latin America, Luis "Louie" Rosa. Over his career, he would sign a lot of major league players. After attending a fall event in Orlando for a few days, I went to Puerto Rico to meet Louie and take a tour of Puerto Rico, Venezuela, and the Dominican Republic. We were slated to have tryouts in all three countries, with two days in San Juan, Puerto Rico before proceeding on to the Dominican Republic.

The next couple days after a few tryouts, we signed some players in the Dominican and headed to Venezuela. We got to Caracas and right away you could tell this was a flourishing city. That was in the heyday of the country before they experienced the problems they have today.

We checked into the Hotel Bravo, a small local hotel with rooms the size of a walk-in closet, no air-conditioning, and no television. No one spoke English, and I got on Louie about why no Sheraton or Marriott were in these countries. He said he thought I would like to try this experience of penurious hotels. Wrong. I'm just a pampered American.

We were in a cool part of town, and when I got up in the morning I strolled downtown. It was like being in any major city, with people hustling everywhere and dressed in business attire.

I found a small cafe and settled in for a few cups of coffee. After ordering, I was brought a little cup with coffee and cream that only took a few swallows. I ordered three more before it hit me. I didn't know the power of Latin coffee and those four cups had me bouncing around for days. Sleep became a problem, and I learned my lesson for future trips.

Later that day, we went to the local ballpark to meet with the owner of the La Guairá Tiburones, Pedro Padron. Pedro had an interesting system of developing players that would be future members of his team. He signed several young kids who would live in dorms at the ballpark and work out each day in the stadium before the game at night. He wanted these kids to sign and go to the United States to become good players, and then return to La Guairá for the Venezuelan Winter League.

When we got to the park, Pedro took us to the field to watch these young kids go through their workout. It was a good group of young players, but there was one kid at shortstop that was *really* interesting. He was highly active with quick feet and first-step reactions. He had a good throwing action and an arm you knew would get better. His swing from the left side had an even path to the ball. He was yelling encouragement to the other players and looked to be having a lot of fun.

When the workout was over, we told Pedro that we wanted to talk with him about some of his players.

I told Louie we needed to sign the shortstop even though he was only 16. Louie agreed, but said we may have to sign another player or two to get him. No problem. We needed to do it.

That night after the winter league game started, Louie and I met with Pedro down in the training room of the clubhouse. Over a training table with Louie and I on one side and Pedro on the other, we started negotiating.

"We want the shortstop," I said with Louie interpreting.

"Alright, but you must sign more," Pedro replied.

After some give and take, it was decided for us to get the shortstop we would have to sign three other players. Easy agreement. For $5,000, we signed the shortstop, a third baseman, and two outfielders.

The shortstop was Ozzie Guillén, who would be the American League Rookie of the Year in 1985 and played 16 years in the majors, earning three All-Star selections.

We left the next day after spending the night at a beautiful hotel resort in La Guairá. It had been a successful trip and a real learning experience for me that would help me through the rest of my career. It was basic scouting, and there was no one tipping you off or giving advance notice about players, such as it is today.

When I arrived back in San Diego and got to the stadium, I found out quickly that I had messed up greatly. I didn't know anything about the visa allotment each club had and came back with eight players signed without knowing what visa slots we had left.

Jim Weigel, our minor league director, couldn't believe what I had done. I now know he was right about me not checking on visas first. It was ok to sign a few players without telling him but signing eight players really put him in a bind. Jim figured it out, but I never signed anyone that needed a visa again without checking first.

After January 1, 1981, before the domestic amateur scouting season started, we took a team of our young minor league players from

Latin America along with some pitchers from the United States to play in a week-long tournament in Guatemala. Louie, Jim Weigel, Manny Crespo, Jim Zerrila, and I took the team down there.

Weigel and I met the American-born players as we were coming from Los Angeles. We were on a Pan Am flight that seemed to take forever, and as we were getting ready to land in Guatemala City, we looked out the window and saw soldiers with big guns hiding in the bushes to the side of the runway. There was a civil war going on in neighboring El Salvador, and it seems some of it spilled over to Guatemala. *Swell.*

We were put up in a nice hotel and all our young players were excited about the tournament. We opened with a night game against the home team, where a good-sized crowd watched, creating a great atmosphere. Little did we know that it wouldn't last.

The local team loaded up with players from Central America and beat our young kids who were nervous. The natives were upset.

"Padres minor leaguers in Guatemala, 1981"

Even though we won our next six games in a row by large margins, the people were still mad. Unknown to us, our team had been advertised as the major league Padres, and not a team of minor league players. The newspapers said we were imposters. Even with all this and our team being the youngest present, our kids kept getting better and dominated.

After the final game in which we beat the local team that beat us soundly the first game, the fans got restless. They were trying to grab our equipment and we hurried everyone into the clubhouse. The fans were getting loud and rowdy outside, and police had to come to escort us to the bus.

As we got on the bus, people outside were banging on the sides and our kids sat in total silence. These kids had never been through anything like this. We made it out safely, and when we got to the hotel, we told the players to stay close.

For Weigel and me, it was the second tense event that we had encountered.

We had heard about a town an hour or so outside of Guatemala City that sold Jade, a rare gemstone, and on an off day early in the week, Jim and I decided to go. We were provided a driver and off we went. It was a neat town, but you could see bullet holes in several buildings. The rebel activity was clearly in the area.

While heading back to the hotel, we were stopped by a group of soldiers with bulletproof vests and big guns at a military roadblock (all guns look big to me when someone else is holding them). The soldiers were looking for something, and suddenly, we noticed they were looking right at us. It was at that time you realize you don't know the driver and who he may be involved with, as well as not knowing what anyone is saying. However, they let us go after a while. Another not so wise choice, but we did get the Jade.

During our last night in town for the tournament and after the bus fiasco, we went to the bar and got into a conversation with some Americans who we noticed were at the bar every night. Turns out they were Marine guards there to keep tabs on us, as we were high-profile American citizens in the middle of potential rebel spillover. We were followed when we left the hotel and never knew it.

They were great guys who invited us to the U.S. Embassy to meet the chargé d'affaires for the United States before we left for the airport. We met the chargé d'affaires and his wife, and enjoyed talking with the Marine guards, making for a cool experience. After our meeting, we left for home.

Getting back to the United States meant it was time to get started looking at players for the upcoming draft. Our main emphasis was to concentrate on getting as many athletic position players as we could. It was a solid draft year, and we had the sixth selection in the first round. This draft would produce a few good major leaguers in the first round, including Mike Moore, Joe Carter, Dick Schofield, Kevin McReynolds, Daryl Boston, Bob Meacham, and Ron Darling.

We were preferably looking for a college position player that may be closer to the majors than a high school player. With that approach, we spent a large part of our spring watching Carter, McReynolds, and Meacham. Although Moore and Darling were fine college pitching prospects, we needed position players.

I will add that Darling is one of the best athletes for a pitcher I ever saw. He was a rather good runner with a solid running stride, and an obviously strong arm. He had a good, level swing, and made sound, line-drive contact. Although a prospect as a position player, it wasn't at the same level of prospect he was as a pitcher. It proved so after a 13-year career as a pitcher in the majors.

We saw all these players many times over the course of the spring, and it really came down to two names for us: Carter and McReynolds. Both were complete players and could play center field. We would be happy to have either one, and drafting sixth we thought we had a good chance of getting one of them. As the spring went on, it looked as though Carter would go in the top five, and McReynolds would slide after he hurt his knee and needed an operation at the end of the season, which made our decision easier.

We would've loved to have either Carter or McReynolds, and in our meeting there would be solid cases made for each, but now it was whether we would gamble on Kevin's knee or not. I saw him play several times, as did our crosscheckers and the scout whose territory included McReynolds at Arkansas, Brad Sloan.

It amazed me that Kevin played with a very noticeable limp but was still better than everyone on the field. He was an above-average runner, who even though wasn't at top speed could still run well. He had a center-field arm and great instincts defensively. At the plate, he had a quick starting load of the bat with a short, level swing and quick path to the ball, along with well above-average power. When he made contact, it sounded different and had that sound you don't hear often. The more you saw him, the more you wondered how he would get to us, even with the injury.

It became apparent that he was our guy if he got to us. The scouts were all on board, and Jack McKeon and I decided to meet with Kevin and his family before the draft.

Kevin lived in Little Rock, Arkansas, and grew up an outdoorsman. He asked me once if I ever went "frogging" and of course I had no idea what he was talking about. He had a laid-back approach, and it's probably that approach that helped make him such a good major leaguer.

When we arrived at the house, we started a good meeting, but I noticed early on that most of the conversation was with his father, Jack, and myself. Kevin was sitting in a chair watching television, with his leg propped up in a full leg cast from the recent surgery. I thought to myself that this kid knows what he wants to do and how he wants to do it. We finished the meeting with a feeling he would sign, but my own thoughts were that whatever signing bonus Carter gets, Kevin will want the same.

Before the draft, we needed to get medical clearance to select Kevin. Our team doctors were from Scripps Medical Center and the player's report would be referred to a specialist of said surgery. After they looked at all the information, I was told that he should be fine to sign, but it would take a year for him to get his speed back and at worst, he may lose a tenth of a second to his running speed. They were right on, as that is what happened.

When draft day came around, we were ready.

It was one of the smoothest drafts I was a part of because of our staff. They worked hard and enthusiastically together, arguing, and swearing at each other, but were united at the end of the day.

There was no limit on the number of rounds you could draft, and we probably had 250-300 names on our draft board. We ended up drafting 37 rounds with those 250-300 names, where today clubs often have 500-1,000 names to do the same thing in 40 set rounds.

In those days, the draft was done by phone with a speaker attached to the phone. When a selection was made, you had to write it down so that you knew the player had been selected and you didn't try to select the same player later. It still happened, and many times a team would announce a selection late in the draft that had been taken in the first few rounds. It could be embarrassing. During this draft, I found another way to be embarrassed.

I was making the selections over the phone, and after this draft, I never did it again, letting someone else do it. When the Commissioner's Office, who ran the draft, said, "Next selection, San Diego," I picked up the phone and announced, "San Diego selects McReynolds, Kevin, outfielder from University of Arkansas."

I was so excited after making the selection that I hung up the phone, disconnecting us from the draft. Now I panicked.

We called back and got through about 20 minutes later. Bill Murray, who was running the draft, asked, "What happened?"

"Mechanical issues out of our control here and we missed the last 18 selections," I replied.

You could tell everyone was ticked as I told them of our "mechanical issues." However, it was my fault, but no one knew.

We got a pitcher, Bill Long from Miami of Ohio, in the second round, who went on to have a good six-year major league career. In the third round, we took Tony Gwynn.

We thought Gwynn could slide a little further, but we didn't want to take a chance. Later in the summer, I would be criticized in-house for taking Gwynn over Sid Fernandez, a prep left-handed pitcher from Hawaii. It was said that I took the safe route and that wouldn't happen again. That hurt.

In the Secondary Phase of the draft, where previously drafted players are selected, we picked John Kruk out of Allegany College of Maryland in the third round. He signed quickly and reported to Walla Walla to start his career. Kruk was an outfielder who ran well and had good overall tools. However, it was his bat that showed best. He had an extremely quick start and swing. He made hard, solid contact and would develop power as he got older. An excellent professional hitter who reached the majors and continued to just keep hitting, he had a 10-year career and earned three All-Star nods.

We ended up getting six players from the draft that went on to the majors, and along with the signing of Guillén prior to the draft, my first year turned out to be the best as a scouting director I would have. However, drafting players is one thing, signing them is another. The money wasn't anything like present times, and the scout's personal relationship with the player and families helped tremendously. The first round could still be tough though.

A short time after the draft, McReynolds and his family arrived in San Diego to start the negotiating process. Our people were sure we could sign him, and probably for less money because of his injury. I kept saying I think he wants what Joe Carter got from the Cubs, but our people were so sure we would sign him that they scheduled a press conference for late in the process of our meetings.

When we had our initial meeting at the stadium with Kevin and his family, our offer was somewhere around $80,000. Kevin said no, and he wanted what Carter got: $125,000. We each regrouped, and then reconvened for a second attempt at getting it done.

This time we came back with $90,000. Kevin stood up on his crutches and asked if our travel agent could get them a reservation to go home.

Again, we reconvened and asked them to stay a little longer.

Our staff talked it over and decided to give Kevin close to what Carter had received. We all met again and offered him $115,000. He accepted.

The press was on their way and would be there in an hour. It ended like I thought it would, with the best thing being that he was now a member of our organization.

In September, we had Kevin and Frank Castro, who we selected in the sandwich phase of the draft, come to San Diego to see our doctors to follow up on their injuries. Castro was a catcher who could really catch and throw but had some arm problems that put him in an arm sling. Kevin was still in his leg cast. Both sat in my office, and I was thinking of how glad I was that nobody could get a picture of this. Our first and second picks, sitting with a leg cast and arm sling. If that were today, it would be in every publication and website, leaving me in big trouble.

Towards the end of the season, Ballard Smith and Jack McKeon approached me about the possibility of joining the Scouting Bureau. I was against it. I thought we had a quality draft and a staff that was as good as you could find. I did agree to go with Ballard and Jack to the Newport Beach office of the Bureau to talk with them and see their operation. It was cool going in one of Mr. Kroc's McDonald's helicopters that picked us up at San Diego Stadium and took us to Newport Beach. Plush helicopter that went right along the California shoreline, all the way to Newport Beach where we saw mansions I never knew existed along the coast.

I had great respect for Jim Wilson and Don Pries, the Director and Assistant Director of the Bureau. They were outstanding baseball men who had done a lot of things in the game. They presented what the Bureau could offer, and I wasn't against what they could do for us. I was against trimming a staff to join. When we got back, I thought the club would go with my wishes.

A few weeks later, Jack called me into his office and said the decision had been made to join the Bureau. They never conferred with me before the final decision, probably because they knew I wouldn't change my mind. I was told that it was done, and I would have to let 18 full-time and part-time scouts go.

After settling in, I started the process of talking with the scouts.

After talking to about eight scouts, I decided I couldn't do it. This was a great staff, and I can't tell them their reward for what they had accomplished was dismissal. I resigned.

Even though I quit cold turkey, I appreciated the opportunity that Ballard and Jack had given me.

Before leaving, I rewarded the top scouts with three-year contracts. This probably wasn't something the club wanted, but they had earned it, and kept producing for years. Luckily for them, Sandy Johnson replaced me as scouting director, and was a long-time baseball man that appreciated veteran scouts.

Showing my lack of common sense and worldly experience, I quit without having another job. Fortunately, Bob Quinn with Cleveland and Danny Menendez with Montreal offered me jobs.

I ended up taking a scouting position with the Montreal Expos, and was going to make more money with them as a scout than with San Diego as a scouting director. I had a clause in my contract that said if the team drew over two million fans in Montreal for the season, I would get a $3,000 bonus. The next year when I looked at the daily sports page for the major league scores, I looked first for the attendance at Expos games.

I needed the money and was on to my next chapter.

SAN DIEGO PADRES – OZZIE SMITH

In 1977, I shared a five-state region with my lifelong friend, Cliff Ditto, after making the move from Texas to Northern California to Southern California in just a few months. Our region covered the hotbed of talent that is Southern California, California's Central Coast, and other states in the Southwest.

I would end up going all over our five-state region in that memorable spring of 1977. Cliff stayed local most of the time and then travel to Walla Walla, Washington in the summer to serve as our Rookie League manager. Cliff and I would end up signing three major leaguers this year. All exceptionally talented in their own respects, but none that matched the talent of one Osborne Earl Smith, now better known as "Ozzie".

Prior to my arrival in Southern California, Ozzie was a two-sport athlete at Locke High School in East Los Angeles. On the diamond, he was a gifted defensive shortstop who played alongside future Hall of Famer, Eddie Murray, and as a talented point guard he shared the hardwood with future NBA all-star Marques Johnson. I believe his original goal was to play college basketball.

After high school, Ozzie attended Cal Poly San Luis Obispo on an academic scholarship and was a walk-on to the baseball program. Not long into his freshman season, the starting shortstop broke his leg, and Ozzie took the starting role. He held onto it through his senior season.

Over those college years, Ozzie developed into a slick, acrobatic shortstop with the quickest feet and softest hands I have ever seen on an infielder. He made the in-between hop look routine and never seemed to be out of balance. The biggest question was his bat. Cal Poly's coach, Berdy Harr, and assistant coach, Tom Hinkle - whom I ended up hiring later with different clubs - were teaching Ozzie how to switch-hit, which added to the uncertainty.

That's the question you have with almost all young players, but when you're not a real strong person that's just a question. In college Ozzie was short with a very slight and slender build, basically as you saw him his entire career. He didn't change a lot. To his credit, Ozzie turned out to be stronger than a lot of people gave him credit for.

I think if a person were honest, the question was how much he would hit over a 162-game schedule and how would anybody know? He wasn't a really strong kid, he was learning to switch-hit, and he wasn't a flyer, but he had such quick feet. The feeling was from the left side he could get down the line well.

Hitting was the only question with Ozzie. You didn't question whether he was going to play in the big leagues. It was what role would the bat let him play? And I think if anybody told you different, they would've taken him first overall and wouldn't have let us take him in the fourth round.

In my report I wrote about what great quickness, athletic ability, and fielding ability he had. I wrote that if he hits enough, he plays every day and if he doesn't, he is a utility player for a long time with his defensive skills. He was an average runner with the quickest first step I ever saw. His arm strength was average to a little below average, but the quickness of his arm was as fast as you're going to see. That makes up for a lot of extra arm strength.

You look at David Eckstein. He couldn't throw but look how quickly he got rid of the ball. Ozzie could throw out the best runner or the worst runner by a foot because his arm was so quick at releasing the ball, and he was very accurate with his throws. That's where sometimes people will get confused when a person doesn't have a real strong arm. They don't realize how important the release is, and Ozzie's was as good as anyone.

Somebody sometime later wrote up that it was a horrible report, and I got a kick out of it. I say and laugh to myself or others, "Yeah, it was so horrible, but we got him. So, what was everybody else's report like?"

Ozzie was drafted his junior year in 1976 by the Detroit Tigers in the seventh round and turned down an $8,500 signing bonus to return to Cal Poly for his senior year. During that senior campaign, he had become not only an excellent fielder, but an explosive runner. He continued to hit around .300, steal plenty of bases and play exceptional defense.

The thing about Ozzie is that he was a consistent hitter throughout his entire career. Even though he hit maybe 30 or 40 points lower than he hit in college, considering it's the major leagues, it's pretty gosh-darned similar. He just hit from day one, and who would have ever known?

When the 1977 draft rolled around, we selected Ozzie in the fourth round.

Our biggest problem was we didn't give much in bonus money, because we didn't have a lot of money to give. We operated on what we made, and when you only draw around 3,000 a night, you don't operate with much.

We were never a high revenue team and never had a lot of money. We weren't just thrifty with one player; we were thrifty with them all because of our lack of funds.

As you look through the records, you'll see the low budget we worked with. Even in 1974, when Mr. Ray Kroc retired from running McDonald's and bought the Padres at the last minute in lieu of a group from Washington D.C., the club only sold for $12,000,000.

What we didn't have in money, we had in opportunities for quick advancement through the organization. It was something we preached to college players regularly and it was about as good as any opportunity inside baseball.

I think when players look back, they see that the opportunity in San Diego got them to the big leagues where they could make more money than they ever would with a bonus.

We approached with quick advancement number one, especially with the older kids and even with some of the younger ones, but even more so with the college kids. Kids were getting the majors in a hurry with the Padres in the 70's.

We were a small staff then and in Southern California, where the ballclub is, there were probably four or five of us that saw Ozzie play at Cal Poly, with Cliff and I seeing him on a regular basis. He was well known though from playing in college summer leagues in Clarinda, Iowa, and playing in the NBC Tournament. Ozzie wasn't a secret.

Even though he was a senior, I thought taking him in the fourth round would allow us to get a little more money to offer him and lead to a quick agreement.

After the draft, I called Ozzie and made an appointment to meet him in San Luis Obispo, believing the potential bonus and opportunity to move fast through our system would help get a deal done. Then again, I had yet to get the hard say on a bonus offer from the office.

I was living in Huntington Beach at the time and started the four-hour drive up Pacific Coast Highway to San Luis Obispo because he was still living there with school ending. While driving the coastline of California, I continued to think about how he was offered money before and knew what we could offer was less.

I had chatted with Hinkle, just to see if he knew what Ozzie's expectations were, and he felt Ozzie was ready to go because he was a senior. It put me at some ease as I thought about my approach with him face-to-face. I had a good feeling that negotiations would go well. Little did I know it would be a long day ahead.

I met Ozzie at a coffee shop in downtown San Luis Obispo where we shook hands, took our seats in a booth, and began the conversation that leads to any negotiation. As I was sipping my coffee, the conversation was going well. It was the standard informal conversation where you tell a player about the organization, where they would play once signed, the opportunities available, answer questions the player has, and then... boom. You get into the contract, and into the bonus.

One thing I learned about when you try to sign a college senior is normally in the beginning there is disappointment. Very seldom is it ever the money they expect. I was just thinking of how I could make him understand the possibility of advancement with us and that he could move quickly.

I never experienced inconsistency with that practice and throughout my career as a scouting director where I stressed consistency. Players hardly ever like the bonus they get, but if you are consistent with what you give to players, they will normally accept it. I never wanted a player to come back to me and say I lied to him. It was important to me.

The one thing a player will accept, even if they don't like the money, is that you've been up front with them on how you dealt with them. You didn't try to give them less and give more to somebody else in their same situation.

You go through your head with any player how you're going to approach a negotiation and if you do hit a bump in the road, you know you have to change gears and adjust accordingly. I played it out in my head, and you think you've been through so many of these before that you try to anticipate what you're going to hear and the reaction you'll receive, but you never really know until you get there.

Here I was with Ozzie and the first offer. $4,000.

If you saw him play, Ozzie had a constant smile and was always a happy guy. It was no different during the conversation. That was, until I told him about the bonus we could offer. The smile quickly disappeared, and his face dropped.

I honestly thought in the beginning it was going to be received better than it was. It wasn't. I think it showed the makeup of the player how they reacted to the bonus, and in Ozzie's case you could see the pride in a positive way.

You could see him thinking to himself. Just the year prior, he was in this same position, but with $4,500 more being offered. He had turned that down and became a better player than he was then. Why was he getting offered less money when he was a better player now?

This was hard to combat, but I was with a team who didn't have a lot of money. Again, I hit him with the opportunity to no avail.

I could tell Ozzie was not happy. Most kids after their senior year want a little cushion to get started. It was late in the morning, and we decided to take a break.

We agreed to meet in an hour over at his apartment near the campus. He was going to think about where we were. I stayed at the coffee shop and ordered another cup of coffee. There wasn't much I could do other than call our office to see if we could up the bonus.

In these negotiations, you sometimes just have to wait. You let the player get his thoughts together and talk to the people he needs to talk to. There wasn't anything I could do. I knew my parameters, and just waited.

After an hour, I made the 10-minute drive to Ozzie's apartment. Over the next hour or so we went back and forth and didn't make a lot of headway. Ozzie wanted $10,000, the same he had asked the year before from Detroit. I told him it wouldn't happen.

I had to keep stressing the opportunity that he would have. It was still hard for me though, as it was with all players I signed when there wasn't a lot of money involved. I never believed in spending more money than a player's value merits, but he was worth more like most players we signed.

We upped the bonus to $5,000. Once again, the smile vanished.

Ozzie said he would consider it, but he needed to call his mother and people he relied on. We took another break and I drove back to the coffee house for another cup of coffee. By that time, I had become a regular.

After another hour, I returned to Ozzie's apartment in the late afternoon. This time, it was a short visit. We agreed on the $5,000 signing bonus and instantly, Ozzie Smith was a member of the San Diego Padres.

Ozzie, like all good players I have been fortunate enough to negotiate with, did so like they played, tough but fair. When he signed the contract, I think it was a relief for us both.

After he signed, he was like all kids when they sign their first pro contract regardless of how negotiations go. He was ready to go. He was excited about going and playing, and he'd be on his way to doing so the very next day.

Back then scouts bought the players an airplane ticket to the team they would be reporting to after they signed their contract. We carried air travel cards that were good for any airline. Just down the road I checked into a hotel and made three phone calls. One to the office to confirm the signing, one to the airline to buy a ticket, and one to my friend, Cliff, who would be managing a new shortstop the following day.

After making the phone rounds, I drove to the airport to get the physical ticket, and then returned to meet Ozzie. I handed him a plane ticket to Walla Walla, Washington. The next day, Ozzie was off to begin his professional baseball career with our Rookie Ball affiliate, the Walla Walla Padres of the Northwest League.

As I handed him the ticket and prepared to leave, Ozzie stopped me.

With robust confidence and that signature smile, he looked me square.

"Bob, I will show everyone I can hit," he said.

Ozzie knew that it was the question that people had and would determine what role as a player he would have. To this day, I remember that confidence. It was evident in the smile he always seemed to have on the baseball field.

You just believed in him. There's something about really good players and their confidence. You see it with Derek Jeter. He had a smile on his face. You see it with Mike Trout. He has a smile on his face. And you saw it with Ozzie. A smile on his face. Not because of anything other than they love to play and they're confident that they are good. With Ozzie, it was just another thing that made you think, "This kid is going to do it."

The next day I began driving back south to Los Angeles where I had to meet with a lot of other players.

On the drive, I couldn't help but feel good. Anytime you sign a player like Ozzie, even though he's a college senior, you knew he had the kind of talent to get to the big leagues and it made you feel good.

Despite my feelings, you must automatically start thinking ahead and don't have the luxury to feel more than just brief happiness. We had drafted Brian Greer with the eighth overall pick in the draft, and I had to get to La Habra to begin negotiations.

We used to draft a lot of college players out of Southern California because the strength of amateur baseball was basically California,

Texas, and Florida. Maybe a few others spread around the country, certainly not like it is today.

We would sign a lot of players out of Southern California to fill out rosters. In a slow year, it was six players, and a big year was nine or ten and you had to sign them in a relatively short amount of time. In 1977, we had 11.

In those days, a scout signed players unless it got to a real jam and on occasion it went higher up the ladder to the front office. Some negotiations went quickly, like our 10th-round pick and future major leaguer, Ron Tingley, and others took time. I did a lot of thinking on the drive, not just about Ozzie and Brian, but the other guys we needed to sign.

Ozzie's first summer with the Padres organization was spent with our short-season affiliate in the Northwest League, the Walla Walla Padres. He had success, not only with that fabulous glove, but with his bat and running game. He hit .303 and stole 30 bases: a great start to his career. His abilities were already starting to garner attention.

After Ozzie arrived at Walla Walla, Cliff would tell me, "Ozzie is leading these kids and he's an obvious leader in the clubhouse."

Those are things that you never know about until you have the player with you.

That winter, Ozzie played a few games on our Scout League team. This is where he caught the club's attention and I was told to bring him to San Diego so our manager, Roger Craig, could see him work out and see if he was a kid we could bring to spring training with the big club. I made arrangements to pick Ozzie up and headed south down the I-5.

We did this a few times over, and during the times I picked up Ozzie for our journey to San Diego I had the privilege of meeting his mother, Marvella. She had encouraged Ozzie during his college career, had a great personality and like her son, was always smiling.

Marvella was one of the most marvelous women you could ever meet. She was so positive and supportive and obviously a strong person. I remember the times I did talk with her, we always laughed. She was such a fun person, and you understood the impact she had on Ozzie's great attitude for our game and his obvious love of being on the baseball field.

It added to the treat of driving Ozzie to San Diego, but the biggest treat was the impression he left with the club during the visits. It didn't take many visits before a decision was made to bring Ozzie to spring training with us in Yuma, Arizona. In Yuma, Ozzie continued to make impressions and impress to the point of the organization making a large move on the infield.

The Padres had drafted Billy Almon out of Brown University with the first overall selection in 1974, and he was coming off a strong 1977 rookie campaign, hitting .261.

Billy was a taller and leaner athlete, reminiscent of the days of Mark Belanger and Johnnie LeMaster. That used to be the way a shortstop was built; long and lean, very loose. Not acrobatic like it's become over the years. Billy could really run, really throw, and had a chance to hit. Not for a lot of power, but he had the chance to be a good line-drive hitter.

His first year in the majors, he made quite a few errors but most of them were throwing errors and you never count that against a young middle infielder. Not very much early, at least. He was a good athlete and he had a decent first year with us. He had good range defensively and a solid arm. When he was drafted, he was going to be our shortstop for a long time. Or so we thought.

Both Ozzie and Billy reported to Yuma in 1978 and everyone thought Almon would be our shortstop while we were just looking at Ozzie for the future. As spring went on, Ozzie made such an impression with his defense and his ability to put the ball in play that it was decided Ozzie would be at shortstop and Billy would be at second base.

Even though the Padres supplied opportunity and quick advancement to those that earn it, Ozzie brought it to a new level. Nobody cared where he was drafted or how much he got. He was someone who could play and was going to move fast. So fast, he skipped from short-season ball to the majors in a matter of months.

As a scout, I was delighted. He had such a good spring training. It's easy to say about a Hall of Famer, but he just fit the position so well. I think you saw a team where pitchers knew if a batter hit it to shortstop, they were out. It was just a great feeling. Billy is a great guy and a great talent, but shoot, I was excited as could be!

Ozzie went on to have a great rookie season where he finished second to Bob Horner in Rookie of the Year voting. I, of course, thought he should have won.

That rookie year he made one of the greatest plays I've ever seen at shortstop when he went to his left to dive for a ball and the ball hit a rock, headed over his right shoulder as he was falling, and then Ozzie reached up and barehanded the ball and proceeded to throw out the runner. Balance, coordination, and instincts like I have never seen.

That first season, Ozzie hit .258 and stole a club-leading 40 bases. He was on his way to greatness, and the 1978 team finished the season with an 84-78 record, becoming the first San Diego Padres club to finish a season over .500.

A few years later in September of 1980, I was sitting in the press box at San Diego Stadium. We were having a horrible year and another small crowd was in attendance. However, that day was a thrill as Ozzie made Major League Baseball history when he achieved the most assists in a single season for a shortstop. He would go on to set both the single-season (621) and career (8,375) marks for assists by a shortstop.

That afternoon in San Diego was probably my first as a scout where you have something happen for a player you were involved with and you're maybe the only one that really cares. That's okay. It's a satisfaction that you look for when you become a scout. It was like when Francisco Rodríguez set the all-time single season saves record and I was sitting in the ballpark and while leaving I said, "That's pretty cool." But you know that's as far as that's going to go. A silent satisfaction, and that was my first chance for that.

In the winter of 1981 at the Winter Meetings in Dallas, there was an upcoming trade that would change two organizations for the next decade. Jack McKeon was San Diego's general manager, and Jack really liked a high-contact shortstop for St. Louis, Garry Templeton, who was an exceptionally talented player. San Diego also needed pitching, and instantaneously, they were trading Ozzie to St. Louis for Templeton. The final deal would include four other players.

I had already left the Padres by the winter, but as a scout, you feel disappointed.

One thing I learned later from Mike Port, the general manager of the Angels in the late 1980's, is anybody you sign and develop that you trade, the player you get in return becomes a product of your minor league system. Ever since that conversation with Mike, I have been comfortable when we trade young players that we signed and developed and later had to trade.

Ozzie's best years in the majors came after he was traded to St. Louis in 1981. Both Ozzie and Garry did well for their new teams, but Ozzie continued to excel and take his game to a Hall of Fame level playing for Whitey Herzog. And of course, he showed everyone he could hit.

Ozzie became a 15-time All-Star over his 19 years in the majors and won 13 consecutive Gold Glove awards from 1980-1992. He hit .262 over his career, which included a season in 1987 when he was awarded a Silver Slugger Award after hitting .303. His 580 stolen bases are the 22nd-most all-time in baseball history.

Doing a backflip when he went to the field, Ozzie showed he loved to play. He was also the most instinctive shortstop, who even among greats excelled.

Ozzie became the first Hall of Famer I had signed as a scout, elected in 2002. He spent most of his career with the St. Louis Cardinals, but it was still as good a feeling as you can have. It's a satisfaction of all the time you've put into the game and all the mistakes you've made, but all the effort has paid off.

You're happy for the player, but it's a good feeling that you have for a little while, and then you move on to find the next millionaire.

As time went on people used to tell Cliff and I about how we had done such a great job signing Ozzie, and we used to smile at that. Yes, we obviously liked him more than others and were extremely happy to get him, but do you think we would have waited until the fourth round and 86th overall pick before selecting him if we knew he would be in the Hall of Fame?

If everyone knew he would hit like he did, he would have been the first player selected in the draft, and I'm proud that we got him. We would laugh about it and it surely shows you must have some luck in this game to have success and you better be humble when things go your way.

There was at least one person who genuinely believed that Ozzie Smith could hit, and that was Ozzie himself.

"Bob, I will show everyone I can hit."

No truer words were ever said.

"Ozzie Smith doing signature backflip"

SAN DIEGO PADRES – TONY GWYNN

In 1981, my first year as scouting director with the San Diego Padres, we drafted sixth in the first round with an extra pick at the end of the round as well. We knew it was a good year for college players and we thought we may be able to draft some good young position players who might help us sooner rather than later, as we were really struggling in the major leagues.

We had signed some young kids from Latin America prior to the draft who we thought might have a chance, with Ozzie Guillén being the player we had the highest hopes for, and with the upcoming draft, we thought we could get better quickly.

When the dust settled, it turned out to be the best draft I have ever been associated with. We had a veteran staff, with more experience than I possessed, who did a great job. Ken Bracey, Cliff Ditto, Al Heist, Brad Sloan, Billy Bryk, Bob Miller, Denny Galehouse, Gary Sutherland, Jack Hays, and others did as good a job as any staff that I have ever been associated with.

To sign Ozzie Guillén in the winter and then to get Kevin McReynolds, Bill Long, John Kruk, and *of course*, Tony Gwynn, in the spring was the work of these outstanding veteran evaluators. To get three All-Stars, a Rookie of the Year, and a multi-time batting champion and Hall of Famer out of one scouting year was a thrill.

I was 27 at the time, and if I didn't have these professional evaluators around me, it could have been a disaster. Not only did they make good scouts, but they worked hard and were as loyal as any young person could be surrounded by. Even though this staff only lasted one year, the impact of these guys was felt by the Padres for many years to come.

The 1981 draft featured a good class of amateur talent, with players like Mike Moore, Joe Carter, Dick Schofield, Ron Darling, John Franco, Kevin McReynolds, Bobby Meacham, and others. We were focused more on the position players, and particularly, ones that could have a near immediate impact at the major league level. The three players we closed in on at the end were Joe Carter, Kevin McReynolds, and Bobby Meacham.

Meacham played at San Diego State, along with a basketball player who played the corner outfield named Tony Gwynn. San Diego State was a premium program that was producing quality major league players at a regular pace, with Jim Dietz as the coach.

Jim had assembled a lot of talent and been extremely helpful to me and the club over the years. He always liked to get talented athletes from other sports to play baseball and Tony was the latest to play for him. Years later, Jim convinced me to draft Marshall Faulk when I was with the Angels.

Tony had been a successful point guard in high school and on the Aztecs' basketball team. He set the SDSU assists records and was drafted as a senior by the San Diego Clippers in the 10th round of the 1981 draft (on the same day he was selected in the MLB draft). Tony received multiple scholarship offers for basketball from major programs, but not even one for baseball, and his success as a college baseball player would likely have never occurred if not for Bobby Meacham.

Two outfielders from the team were involved in an accident when an automobile struck them while riding their bicycles, and Jim began a search for replacements. That was when Bobby convinced Jim to let Tony join the team, after noting the two had played against each other in high school. Because Jim trusted Bobby, Tony was given the chance to play with the Aztecs, who Jim had never seen play in person.

Because we had Bobby high on our list in the top group, and San Diego State was in our backyard, Gary, Cliff, Bob, Jack McKeon and I got to see Bobby play often, and also gave us an opportunity to observe Tony. After a while, we were there to see Tony as much as Bobby.

We became extremely comfortable with Tony, not only as an athlete, but as untapped potential to be a good baseball player. Most of my staff and myself were taught the Branch Rickey way of evaluating, along with Jack's philosophy from Kansas City of drafting athletes.

Our approach was starting with a good athlete, who from the feet on up, everything worked well. Tony had quick feet, great balance, strong hands, and substantial aptitude. He kept getting better as the season went on. He was obviously behind the other players because of lack of playing time, but he just kept getting better and better and better. That made him a player of interest for us all and helped when we decided that he was worth fighting basketball for.

During the season, Tony showed the desire to work hard and become a good ballplayer. At the plate, he exhibited great balance and hand-eye coordination. His ability to keep his hands back until the last moment made him such a good contact hitter of the ball on the left side of the field. He could also turn on a pitch on the inner part of the plate and make solid contact to the right side.

He had the ability to keep his eye on the ball until late which allowed him to approach a pitch as well as anyone you could see at his age. He was a natural line-drive contact hitter who in my opinion, had he wanted, could hit with power in place of consistent contact. It was a natural feel for hitting.

His other abilities are often overshadowed by his hitting ability. In college, he consistently improved his fielding, throwing and baserunning. Years later, after he signed, he worked hard in all these areas to become a solid major league defensive right fielder, winning five Gold Glove Awards, as well as becoming an excellent baserunner. When you look at his stats over the first decade of his major league career, you will notice he stole a lot of bases (238 from 1982-1990). He became not just a great hitter, but a complete player.

The first day of the draft, we took Kevin McReynolds with the sixth overall pick, Frank Castro with the 26th, and Bill Long with the 32nd overall pick in the second round. When we got to the third round, we felt comfortable that this would be the time to select Tony. We thought it might be a little higher than most clubs had him, but we couldn't take the chance of waiting any longer.

We knew all along that we would take Tony in the third or fourth round. In those days, you knew your opposition a whole lot better because scouting directors would stay in their roles for 10, 15, or 20 years. Clubs developed a pattern or type of player they preferred, as well as the team needs, so you had an idea of who teams drafting around you may be targeting. Tony hadn't played much because he came out late, and we had an edge being close to San Diego State.

You put all this information together and we felt that we could get him in the third or fourth round.

I remember, after the draft was over, I was questioned why I selected Tony instead of Sid Fernandez, a high school pitcher out of Honolulu, Hawaii. Fernandez was a fine talent who started off with quick success and ended up having an outstanding major league career. We were criticized for not taking Sid, and the reason being that Sid was a high schooler and Tony was a college senior who's signability would come cheaper, and we were saving money.

It still bothers me to this day. First, Tony wasn't an easy sign, and second, we wanted to get as many good position players as we could. Often, people just don't have patience when it comes to players to wait and see how everything unfolds.

I left San Diego at the end of that year and didn't read any articles until I started looking back and saw that I had been ridiculed for not taking Tony in the first round, while other people in the organization were taking credit for him and blaming me for taking him in the third round. One article even said I was threatened to be fired if I didn't take him, but that is not the way it happened.

Tony would go on the be a great player and things began to be said where me and the scouts weren't in the picture. I was talking to someone years later who was doing some history on the Padres, and they asked if it was all true. Whether I had been threatened to take Tony, with the risk of being fired.

"I was 27 years old," I told them. "I'm the youngest scouting director in baseball. It's my first year. And I'm going to tell the general manager, and people above him, 'No, I'm not going to do what you want.' C'mon. Give me a little credit."

They should have come to us and said that that scouting staff deserves a ton of credit because they got players the quality of

Kevin McReynolds, Bill Long, Ozzie Guillén, John Kruk, and Tony Gwynn. To get those caliber players from the amateur ranks, they should have said that scouting group did a fantastic job. Instead, we were ridiculed.

I don't get bothered often, but this bothers me. Forget about me. Look at that group of guys that were in the draft room. Ken, Cliff, Al, Brad, Billy, Bob, Denny, Gary, and Jack Hays. These were big guys in the amateur field, and it bothers me that people don't understand that when you're in an organization at a high level, you get credit for everything, both good and bad.

Those guys out there busted their ass. They knew the opposition and they knew where we could select Tony and probably get him safely. For those in the organization to ridicule you or take credit for their doing really rubbed me the wrong way.

Before Tony started his professional baseball career, we needed to get him signed and not pursue basketball as a career. Gary and Cliff went into his parents' home in Long Beach to make the initial offer of $15,000, which was quickly declined.

Not long after, Gary and I traveled to the home of Tony's parents. In the middle of our conversation, Tony received a phone call with someone pretending they were from the San Diego NASL soccer team and that they had just drafted him, which of course, wasn't true. Though, with the kind of athlete he was, I'm not sure I would have been surprised.

We continued with chatting and finally landed on our second offer, around $20,000. This upset Tony's father, Charles, who was a wonderful man, and the conversation was headed in the same direction as the first. Charles wasn't pleased and the conversation began to get heated. Meanwhile, Tony's younger brother, Chris, who played 10 years in the major leagues, sat with a giant smile on his face. Chris was a jokester who you couldn't help but enjoy the company of.

Without physically throwing us out, we realized that today may not be the best and it was time to reconvene later. As cheap as we were in those days, I can't say that I blame Charles or Tony.

Tony was a college senior, and although he had an option in professional basketball, he didn't have a lot of leverage in baseball.

After a few weeks though, we were able to work out a deal at $25,000. Tony came to the stadium, signed his contract in my office, had a brief press conference, and was then on his way to our Northwest League affiliate in Walla Walla, Washington, to start his professional baseball career.

I think for Tony, even though he had the basketball option, he realized he had a better chance for a more successful and longer career in baseball.

He went to Walla Walla in the Northwest League, started hitting immediately and never stopped his entire career. In 42 games, he had a league-leading .331 batting average and hit 12 home runs, second-most in the league, to win Most Valuable Player honors for the Northwest League. After that month-and-a-half stint with Walla Walla, he was promoted to Double-A Amarillo of the Texas League and hit .462 over 22 games.

The next year, Tony spent just 93 games with our Triple-A Pacific Coast League affiliate in Hawaii, before being promoted to the major league club, and never played anywhere else. He hit .289 that rookie year, the only season he ever hit under .300. His instincts for the game of baseball were tremendous and he made difficult things look easy.

That first year in the minor leagues, coaches would tell me how he helped younger players and had such a positive approach to playing the game. During the offseason of that first year, he even played some games on the Southern California Padres Scout Team and had such a great influence on the young guys then.

Tony was like a lot of great players. He loved to play, and always had a smile on his face. He was a great influence on those around him.

His career took off from the get-go, and he became the face of the San Diego Padres franchise. He kept improving and after 20 years at the major league level, he never stopped swinging the bat.

Over his career, Tony became the Padres all-time leader in games played (2,440), batting average (.338), runs scored (1,383), hits (3,141), walks (790), runs batted in (1,138), and stolen bases (319). His career .338 batting average ranks 11th best over the past century and is second-best to Ted Williams since integration in 1947. He holds National League records for most batting titles (8), most seasons leading the league in hits (7), and most consecutive seasons batting .300 or better (19).

Tony was a 15-time All-Star, eight-time National League batting champion, five-time Gold Glove winner as well as a Roberto Clemente Award winner, Lou Gehrig award winner, and Branch Rickey award winner.

Noted Baseball Statistician, Ryan M. Spaeder, has shared many great statistics from Tony's career such as:

- Tony Gwynn faced Greg Maddux more than any other pitcher in his career, with 107 plate appearances. Maddux never struck him out, and he hit .415.
- Tony Gwynn struck out three times in a game once. He would score the winning run later in that game.

- Tony Gwynn would have to come back and go 0-for-1,183 for his career batting average to drop below .300.
- Tony Gwynn reached base in 2,069 of his 2,440 games (84.8%).

I have never seen a hitter that understood the strike zone and his zone better than Tony. The ultimate professional hitter.

A big event for me was when my wife, Karen, and I were invited to attend the last game that he played in San Diego. It was a thrill to be part of the on-field ceremonies for him after the game.

He loved the game, and to play his entire career with the Padres was an incredible feat.

In a fitting follow up to his playing days, he became the head coach at San Diego State, which was a title he held for 12 seasons, while he assisted in the development of some of today's stars, such as Stephen Strasburg.

Tony was a wonderful person who I don't believe you'll ever hear someone say something negative about. He loved baseball and he loved San Diego.

MONTREAL EXPOS

"Randy Johnson receiving Professional
Baseball Scout's Foundation Award"

After I resigned from the Padres, I didn't have a job and had a wife and a child to support. I wasn't smart enough, or consulted anyone, to know that you need to have a job in place before making a move like that. As I think back, I wasn't nervous like I should have been, and I remember my father being concerned for our well-being.

I contacted all the clubs to see if there was anything available and waited.

Paul Snyder with the Atlanta Braves was the first person who tried to create something for me. He called and said, "I am creating a job in California for you that will pay $20,000, so that you know you will be able to take care of your family. I know you will get something more, but you know you have this."

It was a regional scout position that meant as much to me as any job I was ever offered or accepted.

Paul is one of the most respected men in baseball and was the top scouting director in the business at the time. To hear that from him meant the world to me, but he was right though, saying I would find something more.

Bob Quinn with the Cleveland Indians was in contact with me frequently and working hard to put something together as a West Coast supervisor. Bob is a long-time baseball man who said I would have the freedom on the West Coast to operate and have good input on players. This job looked to be a good fit for me, and I thought I was going to take it.

Within a week of thinking I would accept the position with Cleveland, I received a call from Danny Menendez, the scouting director with the Montreal Expos.

Montreal was going to offer me a job in Southern California as a supervisor, where I would have the ability to see players on the West Coast. Even though I would find out later that my philosophy on scouting and theirs was a little different, they offered me more money than I would have made if I was the scouting director in San Diego.

I was going to make a base salary of $27,500, with a clause in my contract that would pay me $3,000 if the Expos drew two million fans or more. The Expos drew well in those years, as they had a quality team, and I received this bonus three of the four years I was there. Considering I was making $15,000 two years prior, I felt like I was rich.

It was hard to say no to Cleveland, as their job was interesting to me, but the difference in money was $7,500, and I couldn't walk away from that.

After I accepted the offer from the Expos in November of 1981, they had me attend the Winter Meetings in Hollywood, Florida, to meet with all their people and get acclimated to the position and organization.

The Winter Meetings are an annual event for baseball, where both the major league teams and minor league teams attend. It is there where teams discuss items for the upcoming season, meet with affiliates, trades are discussed and often are completed, and any miscellaneous items that pertain to baseball business are taken care of.

Montreal had just won its division and had a stockpile of good young players. I was excited to join the team and was impressed by the professionalism and vast baseball knowledge they had on their staff.

Danny Menendez was a wonderful man who was the cousin of Dave Garcia, a former major league manager and coach, and a dear friend of my family. Danny made me feel right at home.

I was introduced to Jim Fanning, who was the manager at the time, and three scouts who were the club's national crosscheckers and some of the finest people I ever met in baseball: Whitey Lockman, who was a star with the New York Giants and was on base when Bobby Thomson hit the home run to win the pennant against Brooklyn in 1951; Eddie Lopat, who pitched for the great New York Yankees teams in the 1950s; and Earl Rapp, who played in the major leagues briefly and was a star in the Pacific Coast League for many years.

John McHale was the general manager and was great to me. He carried himself in a way that you knew who was in charge the minute he stepped in a room, without even saying a word. He had a good playing career and was the ultimate professional.

I learned a lot from John and Jim, mostly on how to approach a job, and most importantly, how to treat and respect people even when you are at odds with them. It was a class group of people to be associated with.

One night at the Winter Meetings, I was interviewed by a local radio station in Montreal. The next night at the club reception, a man came up to me and said, "Hi, I am Charles Bronfman, and I enjoyed your interview on the radio last night. Welcome to the organization."

Charles Bronfman was the owner of the Montreal Expos and one of the wealthiest men in Canada. He owned Seagram's liquor and mass shareholdings across the country.

I would learn from the few times I was around him that he had a comforting effect on people, and I believe it made it easier to concentrate on the task at hand. If there was a problem or a lot of pressure, it was felt at the top and didn't trickle down. He was an exceptional owner who created a great place to work.

I worked with Jack Paepke and Bill Schmidt in Southern California. Jack was a former two-way minor league player in the Dodgers and Pirates organization, catching and pitching alongside my father for two years, and later went on to coach and scout for the California Angels. Bill would go on to have a successful scouting career and is currently the vice president of scouting for the Colorado Rockies.

My great friend Cliff Ditto was hired to work with us in Southern California, and the following year, Tom Hinkle joined us.

Montreal didn't sign a lot of players from California, but the ones they did ended up being rather good ballplayers. They had drafted and signed Gary Carter, Ellis Valentine and Bob James, and Jack had signed Tim Wallach three years prior to my arrival.

That first year, the Expos didn't have a first round pick in the 1982 draft, which produced several major league players, but only a few became stars like Shawon Dunston and Dwight Gooden.

When I went back to Montreal for the draft meeting, it was a great experience, as I had never been before.

Everything about the European-style city was alluring. The old buildings, cathedrals, back alleys, and women were all beautiful, and the city was clean everywhere you went. Subways were clean and women walked the streets at night because they felt safe, and this multicultural city made you feel like you were in the heart of France.

Montreal is also where I got hooked on Mille-Feuille and Napoleon pastries. Every time I went to Montreal, I would stop by a little bakery and pick one up. It is the lightest dessert I've ever had, and it would just melt in your mouth. There was always a surplus as the French Canadians would make these pastries the same way we make glazed donuts in America.

After arriving in Montreal for that first draft meeting, I went to the register at the front desk of the hotel I was staying at. The clerk saw my name and assumed with a French name like Fontaine, that I would speak the lingo. Wrong.

When I stopped him from speaking in French, he got mad and handed me my key.

I knew there was friction between the French and English in the province. I remember being told that the French speak English, and the English speak French, but they don't like to speak the other language to each other. With everything in French, it was sometimes a little confusing, but as an American, I got along with everyone.

One time I was taking a cab somewhere in the city, and the cab driver was telling me how bad the French were, even though he was French-Canadian. He went on and on, and it was quite interesting, but when we got to my location, I paid the fare and gave him a tip. After, I said thank you, I told him, "By the way, I am French."

"No sir, you are not," he replied in his broken English. "A Frenchman would never tip a French Canadian."

Off he went.

I know things have changed since those times, but it was an experience.

We got a few players from our area in that 1982 draft, with Rene Gonzales of Cal State Los Angeles in the fifth round leading the way. Rene signed right away and reported to our Double-A affiliate in Memphis, Tennessee, to start his professional career. Rene was a soft-handed infielder with a good arm who could *really* play shortstop.

We continued to have a Scout's League team with the Expos in Southern California during the winter months and were able to keep the minor league players in the area playing until they left for spring training. Rene was always there and worked hard to be the good player he became. He learned to make enough line-drive contact to spend 13 years in the majors, mostly as a utility player.

After the 1982 season, my boss, Danny Menendez, was moved to another position and Jim Fanning moved from manager of the team to scouting director. Pat Daugherty became Jim's assistant and Bob Gebhard became the minor league farm director.

Pat was a long-time coach at Indian Hills Junior College in Iowa and was one of the most successful Rookie League managers in baseball. He was a quality baseball man who was also one of the funniest people I have ever been around.

Bob was a former major league pitcher and coach for a while, and then became the first general manager in Colorado Rockies history in 1991 and took Pat along with him to become the scouting director.

The Montreal staff included many veteran scouts such as Red Murff (who had signed Nolan Ryan as an amateur in 1965) and Bob Oldis (who played for the 1960 World Series champion Pirates and was one of the funniest men I've ever met), and with the crosscheckers they had, it was a very experienced scouting operation.

When Jim took over the department, he put more emphasis on statistics to go along with the actual scouting, and this was different than I was used to. Certain stats, like strikeouts and velocity for pitchers and home runs and performance for hitters, were often given more importance than mechanics and projectability.

Clubs had done this for years, and with some success, but they would incorporate the scouting. I was often at odds with some of our preference lists, but Jim always gave me my say and never held my opinions against me, even if it was against the whole group.

Whitey, Eddie, Earl, and Pat were all sound baseball men who gave their own opinion, and then would unite with whatever the decision was. I often would keep hammering my opinion, even when it wasn't going to change anything.

I was young and *of course*, always thought I was right, but Jim and these guys all listened to me and really made me understand the importance of letting people express what they believe. I look back and even though I agreed with them all more often than not, there must have been times they wanted to throw me out the window.

Whitey had a good feel for hitting and he really tried to understand what a scout was saying about a player when he would observe the player and not see the things the scout saw. He was a scout's crosschecker, who always sided with what the area scout said, and was an exceptionally good evaluator. Eddie understood the makeup of what it took for a pitcher to succeed, regardless of the type of stuff he had. Earl was a grinder who looked at the positive in a player.

This was a special group, not because they were good players and evaluators, but good people who really appreciated the scouts. They worked hard and got along even when they disagreed. We joked constantly and shared many laughs together, often ending with Earl shouting, "Whitey, you son-of-a-bitch." We had a lot of fun, especially when it came time to have a cocktail.

Jim liked to have long meetings before the draft, and for a couple of years we would start our meetings at the College World Series in Omaha, Nebraska. We would meet from 9 a.m. to 3 p.m., go to the ballpark to see a doubleheader, go out at 11 p.m., and do it all again the next day.

We did that for the first three days of the College World Series, and then went to Montreal for a week to finish up.

I remember leaving Omaha at 6 a.m. for a flight to New York and changing planes to go to Montreal. Our plane was late into New York, so they let us take the stairs down off the plane and walk the tarmac over to the plane headed for Montreal. Our luggage didn't make it, but it didn't matter because it was a long time before we ever got to a hotel.

When we arrived in Montreal at 6 p.m., after 12 hours of travel, Jim said let's go to the park for a little while. We had all thought we would go out and have a nice dinner and night off, but that didn't happen. We went to Olympic Stadium and started to meet.

After a few hours, around 10 p.m., Whitey asked, "Jim, are we planning on having dinner tonight?"

Jim looked surprised and said, "I guess it is dinner time. We can call and have some chicken delivered."

A big sigh went up in the room.

We were used to John McHale taking us out for a nice dinner, particularly French food. Montreal is one of the greater dining cities there is, and we were eating greasy fast-food chicken in a box.

Jim never wanted to miss a thing, and he never was caught up with the time of day.

One thing though was that the guys knew where the liquor cabinet was in the office, and when we were done for the day, they would say, "Time for a cup of tea." Code for a cocktail.

We worked hard, but we had fun.

We would take the subway to the ballpark every day to meet and for the draft itself. One time, on the first day of the draft, we met in the lobby of the hotel and started to walk to the subway. When we got to the station, it was padlocked shut.

Turns out the night before, the workers decided to strike for a day and there was no subway service. It was a one-day strike, but it *had* to happen on draft day.

Since everyone was taking cabs with the subway closed, we were lucky to find a taxi and make it to the park just in time for the draft. I guess those one-day strikes used to happen quite often from what I was told.

In the 1983 draft, we selected one player from our territory that made it to the major leagues: Bill Moore, out of Cal State Fullerton. Bill was a wrong way player (bats right, throws left) who was a good defensive first baseman and hitter and made solid line-drive contact. He made it to the majors for six games in 1986, and after his playing days, became a highly successful scout and crosschecker for the Toronto Blue Jays and Philadelphia Phillies.

He wasn't an easy sign even though he was a college senior, as he turned down our offer to go to a college summer league to play, but then reconsidered. I think he just thought I was cheap, but actually, Montreal paid its players a lot more than San Diego did.

There was a college pitcher that we drafted that I didn't have on my preferential draft list (the list of players we have interest in ranked in order of preference). He had a good arm, but also had a lot of mechanical issues that I thought would keep him from reaching the major leagues because I could never see him having enough consistency in throwing strikes.

He did have a fine arm with an above-average fastball that would read in the mid 90's on a radar gun, along with a hard-breaking curveball. Our guys saw him at the College World Series where he lit up the gun, and that was someone they wanted, even though I didn't have him turned in. After he was selected, I was told to go sign him.

I would like to say that it is hard enough to sign a player that you have a lot of interest in, but to sign someone that you don't have *any* interest in is really tough.

I made an appointment to meet with the player and his agent to start the negotiation. After I made the initial offer and they countered, we were quite distant in numbers. I left and told them to let me know if you decide to get in our range or best of luck to you.

I was taking a chance because I knew how badly Jim wanted to sign him, but what they were asking for was way out of line. I thought we could either wait them out to get their figure down, or maybe he would go back to school. He was a nice kid, but I didn't want to put a lot of money into him.

I didn't hear anything from them for about a week and by now, Jim was checking with me regularly to see if I was close to getting a deal done. Finally, he just told me on a Friday to call them, go over on Monday, and give them what they want to get him signed.

I just couldn't do it that day and thought I would call on Sunday to set something up when my phone rang. The player's agent called and said they wanted to talk again and asked if I would come over.

This is where I took a big risk and said, "I will be happy to come over, but if you are still looking for the money you talked about before, I'm not coming."

I was assured they weren't and that we could get something done.

On Monday, I met with them and sure enough, we got a deal done where I felt it should be. But it was about $8,000 less than what I was told to get it done for.

When I called Jim and told him, he said, "Great, so you have him what we discussed?"

"No, I got him for $8,000 less."

Jim was so happy that he told me I could take my family on my next trip, and the club would pay for it. It was a kind gesture on his part. Jim was a wonderful man to work for, and really treated his scouts right.

By the way, the player never made it to the majors, as he didn't have enough consistency throwing strikes. Occasionally, I was right.

The 1985 season would prove to be the most productive of the time I spent with the Expos. It would also prove to be my last year with them.

Murray Cook took over for John McHale as GM for the 1985 season, and at the end of the year, Murray hired Gary Hughes as the new scouting director. Jim was assigned to another department.

Murray had previously been the general manager of the Yankees and the farm director with Pittsburgh for over two decades. Baseball was a fraternity at the time, and though I didn't know him well and went on to know him better after his days in Montreal, I really liked him, and we became good friends.

Before Gary Hughes was hired, I had applied for the job, along with others. When Gary got the job, Murray called me to tell me that I didn't get it. He told me that they had decided to go in another direction, which are famous words for saying I don't want to give you a reason.

"What direction is that?" I asked, and he just repeated it again.

I wouldn't let it go, so I asked again, "What direction? I can change directions."

Murray finally told me that he had worked with Gary, trusted him, and they thought the same way.

I have always liked Murray and that's why I probably felt I could push it, but I appreciated the honest answer as Gary was a qualified person, but I wanted a reason. I think it ticked Murray off some though.

Gary and I have been friends for a long time, and when we were put into the Baseball Scouts Hall of Fame in Sioux Falls, South Dakota, we were put in together. Our plaques are side by side and they honored us on the same night.

The four years I spent with Montreal were very educational for me, and particularly important in my development as a baseball person and director of a department. It was a first-class operation that appreciated and encouraged honest input, and it was loaded with veteran baseball people that had a plan and philosophy.

Jim had a big influence on me and on how important every opinion is, even if it is different than yours, and to treat everyone with the same respect that you would hope to receive. He had great patience and an even demeanor, which is so important. He backed the scouts as much as anyone I had ever been around in baseball.

It wasn't a team where I shared all their beliefs and philosophies, but I was proud to be a member of the organization, and very appreciative of what I learned there.

MONTREAL EXPOS – RANDY JOHNSON

"Randy Johnson pitching for USC, circa 1985"

The first time I saw Randy Johnson was in the spring of 1982. He was a tall and lean pitcher at Livermore High School in Northern California who you had to project and envision many years in the future. That projection all turned out to be true.

The first thing you notice about a guy like Randy is his stature, and man, was he ever tall. He was an intimidating figure on the mound even though he hadn't yet filled into that massive 6-foot-10 frame.

At Livermore, Randy didn't throw all that hard. It wasn't worrisome because you knew he'd throw a lot harder down the road (which he did). He didn't know he had it working for him, but he had a lot of deception because of all the moving pieces from a guy his size and that made him very tough on hitters even though he was only throwing in the upper 80's and low 90's. What truly separated Randy was his competitiveness that made him tough on hitters. He didn't just want to win, he wanted to beat you.

His biggest trouble was finding consistency in his delivery and repeating proper throwing mechanics. It's a common theme for taller pitchers like Randy who find it harder to get the whole body working together to maximize your throwing ability.

Anytime you get a tall pitcher it normally takes them longer to get consistency and the ability to repeat, not only in their delivery but with their stuff because they have so many moving pieces they have to get in order.

A shorter, more compact pitcher doesn't tend to have these problems and that is why you see a shorter high school or college pitcher be able to repeat. You have to let the taller kids grow a little and get all their coordination, which can sometimes take into their mid-20's. But when it happens, they begin to dominate.

Randy's primary mechanical problem was that he had little arm extension in the back and rushed his release point. As he got older and pitched more, he got more extension not only in the back but out front. You would see him try to overthrow because he threw harder than most kids at that age, and when you do that you make a lot of inconsistencies to your delivery.

Another unique display from his mechanics was his arm slot. Plenty of guys throw from a three-quarter arm angle and Randy threw from a slightly lower three-quarter slot. However, for most guys, when you throw from that angle you're throwing from nearly under or around six feet off the ground from the release. With Randy being 6-foot-10, that release point was still around 6-foot-6 but still funky, making him deceptive and hard to pick up.

Aside from the mechanics, you saw a tall kid with a quick arm and strong wrist. This made him easy to project even if you believed it may take a while before it all comes together.

Randy was drafted later that year in the fourth round by the Atlanta Braves and turned down a solid offer of $50,000 to attend the University of Southern California on a full athletic scholarship.

Plenty of teams had interest in Randy out of high school, us included, but even then, I'm sure it wasn't a slam dunk he would sign. Atlanta was particularly good with high school players back in that era because they understood projection and had a lot of success with high school players. For most clubs, the thought was that he needed the three additional years of playing college baseball to grow and fill out his tall frame.

When you're growing into a large frame you need to constantly get stronger and need to constantly throw to build up your arm. What happens, and I learned this later - especially Randy's first year - the taller a kid is, because you throw so much, the arm will develop faster than the body. The arm can strengthen simply by throwing a lot of pitches and it takes less time to strengthen the arm than it takes for the body to fill out and gain strength.

During his time at USC, Randy continued to develop not only with his stuff getting better, but his delivery became more refined. The more he was able to repeat his delivery the stronger he got, and the stuff got better with it. His arm extension in back and out front was getting better and giving him more arm speed and velocity to his pitches, putting him in the 90's with ease. His balance over the rubber still needed work and as he tired, he would get erratic with his control. But when he was in the zone, he'd blow it right past guys.

He would get through two or three innings where he would throw really hard and then it would start dropping off. Again, a lot of that comes with strength to come and it hasn't gotten there yet. The taller you are, the longer is usually takes to get to the consistency that is needed. His best velocities would come in his mid-20's, but it wasn't there just yet in his early 20's.

We kept track of his progress as he approached his draft-eligible junior year. He was usually the Sunday starter or came out of the bullpen the first two years, but showing improvement is all that mattered to us.

Going into the spring of 1985, he was certainly one of the best players in the area and would be garnering a lot of attention. He was starting to fill into his frame some and generating more velocity on his fastball even though he lacked consistency. He was slated to be the Trojans' third starter that spring behind Brad Brink and Steve Bast, at a baseball factory that for many seasons produced several major leaguers under their coach, Rod Dedeaux.

When the season started, Randy began with better velocity on his fastball and a sharper breaking ball than he had the previous year. His delivery still left a lot to be desired and he lacked the consistency to repeat properly, but nevertheless, was getting better. He had lengthened out his delivery to get more use of his body and was getting more extension with his arm in the back and out front, generating more arm speed with the ball coming out of his hand easier. At that size, if you keep a good angle to the plate, the ball is coming out of the hand closer to the hitter, which gives the hitter even less time to pick up the ball.

The problem remained, though, that he struggled to throw strikes. His junior year, he walked 104 batters in 118 innings. He also had trouble maintaining his velocity after a few innings mostly due to throwing so many pitches. In his three-year career with the Trojans, he walked 188 batters in 243 innings, while striking out 206. Even with these erratic statistics, he was showing steady progress and still had so much room to project he would get better.

It wasn't a matter of throwing first-pitch strikes or putting guys away. He could put guys away if he put it over the plate. His stuff was outstanding even then because of the newfound velocity, the deception and the developing breaking ball, but it all has to do with consistency of command. It gets back to the mechanics, but with the improvements he was making you could see the makings of where he could lower that walk rate, and he did.

In today's world of analytics, it's unlikely he would have been drafted nearly as high as he was. With the number of walks and the age of a college pitcher, although the velocity was good, it wasn't 100 mph and that would have worked against him. You could take a 5-foot-11 high school pitcher who threw 96 mph and didn't walk anyone and the draft model may come out ahead. We had little statistical data (which in this case was good) outside of the standard wins, losses, ERA, walks, strikeouts, etc. We had no analytics and little video so you had to go with your instincts, reference, and that you believed he could be helped.

During the season, Cliff Ditto, Tom Hinkle, and myself made sure that one of us was at each of his starts to make sure he stayed healthy, and we could effectively evaluate his whole year. Cliff had good contacts for information at USC, Tom knew coaches from other schools who could provide information, and I had seen him since high school, so I had the best reference of his overall improvement. We all had something different to add to the equation.

It gave us a good idea of Randy's strengths and weaknesses from all angles and less surprises. I hated surprises, good or bad. I always wanted to know what the guy might be capable of doing and what he might not be capable of doing. I think when you have three different people coming from a different angle like this, it leaves you less unknowns and made us feel comfortable.

We had all seen him so much and talked about him constantly. We talked about makeup and how far Randy had come in three years. How his stamina is, what happened in this outing or another. Sometimes he would only throw two innings, but a lot of times in a two-inning outing, you might still have had good moments you can build off, so we talked about these things. We didn't leave any stone unturned, and we liked this kid. We all grew up the same way to project and project certain things, so it was an easy thing for all of us.

All our upper-level staff members within the Montreal scouting department - Jim Fanning, Whitey Lockmann, Eddie Lopat and Earl Rapp - saw Randy pitch and were on board with trying to get him in the draft. It took little convincing as they all saw the potential and the trust of our pitching instructors in the organization that we felt could help him as a professional.

We had good veteran instructors and managers in our farm system that could take a delivery and help it quickly. They could get pitchers balanced and get them to do the things they needed to succeed. It was a good feeling knowing that if we got a kid from the amateur ranks that he was going to go to people that knew what they needed to make the pitcher better. Montreal through those years developed a lot of players and were among the best organizations in doing so.

There were rumors among the scouts in Southern California that Randy was too tall to be a starting pitcher and wouldn't be able to pitch deep into games. A lot of people believed those rumors. Scouts like to talk and once they start talking, they end up letting out a lot of stuff. Because of Randy's inconsistencies in his delivery, these rumors kicked around and to a point, you understood.

It's a good thing we weren't smart enough to listen to those people in this case. I was pretty stupid about listening to people and pigheaded (I'm still pigheaded). I believe in what I was taught and one thing I was taught by my father early on is that if you see it once, they own it, and don't forget it. When you see a guy like this do it right once, you can't forget it. When you see somebody like this you want to exhaust every avenue to see if he can be in the most important role.

There were also questions about Randy's makeup which still leave me wondering what it could have been. Randy was a quiet kid and maybe people didn't get to know him and sometimes that can be the case. It may have been in this scenario or it may not have been, but there were organizations that did question his makeup for whatever reason it was.

We didn't talk to kids very often before the draft and I think when people don't get the chance to talk to a player a lot, they begin to ask questions about why that player won't talk to them. I don't know. I don't know if people thought he wasn't tough enough, but that couldn't have been farther from the truth. His nickname, "Big Unit," came from Hall of Famer, Tim Raines, who gave him the nickname after the two collided headfirst and Tim yelled out, "You're a big unit!".

All I know is that when he was on the mound, he was an extremely aggressive and tough competitor and I know I never had a problem with it. I still believe makeup evaluation is instinctual and when you're looking at a player you can get a better read from that than you can from any handwritten or personality evaluation test.

When the 1985 draft came, we were able to select Randy in the second round, 36th overall. I'm still not sure how far past where we selected him someone would have taken him. You would think not long, but he didn't have the year people expected and statistical-minded clubs would have struggled with the walks he allowed.

My gut tells me he never would have gotten to us in the third round. You never know, but I doubt it. Honestly, I was concerned he may not even get to us in the second round because there were organizations out there that thought like we did. There were plenty of teams interested in him around the same range as the 36th pick.

When all is said and done, it doesn't really matter, because we got him and that's all that counts.

Following the draft, I contacted Randy to set up an appointment and come meet with him and his parents about signing with the Montreal Expos.

His parents had retired to a little suburb just west of Grass Valley, California in Gold Country of the Sierra Nevada Mountains. I had once lived about 25 miles away in Auburn. A wonderful old town up in the hills surrounded by pine trees that take you back to the gold mining days.

Tom and I made the trip a few days after the draft to see Randy and his parents in a gated golf course community of Lake Wildwood, where to this day, I believe Randy's mother still lives.

Randy's parents were good people. I know Randy was awfully close to his father, Bud, who was a policeman in Livermore. Carol, his mother, was a stay-at-home mom who helped raise Randy and five other children. Genuinely nice people.

Sitting around a large family table, we had a very productive first meeting with his parents asking most of the questions about our organization and professional baseball.

"Where are your minor league teams located? Where would he live? What kind of insurance do they have? What are the college scholarship plans?"

They did a good job of covering all the areas you would want a parent to ask.

When we finished the discussion and answered their questions, it was time to make our initial offer. During the conversation, Randy didn't say much and would ask the occasional question you'd expect a player to ask. When we got to the offer though, Randy pulled up his chair a little closer, leaned forward and in so many words asked, "What have you got?"

You somehow got the impression he knew what he was doing.

I made the offer, around $35,000. Randy sat back, declined the offer, and proceeded to tell us why. He started to list players name after name who had been selected near his spot in previous drafts and what bonuses they received. He knew this info by heart and didn't miss a beat.

I realized we needed to regroup and Tom and I needed some time. I told the family that we will get back with them and decided to meet a few days later.

When Tom and I got into the car outside the house I asked him, "Do you have any idea if any of those numbers he said were true?"

"I have no idea," Tom replied.

Back then, you didn't have publications that told you how much kids signed for out of the draft. Clubs didn't tell you anything. It was all secretive and under wraps. Those numbers were not readily available so we didn't have any idea what the other picks got and were just told to simply go sign him for "x" amount of dollars if we could.

Though we didn't get a deal done, we left the meeting in a good mood. People tend to understand that you have a starting point in negotiations and very seldom do you get it done the first time but hope to be closer. All was fine.

We left the Johnson's and made the half-hour drive to our hotel back in Auburn. I went up to my room and immediately called Jim to tell him about the meeting and with what info Randy had hit us with.

Jim listened as I repeated the bonus money Randy said other players received. Jim was quiet the whole time and I started to get a little worried with all that silence. Usually while you're talking with the scouting director, they'll interrupt you and say what about this or that, but Jim said nothing.

Right at the moment I started to think, "Oh man, I'm in trouble," the silence broke with a chuckle on the other end of the line.

"Bob, the kid's right on with those numbers," Jim said.

A few days later back at the Johnson residence, we offered Randy $60,000 and he agreed. We had signed him, and if it wasn't for what he was asking, it was close. When you give a kid pretty much what he asks for, it goes smoothly.

Shortly after, Randy Johnson was heading off to Jamestown, New York, to start his professional career.

It was in that negotiation that Randy gave us a glimpse of what was to come. We didn't know it then, but when you start as a scout you are told ability and makeup are key. My father taught me the way a player negotiates is the way he plays the game. If a player is timid, worried he might not make it, or asks for much more money than he should receive, you should be tentative about signing him. But, if a player is knowledgeable, fair, aggressive and wants a successful outcome, they have a chance to be highly successful. Randy was prepared, fair, aggressive, and wanted a successful negotiation. As his career unfolded very few were as prepared, fair, aggressive, and successful as Randy.

Looking back over all the negotiations I was a part of, Randy, Ozzie Smith, Tony Gwynn, and Jim Abbott were as tough and fair as you could get. They all carried it on the field. Every good player I could think of that ever succeeded, they wanted to do it this way.

With agents handling most negotiations today from high school to the major leagues, you don't get a chance to see this important side of the player anymore as a scout. For many players, the initial bond they had with the scout that signed them was an important and trusted connection. I think for some, these negotiations were as important for the family as they were for the kid because they knew somebody they could talk to that was in the organization. Until a player had been around a long time, they didn't know the general manager or farm director of the team.

You don't have these connections and trust nearly as often today as when scouts handled all the negotiations. I would say there are times now when a player hasn't even met the scout that drafted him. Not very often, but it could happen because they don't see the scout at the negotiation table. I hate to see that part of the game gone.

After Randy signed, he had some up-and-down times, mostly with his control. I did receive a call not long after he arrived in Jamestown saying that his velocity was down and that maybe we had signed him hurt.

I objected as sternly as I could that there was no way he wasn't healthy. We didn't miss a single start at college that year. We've never known a player better than we've known Randy Johnson. We have all the information. We did all our homework. We didn't sign Randy hurt.

Jim backed us strongly. It was determined that Randy was still growing and getting stronger but wasn't able to have his best stuff going every five days instead of seven. With most professional teams, starting pitchers work in a five-man rotation, pitching every fifth or sometimes sixth day. In college, you have three or four guys in a rotation who pitch once a week and usually on the same day as their previous start. Randy was still green, and all he needed to do is get stronger and get that extra day off until then.

Almost immediately after he returned, he started throwing hard again and striking people out. I think his first game back he struck out 11.

I was upset because we did our job on this kid and didn't sign him hurt. We knew it and Jim knew it. Jim always backed his people.

Randy went on to get stronger in the Expos farm system and even though commanding pitches would take time to master, his stuff, makeup, aggressiveness, drive and commitment to success helped him get to the majors in just over three years. He developed more consistent balance over the rubber and found a consistent release point that made everything better. Everything he needed help on from college, he got help on.

His fastball was thrown harder (reaching triple digits in mid-20's) with late, hard sink and a quick, late break to his slider. He was equally tough on both right-handed and left-handed hitters and for some lefties in the box, they seemed to be totally overmatched, even the best of them. After he gained command of the strike zone, his next 22 years in the major leagues were almost unmatched.

Over his career, Randy was 10-time All-Star, five-time Cy Young Award winner, World Series winner and co-World Series MVP in 2001. He is one of 24 pitchers with 300 or more wins (303), has the second-most strikeouts (4,875) in baseball history, and became a first-ballot Hall of Famer in 2015.

Looking back, there are a couple of times that come to mind with Randy that affected me personally. The first came in 1995 when I was with the Angels and we tied the Seattle Mariners for first place in the division and were forced to have a one-game playoff in Seattle. Of course, the Mariners' starting pitcher would be Randy.

That year everyone had picked us to finish last with a young team, and we ended up building a late season division lead. We fell back late in the year and ended up tying for first place. I knew as soon as there was a one-game playoff, Randy was going to pitch against us.

There I was watching a player I signed pitch against the team I was working for and as much as you want to see a player you signed do well, you want to win with the team you're working for, and man, we really wanted to win. It's the kind of game you want to see him pitch well and you want to see him throw eight good innings, get taken out of the game, and have us win it in the ninth. We had our bags packed knowing that if we won, we would travel to New York for the first round of the playoffs, and if we lost, we were headed back home to Anaheim for the winter.

Randy was perfect through five innings and we allowed one run in the bottom half of the inning. We finally broke through with a hit in the sixth, but Seattle's offense exploded in the seventh after Luis Sojo's ground ball down the right-field line with the bases loaded got caught under a bench. Four runs scored on the play, followed by four more the next inning.

We lost that game 9-1, and Randy threw a complete game allowing just three hits and one run on a ninth-inning home run. He struck out 12. It was signature dominance from one of the game's best pitchers. It sucked for us.

The second time was in 2017 when Randy was given the Lifetime Achievement Award from the Professional Baseball Scouts Foundation. It takes place yearly at a wonderful venue in Beverly Hills, California with plenty of high-end auctions involved to raise money for the foundation. I didn't go often because it was a lot of big money, and scouts don't make big money.

When they had asked Randy who he would like to present the award, he stated that he wanted the scouts that signed him. The idea that after all the years of seeing him so rarely, like when we tried to sign him with the Angels in 1998, meant an awful lot to me. Scouts aren't usually remembered and accept that fact, so that made this incredibly special.

My wife, Karen, and I spent two days with Randy at the event and it was a great night. We had dinner the night before the event and chatted a lot about the Expos days, pitching in general and his excitement of joining the Arizona Diamondbacks organization as an advisor.

It was an unbelievable night at the ceremony where I told this story that you just read. It made me remember Cliff and Tom and everything we went through to get him signed and about how he signed and how that reflected on him as a player.

As I presented the award to Randy at the dinner I said, "Tonight is a wonderful night and a deserving award for you, but for three scouts, this is a career night."

I meant it and I know that Cliff and Tom would feel the same way.

Randy became the ultimate professional pitcher, not only in the way he performed, but in the way he prepared to pitch. He is a model for young pitchers and those to follow. He played the game the way you should play it.

CHICAGO WHITE SOX, PART I (1986)

In 1986, I left the Montreal Expos to join the Chicago White Sox when Duane Shaffer and Terry Logan hired me to scout Northern California and the Northwest while crosschecking players nationally. Even though that amounts to three jobs, this was the year Ken "Hawk" Harrelson became the team's general manager after leaving the broadcast booth. He told ownership that by hiring experienced scouts and paying good salaries, we could scout with six people and have them travel all over. It sounded and looked good on paper, but it would prove to be unsuccessful.

Even though we were spread so thin, we did have a group of experienced scouts with contacts and knowledge that would be an asset. Time was our biggest enemy, as we didn't have enough of it to do the job as completely and thoroughly as we normally would.

Hawk believed that with experienced scouts, you would get better results with fewer people. I think there is truth to that, but six wasn't nearly enough. We were solid through the first 20 rounds of the draft and then we were done. We did the best we could, but just didn't have enough time.

In many cases, I only got to see players in my area once because of my travel to other areas. My area of about 12 states was pretty lean and the weather during the spring made it a tough year. My training from when I started with the Padres in the Midwest really helped prepare me for this, but it still made things even more difficult. Couple that with the crosscheck assignments I had, and it was challenging to get multiple looks at players.

However, working in Northern California and the Northwest is, I believe, the best territory to cover. It is beautiful country with normally a good amount of solid, draftable players. I had this area only briefly on a few occasions, but it was my favorite.

Before the season started, Terry had a staff meeting in Houston to go over our operating schedule for the year. Since this was a new experience, all of us were anxious to get together.

The staff included Terry, who was our scouting director, Duane, our West Coast supervisor, George Bradley, Larry Monroe, Walt Widmayer, Leo Labossiere, and me. All baseball people who had great conversations.

I had met Terry when I covered the Texas region and he was the baseball coach at Brenham High School, an hour outside of Houston. I knew Duane from scouting on the West Coast.

Walt was a well-respected veteran who was known for his pocket drafts. These were names down the line in a draft that he would produce on a 3x5 card in the pocket of his sportcoat when the club was running short of players to select. He would get a lot of those players and many went on to good careers. Tom Kotchman of the Angels always reminded me some of Walt in that he had a ton of success with those lower draft picks.

It was a good group, and I learned a lot from all their ideas and thoughts on scouting.

After one of our meetings at Terry's, we went out for dinner. All six of us plus Dave Dombrowski, who was our assistant general manager, piled into Terry's station wagon. I kept thinking, not to be negative, that one accident could eliminate the entire White Sox scouting staff and their assistant GM in one motion. Luckily, we made it to dinner, where Don's Seafood provided a great meal, and we made it back to Terry's safely.

The 1986 season was still a lot of fun with almost an unlimited travel budget and being involved with most everything that was happening around the country. It was a busy and fun time, and with only six scouts, you knew you would be involved.

When we arrived in Chicago to start the draft meetings, everybody was looking forward to how it would go. We met in a room in the old Comiskey Park that was small and had no windows. With only seven of us total in the room, it at least wasn't cramped.

We had long meetings, but with the scouts we had and the experience they owned, the meetings were interesting, fun, and I thought productive. We had some arguments, but it was based on baseball belief and we all knew how to handle it.

A day before the draft, Hawk came in to talk with us and expressed that we should draft as much left-handed pitching that we could.

We had planned on going in a different direction, but it is the prerogative of the general manager or owner to lead a staff in a certain direction. Every year I was a scouting director, I would ask the general manager if there was a direction they wanted us to go. In almost 20 years I was only asked twice, that if things were even, to try and get as much pitching as you can.

After the meeting, we selected Grady Hall, a left-handed pitcher from Northwestern, with the 20th pick in the first round.

When your first-round pick doesn't work out the way you want, it can sometimes set a trend. We didn't have a horrible draft because we got four of the 21 players selected to the majors. But Grady Hall was not one of them. Hall spent seven seasons in the minors, pitching between Double-A and Triple-A for four organizations, and never made it to the majors.

I don't think it was the way anyone in the room thought we would go if we hadn't been pointed in that direction. Again, no one's fault, as that's the way it goes. I thought Terry did a good job in the meetings and that we probably had the first hundred players lined up as well as anyone. The problem is when you have such a small staff, your conviction on players isn't as strong.

We were able to draft 20 rounds on our staff's evaluation, draft one on an MLB Scouting Bureau report, and then passed in the 22nd round. We just didn't have the depth to go farther.

I got two players in the draft: Bryce Hulstrom, a left-handed pitcher out of Oregon State, in the ninth round, and Mark Davis, an outfielder from Stanford, in the 12th round.

Hulstrom had a good arm and a curveball that could be tough, especially on a left-handed hitter, but he was traded to St. Louis the next year and didn't make it to the majors.

Davis was a highly touted player out of Herbert Hoover High School in San Diego, and even played on our Padres Scout's Team as a high schooler. Davis had a lot of ability, but the interest in him started to slide in college. He still had good tools and was a bright kid with good baseball instincts. I was happy to get him where we did, and he did get to the majors for a cup of coffee.

After the draft was over, we had a lot of pro coverage of the other organizations. Early in the summer, things were starting to go south with the big league team and Hawk brought in Tom Haller to be his general manager while Jim Fregosi took over as manager, replacing Tony LaRussa. We were starting to get a lot of negative press and you could feel that things better start changing quick, or this fun job could go south.

One of my assignments that summer was to cover the San Jose Bees, an independent team in the California League. They had several former major league players who were trying to get back to the bigs, including Steve Howe, a former left-handed reliever for the Dodgers. He would fight substance abuse for many years and had been let go most recently by the Minnesota Twins after five years in the majors.

I was told to watch him throw and find out everything I could about how he was doing off the field. I started my investigation.

Over the next week, I saw him pitch three or four times. He had a solid, above-average fastball and a power curve that was almost unhittable, showing good command in the strike zone while challenging hitters. That was the easy part.

I asked questions of people in the organization to see if he was behaving himself. I was told he was and did all the things the club asked of him. I reported all this back to Chicago, and they asked if I had met him yet, and how his eyes looked. I hadn't by this time but said I would set up a meeting.

Harry Steve, the general manager of the San Jose club, was hoping to sell as many of his players he could to major league organizations and helped set up a meeting with Steve. We met early in the afternoon in Harry's office before Steve went to the clubhouse.

I was looking forward to talking with Steve but wasn't sure how I was going to get a great look at his eyes. I'm sure they wanted me to look and see if they were glassy or red, but I'm no expert on what different substances do to your eyes.

He was a pleasant guy who was easy to talk with, but I'm not so sure I did a good job looking at his eyes, as I kept *staring* at them. I think he knew what I was doing but he was good about the meeting, and his eyes were as clear as crystal.

I recommended that we sign him, and I don't know if we tried or not, but he went on to sign with Texas. He pitched seven more years in the majors with the Rangers and Yankees but had more substance abuse problems along the way. What a shame that he had the problems he had, as he had such a fine arm and there is no telling how good of a career he could have had.

Towards the end of the season with the big-league club 22 games out of first place, Hawk was fired and headed back to the radio booth. The search for a new general manager was underway. Several people in the organization thought they were going to get the job, but ultimately, Larry Himes, the scouting director for the Angels, got the position.

When Larry came over, he told me I would have another year because he knew I worked hard. This would've been the kind of year you enjoyed to the max but knew it was too good to be true, and probably wouldn't last. It didn't.

I was traded to the California Angels in exchange for Al Goldis before I could do any work for Larry.

CALIFORNIA YEARS

"Tim Mead's farewell at Angel Stadium; L-R:
Mike Port, Me, Tim Mead, Bill Bavasi"

CALIFORNIA YEARS – BUILDING A FOUNDATION

"Bobby was old school as it gets. His dad was the head scout with the San Francisco Giants for years – Mr. Fontaine Sr. We all really learned from him too. Bobby would incorporate everybody. When you talk about Billy (Bavasi) and Bobby, they would permit you to do your work, open communication, you never felt restricted in what you wanted to say to them and that it would be taken in the wrong way. Bobby permitted me to scout even after I became a full-time manager in 1984. He permitted me to scout full-time before I went to spring training, which I really appreciated. Bobby was really good, I thought, on the draft board. I thought he was really good in the upper rounds. I used to argue with him a lot at times to get some of the lower guys I wanted, but he just included everybody. The ability back then that I really think we're getting back to within (our current group) is the ability to disagree openly. I think that is probably one of the key components of any successful group, that you can openly disagree. You're not worried about hurting somebody else's feelings – respectfully always – and then you decide what's the right thing to do and move along." – Joe Maddon, Angels manager and former scout and coach.

In November of 1986, I was about to start a long, productive, and extremely enjoyable time with the California Angels. I would spend the next 13 years as scouting director, and later player personnel director as well. I was to be associated with some of the best and most talented people I have ever worked with in every aspect of the game, including the privilege of working for an owner like Gene Autry.

After Larry Himes was hired as the new general manager of the Chicago White Sox, he took about 80 percent of the scouting staff from the Angels with him. Larry had been the Angels scouting director. When Larry approached Mike Port, then Angels general manager, about bringing Al Goldis with him to become scouting director, Mike said no unless they could have me as the Angels scouting director. It wasn't long before an agreement was in place, and Al and I were traded for each other.

From what I have been told and through personal research, this was the first occurrence of scouts being traded. Jerome Holtzman, a well-known sportswriter for the *Chicago Tribune,* wrote an article about it saying that there have been players, managers and even owners traded, but no scouts.

When I got to California it was great to be reunited with Mike Port after our days in San Diego. He is one of the best development and scouting-minded general managers I have worked with. He always backed what we did as scouts unless he thought something was a big mistake or wouldn't work.

Bill Bavasi was the Angels minor league farm director and was familiar to me as I had worked with his dad and brothers in San Diego. Frank Marcos, who would later become the director of the Major League Scouting Bureau for many years, was Bill's assistant.

This was the Angels front office. By today's standards, that would probably be the smallest in baseball, but was about average in size for the time and worked fine.

Right after I was hired, I met Mike, Bill, and Frank in Hollywood, Florida at the Baseball Winter Meetings in early December. My first item of business was to basically hire a staff. Larry and Al had taken most of our staff to Chicago with them, leaving us approximately six full-time scouts and a few part-time scouts. Scouting staffs were usually in place for the next season by October 1, so the available selection of experienced scouts was minimal at best.

Bill and Nick Kamzic, who was the ranking scout with the Angels and who I had known for years, helped me the best they could with available names and for possible scouting positions. Everyone in baseball knew what had taken place and I was getting recommendations of names of people from all different types of backgrounds, from sporting goods reps to coaches to umpires. I was interviewing around 10 people a day, but still had no idea which direction to go.

Towards the conclusion of the meetings, I started to hire scouts and even though it was put together quickly and at the worst time of year possible, we started to develop a solid foundation of a staff that would be very productive.

That first year we were able to add George Bradley and Paul Robinson from the White Sox, and Cliff Ditto from Montreal. Nick, Rick Schlenker, and Rick Ingalls had remained with the Angels through the transition, and along with George, Paul, and Cliff, gave us some stability at the senior level of the staff. But, with so many new people who came from different backgrounds, it took time to get everyone on the same page.

The first thing I tried to instill was that we had a philosophy that would closely follow the Dodgers and Pirates outlook on what to look for in a player, or how I refer to it, the Branch Rickey philosophy. Mike had learned that way, as well as Bill, so it was the right fit for us. We would evaluate by the following guidelines:

A. Position Player: Athletic ability, quick feet, speed, arm strength, bat speed, power.
B. Clean delivery, good arm action, strong wrist, loose arm, velocity, ability to spin a breaking ball.
C. Try to get athletes from other sports.
D. Convert players to be catchers.
E. Rely heavily on gut feel and scout's instincts.
F. Take chances even if we are second-guessed.
G. Make our money go as far as we could.
H. Operate as if we were spending our own money.
I. ULTIMATE GOAL: Have all nine players on the field on the Major League club be homegrown talent from our farm system (Note: We did get eight at one time, which was a real testament to our staff, as I never saw a team with nine at one time.)

Once we finished the hiring process and completed our staff, we held an organization meeting in Anaheim in January. Our scouting staff and minor league personnel met together for the first time as a collective group. In the past, it was my understanding that the scouting department and minor league staff met separately, which is the way most clubs meet today. It would turn out to be one of the best meetings I ever attended.

When we decided to have this joint meeting, we talked about utilizing our personnel so that those who were capable of working in both departments would be encouraged to do so.

Mike Port is an outstanding baseball man who delegated responsibility so that people wanted to work and succeed. We had done this together in San Diego, and you can't utilize staff and personnel like this without the permission of the general manager. His lead in this was something I tried to pass on to any staff I ever led.

Bill Bavasi was the most talented minor league farm director I had ever been around. He listened, used his staff to maximize their ability, was organized, possessed great people skills, and was always open to ideas. Bill wanted a scout with the Rookie League affiliates, whether it was as a manager or specialty coach, if possible. He was completely on board and was one of the orchestrators, pushing for it as much as anybody.

Even though Joe Maddon was our minor league field coordinator, he would scout through March and years later became instrumental in the signing of Tim Salmon, who became the face of the franchise.

We had people like Cliff, Rick Ingalls, Bruce Hines, and others who could contribute to both departments. Tom Kotchman, who was our Triple-A manager, went on to become a scout in Florida and our Rookie League manager, becoming as successful as anyone who ever took that role.

This developed great comradery. We wanted everyone to consider this a player procurement staff that found the players, signed the players, and developed the players to get to the majors. They quickly understood one was only as good as the other in accomplishing this goal.

As the meeting continued, we began talking about setting up a dinner when the staffs were in Anaheim, where they could eat, drink, and talk baseball. I, of course, was thinking Morton's or

Ruth Chris Steakhouse, but Bill said, "Let's meet in the clubhouse at the ballpark and have sub sandwiches and beer."

I thought he was nuts, but he felt it would be a great atmosphere for this. He was right.

The staffs started to mingle, and really gave us a good note to depart on to start the season. We would have many of these types of gatherings through the years and talk baseball, and share ideas and philosophies. These gatherings made us stronger as a group.

A few days before our meeting in the clubhouse, Mike called me into his office and said, "You won't believe the call I just received. Mr. Autry wanted to know if it was all right if he came by the dinner in the clubhouse to say hello to everyone."

Mike and I sat there in disbelief, knowing the staff would be thrilled to see him.

Gene Autry was a famous singer and actor in the mid-20th century. He wrote songs such as "Back in The Saddle Again," "Rudolph, the Red-Nosed Reindeer," "Frosty the Snowman," and "Here Comes Santa Claus." Most of his fame came in country music and cowboy and Western films, where he was always the hero coming to save the day.

Mr. Autry, as all reference him, had a true love for baseball and was a minority owner of the Hollywood Stars in the Pacific Coast League. In 1960, he purchased the Southern California-based Major League Baseball expansion team, which went on to become the Angels. He owned the team until his death in 1998 and is beloved by the fans to this day.

He was a true gentleman, and whether you grew up listening to his music or watching his movies and shows, or not, he was the type of person that everyone knew.

When Mr. Autry came to the dinner, he brought Pat Buttram with him. Pat had been in movies with Mr. Autry and is well known for his role in "Green Acres" as Mr. Haney.

The pair spent a lot of time with us and told so many great stories that left us grasping for breath they were so hysterical. They mingled with everyone and it made those that were new, as well as those who had been with the club, feel like an important part of the organization. When those two walked in the room, it was like Santa Claus had arrived.

After the meetings adjourned, we started on the coverage for my first draft with the Angels. It was going to be the most difficult one I was ever associated with. It was fairly productive and certainly the start to establishing a staff that would create a solid foundation for the Angels for years to come.

Something I learned when I was the scouting director with the Padres was how important treating your staff is. The old saying to "treat people the way you would like to be treated" is *absolutely* true. I found that if you have $10 to spend on an employee's salary, you can get three returns on that money by how you treat them. First, an $8 return if you treat them poorly or as inferior. A $10 return by treating them well but never making them feel completely like a full partner. A $12 return if you genuinely include them in the process and ask for input.

People will accept a decision, even if it is different than what they would like, if they felt they had a genuine say. I believe this and it proved to be true and productive for the time I was with the Angels.

CALIFORNIA YEARS
(1987 – 1990)

Crosschecking was going to be particularly important to our overall operation. I always thought the more opinions you had, the more things, good or bad, you would see with a player and the better your chance for success. It costs more to operate this way, but if you lessen your mistakes, the return for your dollar spent should be greater. I don't like surprises, and the best way to avoid them is to have as many different looks as possible.

We set up a staff structure similar to what I had in place in San Diego, with regional coordinators and national crosscheckers. Unlike San Diego, we started to use minor league managers and coaches that had scouting experience, or lived in warm weather areas, to help us out before they left for spring training in March. After the draft was over, we used many scouts who had field experience to help coach in the minor leagues. This was a practice we started, and the two staffs not only blended, but also made it possible for each staff to understand the difficulties the other faced. We heard few complaints incorporating this philosophy.

With a new approach, and almost an entirely new scouting staff that hadn't worked together, you could sense it would be an interesting year, and it proved to be. When someone new comes in and changes things there is usually some resistance, and this was true here. Some of the few scouts that didn't go to Chicago with Larry were upset, some didn't like my approach, and others were just trying to get used to working for a new club with a different philosophy. When you add in that we didn't get together as a staff until extremely late, it was a rough year.

One thing that would eventually prove helpful with a staff that was comprised like it was is that you get many different views on how a scout evaluates a player and what is important to them. As long as everyone shares the same goal, this gives you a better chance of not missing anything about a player, both good and bad. When you don't like surprises like I don't, this can help the overall process.

The staff worked hard, and we had many meetings during the year to not only keep up on players of interest, but to help the scouts get more comfortable with our system.

Cliff Ditto became an extra set of eyes and legs for me. He could help the scouts he was with to understand what I wanted and why. A lot of times, they wouldn't ask me questions, but would ask Cliff. This made it more comfortable for a lot of them, and Cliff had the personality that made people comfortable.

One of the national crosscheckers had been with the Angels for a while, Rick Schlenker. He and I worked together in San Diego, and it gave me someone who I not only knew on a personal level but knew was an excellent evaluator. Rich and I would have our disagreements through the years, but I could always count on him to tell me what he really thought and why. Often, our disagreements made it easier to understand the overall picture of a player and make it more comfortable, whatever the decision was to be on that player.

I encouraged communication by phone and voicemail. I would keep track in the spring of how often I had talked with a scout on the phone, voicemail, or in person. If a scout didn't have many good players for the year, it would be easy to not communicate often, so with my list of communication I would know if I hadn't contacted someone for a while and I would call, if nothing else, just to check on them and their family. I knew that is what I would like when I was in their spot.

When texting and emails became part of the overall communication process, they took more away from phone calls and voicemail over time. People say it is quicker, and I understand that and often it is, but when describing players or important items, an email or text doesn't describe the emotion of the individual's feelings. People also tend to be braver with the written word over the spoken word, as well as reaction to impulse. Most times when I reacted to impulse, I was either wrong or wish I would have taken time to digest it. I lasted 19 years as a scouting director because I read people, not words. The emotion and gut feel of a scout is what I wanted, and it proved to work for us.

During the transition process, we stressed multiple items for our scouts to focus on.

Something that personally took me a while to get comfortable with was to not be afraid to make a mistake and stay aggressive, and if you don't know something, just admit it, and don't guess. Although I realize no one wants to admit they don't know something, when someone guesses they are usually wrong. I learned this from personal experience. If you admit you don't have the answer to something, it gives you more time to find out the answer.

I believed and stressed to our staff that it is important to concentrate on what a player does well first before dwelling on what they cannot do. When you are looking at a young high school or college kid, they are going to do many things wrong even if they possess good ability. You must remember that in most cases they don't know the right way because they have never been told or taught the right way. If a player shows you an average major league tool, they own it, even if they can't repeat it consistently yet.

Never give up on natural power and speed as it is such a tough commodity to acquire in baseball. Both abilities cannot be taught. Speed and power are game changers. Too many people worry about strikeouts with a power hitter and batting average with a burner. Players with those tools can be taught to do enough with the bat in many cases to utilize their strengths.

I had each member of the staff, and any staff I supervised, make sure to see a major league or professional game in the middle of spring. It is important when evaluating high school or college players that you never lose what the speed of a professional game is. The higher the level, the faster the game. It is important that you can picture a player you are recommending for the draft being able to stay with the speed of the game.

As the 1987 draft season got underway and we covered the country, it became apparent that we had no idea who we would draft, which is not uncommon when you select 25th overall.

Since the Angels had been in the playoffs the year before, our draft slot was at 25. We had also received a compensation pick and had the 31st selection. It was a solid draft year with such standouts as Ken Griffey Jr., Jack McDowell, Kevin Appier, Delino DeShields, and Craig Biggio.

The previous year in 1986, the Angels had five picks in the first round and had added some young talent on the pitching side. Three of their first four picks made it to the majors, with right-handed pitchers Roberto Hernández and Mike Fetters each having long careers. This gave us the luxury to look for the best player available at any position.

A practice we used during my years with the Angels was to have a meeting with all the crosscheckers at the midway point of the amateur season to start narrowing down the players we had the most interest in so we could concentrate our time on them before the draft. I don't believe in spending much time on players you don't care for or probably won't get unless you are trying to throw other clubs off your trail. It is much more productive when you can spend more time on players you feel best about.

Ken Griffey Jr. had separated himself from the pack. A complete player who did everything, but because he was so much better than the competition it was hard to see everything that he could do. History will tell you he became one the elites in baseball history.

Seton Hall's catcher, Craig Biggio (who was drafted three picks before our selection), was a good prospect and played a hard-nosed game. I never realized the versatility Biggio had, even though he was very agile behind the plate, and he went on to have a Hall of Fame career while playing five different positions.

We needed catching in the system which made Biggio desirable, but there was a kid at Cal Poly San Luis Obispo by the name of John Orton that was, and still is, the best defensive catch-and-throw amateur catcher I've seen. Real soft hands and receiving skills, with good body movement behind the plate. A smooth, quick throwing action, with a well above-average arm that had good carry on the ball. As the spring went on, he came into the picture more and more and we thought we would have a good chance to select him.

There was also a high school pitcher that had been projected to go in the upper half of the first round but had hurt his shoulder in a non-baseball accident that didn't allow him to pitch. David Holdridge had one of the loosest, quickest arms, with a sound delivery. The ball came out of his hand easily with good extension out front. He could spin a breaking ball and created good angle to the plate. A live arm that we needed to get medical clearance on from our doctors.

During my 13 years with the Angels, I would be associated with, for me, the best doctor in baseball. Dr. Lewis Yocum was the most realistic, positive, and baseball-minded doctor I ever worked with.

Even if a player may have some expected problems in the future, Dr. Yocum would often tell me the player may break but we can fix him, so if you like him go ahead and take him. I can only think of about half a dozen times in my years with the Angels when he said to definitely stay away from a player. Holdridge was not one of those players, and we got clearance from Dr. Yocum to take him if we wanted.

I always had the regional coordinators and area scouts handle their region like it was their own country. They would have a meeting and pull all their players together in a preferential list. When completed, the coordinator would come to Anaheim for our meeting before the draft, joining me and our national crosscheckers. I felt this process gave all the scouts a good forum to be heard and get their players in a position they were comfortable with for the final list.

We would meet for a week before the draft and put our draft board together with input from everyone. Some clubs meet for two weeks or longer, but I believed you can do it in much less time if you put in a good 8-10 hour day, have a nice dinner, and get a good night's rest. Working a lot of hours when you are tired can cause unneeded mistakes, and I will take an alert and rested staff anytime. Some of the best conversations you can get on a player is at dinner when guys are relaxed.

The meetings we had that first year, however, were the worst and most stress filled I would experience in my 19 years of running drafts. Though it improved remarkably over time, this group did not yet get along well together, and many were fighting what I was trying to do. We even had someone giving our information to another club.

I received a call from a friend who scouted for an opposing team, saying, "Bob, someone is calling our people and reading your draft board off to us every day."

I was shocked and hurt but decided to make an adjustment to the board without telling anyone. I put names up on the board in an order that wasn't even close to what it would be on draft day. I hated to do this for the guys who were just doing their job, but I had no choice. I never was able to find out who did it, but I did change things up enough that another club couldn't get anything helpful from that point on.

The in-room fighting was fine by me, as I normally liked and encouraged people to express their true emotion. After working hard for six months, they deserve that, as you don't want to miss anything. Difference in opinion makes for spirited, emotional, and successful meetings, and should never be looked upon as disloyal if their goal is to do what they think is best for the club.

This first meeting though, because of the things I described and the atmosphere far from united, made it the toughest one I ever had. It got so bad that I had killer headaches the last few days before the draft. I made up my mind that this would never happen again.

By the following year, I had an entire calendar's worth of days instead of months to prepare our staff to be of the same mindset. I wanted a staff that ran on autopilot, and by the second year, we changed remarkably.

When the 1987 draft arrived, we selected Orton with the 25th pick and Holdridge with the 31st.

We committed on Orton because of his defensive traits and the fact he had strength and some power potential with the bat, despite a moderate batting average in college. I had learned through the years that if a catcher was a good receiver and had a strong arm, they would get enough playing time because of that ability, and that would lead to enough at-bats to develop into a productive hitter.

Orton caught for five years in the majors with the Angels, mostly as a backup, but was as fine a defender as you could find. He developed some arm problems, and his career didn't last as long as it could have. He is now a catching coordinator for the White Sox, and those kids are lucky to have someone who was so good defensively helping them.

We thought Holdridge could be a steal, as he was coming back strong after the injury and in the spring. During his second season in 1989, with the Angels in a pennant race, David was traded to Philadelphia for Lance Parrish.

I was devastated, as he had an electric arm and was making progress, but as Mike Port told me, "Parrish is now a product of our minor league system."

That has stayed with me since that time, as it wouldn't have been possible to get a major league catcher of Parrish's ability if we hadn't acquired a young pitcher of Holdridge's talent. It made sense and made me feel better.

David only pitched in one season in the majors, for Seattle in 1998, but you take kids like this every chance you can.

We ended up drafting five players in 1987 that played in the majors, with Mark Holzemer, a left-handed pitcher, and Ruben Amaro, an outfielder, having lengthy careers. Amaro went on to become general manager of the Philadelphia Phillies and a coach for the Boston Red Sox and New York Mets.

One practice we started, and I did it every year I was with California and later in Seattle, was to have our minor league field coordinator, minor league pitching coordinator, minor league hitting coordinator, and Rookie League managers at the draft. We brought them to the draft so that after each selection we made, we could give them a copy of each report on the player, look at video with them, and talk about the player and any item of concern we may have. This gave our instructors a good background before the player ever reported and helped again to bring the scouting and minor league departments together.

We used video a little differently than most clubs. Many clubs evaluate off video which I think can be dangerous. You don't know the speed of the game that they are in, or the quality of competition they are facing. Things on film do not look quite the same as with the naked eye. We used the video if there was something about the player we had a question on, such as the start of the bat, length of extension out front, balance level, and arm action. It can be helpful for things like this, but to decide on ability is a bigger risk than normal.

With 1987 under our belt and preparing for the next draft, I felt more comfortable and confident going in. It was a proper period to prepare, without the task of putting together three-quarters of a staff in December. The staff had a full year to understand our direction and philosophy and what was expected and when. We started off with a much more united approach and in time, it would become one of the best drafts I have been a part of.

The big league club was coming off a subpar year and we had the eighth selection in the first round of 1988.

Going into the year we were looking at the possibility of selecting a college pitcher, and there were some good ones to consider. Andy Benes, a right-hander from Evansville, was a strong-armed kid who would go first overall to San Diego. Steve Avery, a left-hander from John F. Kennedy High School in Michigan, was young but had a live arm and a big curveball. Gregg Olson, a right-hander from Auburn, was a short reliever who had a good fastball and hard breaking ball, and Pat Combs, a left-hander from Baylor, had a good fastball and sharp curve.

The other pitcher of interest was Jim Abbott, a left-hander from Michigan, who had as good of stuff as any of the others but had been born without a right hand, leading to questions about his ability to field his position.

The draft had many other fine players that would come out of it such as Robin Ventura, Tino Martinez, Royce Clayton, Charles Nagy, Ed Sprague, Brian Jordan, and Marquis Grissom.

I knew that there would be a few of our people that wanted a different player to be our first selection, which is a good thing because it means it was a draft with good players. But for me, after I first saw Abbott, it was hard to think he wasn't our guy.

When we had our midseason meetings, I knew we would never have a consensus on the first pick and that I may have to break the tie, which is what happened. When you have the veteran scouts like we had, you hear complete pictures of a player, both positive and negative, and it makes you much more comfortable when you decide which player to select. Rich, Cliff, George Bradley, Paul Robinson, Nick Kamzic, Rick Ingalls, and all others equaled hundreds of years of experience and a ton of success, which was comforting to me when we talked about players.

As the draft approached, we felt Benes and Avery would be gone by the time we selected, and we turned our focus to Abbott and Combs. Some of our guys wanted to consider a position player, but we decided unless there was someone well above the pitchers, we would go with a pitcher.

We had a split camp on whether Abbott would be our selection, but for me, it was the right choice. We still had other players to discuss for the other rounds and the debate continued. Because we would get a college pitcher in the first round, we could take position players after, and we did.

Our philosophy of getting good athletes who had active feet and instincts, along with the ability you look for, paid off. The good thing was the staff discussed, argued, and reasoned on each round just like it was the first round. I always felt that you must approach each round of the draft when you get to it as though it is the most important round. That is key to being successful deep in the draft.

Abbott was the player we ultimately ended up deciding on if he were available. If we did get him, we knew it would be somewhat controversial, but we thought he was the right player for us. Although you think you know who you'll get when you select that high, you never know who may throw a curve and take the player you want.

Luckily for us, when they called our name, we were able to select Abbott. When you get the player you really want first, it is amazing how things seem to flow smoother through the draft's entirety, and that's what seemed to happen.

As the draft went on, we were able to select several position players we wanted. We lost our second-round pick for signing a free agent but ended up with four picks out of our first six getting to the majors.

We selected eight players total that went on to reach the majors, with two becoming starting pitchers, four becoming everyday regulars, one relief pitcher, and a backup catcher. Three of them became All-Stars in Gary Disarcina, Jim Edmonds, and Damion Easley. This group of players were to begin the nucleus of a solid young group of players for the future.

Disarcina was a steady fielding shortstop from the University of Massachusetts who we took in the sixth round. Jon Neiderer, who crosschecked the East for us, was sold on his defense and thought he would be a line-drive contact hitter. Because of the bad weather in the East, he probably slid a little in the draft. Gary had average tools, but his instincts and first step were exceptional. He ended up being that contact hitter and was probably the best routine defensive shortstop you could find. He may not make the highlight film every night, but if you hit the ball to him and were supposed to be out, you were out. Pitchers love pitching with fielders like him behind them. Gary spent his entire 12-year career with the Angels.

Edmonds was an outstanding athlete at Diamond Bar High School, just 14 miles from Anaheim Stadium, who was a pitcher and outfielder. Ingalls and Steve Gruwell, our two scouts that lived in Southern California, believed he was a position player and that the five tools made it too hard to pass on him as an outfielder. There were questions about Jim's shoulder, which led to us getting him in the seventh round. He had good years in the minors but didn't develop big power until he reached the majors, which is something you learn can be common for a young hitter. He was a great defensive player who had an outstanding 17-year career, winning eight Gold Glove awards.

We drafted Easley in the 30th round out of Long Beach City College. Ingalls liked this kid's quickness and chance to play the infield, as well as become a good contact hitter in time. We didn't sign him right away but because we held the rights to sign him until right before the next draft, we signed him in May. He moved through the system in three years and became an everyday player for most of his career. He was a solid defender, good contact hitter, and could steal a base, which he did his entire 17-year career.

Those three players along with Abbott combined for 56 years of Major League experience and six All-Star appearances. I remember many publications saying after the draft that we had an ordinary year. I will take an ordinary year like this *any* time.

The 1989 draft would prove to be a solid one for us, and one where we would take a different approach to how we selected. It was a draft that featured 26 outfielders being drafted in the first three rounds, which was the first time I had ever seen that. Because of this, I decided that we would take the approach of drafting opposite of the draft strength and not only acquire a needed outfielder, but as much pitching as we could get.

I have always believed that you must draft greedy and get not only your share of players, but as much of everyone else's share as you can. When there is an obvious strength in a draft, you draft opposite of it, as you tend to get more quality of the positions that are not the strength and still acquire players of the position that is strongest later. You *have* to draft greedy and make every round count.

We always monitored other teams' first 10 selections so that if we were worried about a team's interest in a player that we liked, we could always check and see how many players they may have drafted at the position of that player. This could give us a possible option of waiting awhile to draft that player or decide that we better not wait any longer. To beat the opposition, you better know the opposition. This was successful for us over my years as a scouting director.

I always found that if you ask a player right before a draft, "If we don't draft you, who do you think will?" that most kids will tell you honestly who they think will, as most have never been prepped to answer that question.

Drafting ninth in each round, we spent much of the spring concentrating on pitching and did alright by getting four pitchers we drafted to the majors, including three of our first four picks.

With so many outfielders being taken, there were some quality infielders that slipped through the cracks like Frank Thomas, Mo Vaughn, Chuck Knoblauch, and John Olerud. The overall quality of the infielders and pitchers in the first three rounds ended up better than the outfielders who were considered the strength of the draft.

Our staff was starting to get used to our way of operating and were adjusting as needed. We never let on what our approach was and spent extra time on pitching. Drafting against what was thought to be the strength was still the right move, but as I look back, I should have expanded our emphasis to the other positions besides pitching and taken a longer look at the infielders.

One of my biggest personal mistakes was during this spring, when I saw Frank Thomas, who played first base for Auburn. Duane Shaffer, who now was one of our national crosscheckers, and I attended a game where Auburn was playing Kentucky. Frank had a rough infield practice, throwing the ball erratically, and you could tell he would be limited to first base defensively. He was a below-average runner, which was to be expected for someone nicknamed, "The Big Hurt." At the plate, he showed tremendous power and good bat speed, but had holes in his swing that concerned me.

My report wouldn't be good enough to take him with our first pick. It didn't matter, because he didn't get to us as he was taken two picks in front of us by the White Sox at seven. The thing that I didn't figure though, was that he would learn good discipline and pitch selection. Actually, not good discipline, but *great* discipline, as he became the most patient and disciplined power hitter I ever saw. He just didn't swing at pitches in the strike zone he couldn't hit until he had two strikes. He not only made a lot of contact but made extremely hard contact and had great power to all fields.

I learned a lot from my mistake and again realized you give players with big power the benefit of doubt because they are game-changers. Frank went on to be one of the game's greatest power hitters and was elected to the Baseball Hall of Fame in 2014. As I said before, when I make mistakes, I don't mess around.

We had our draft meeting on Catalina Island in 1989, same as we did in 1988. Catalina Island is a 76 square mile island, 22 miles off the Southern California coast, with two main ports with the primary port, Avalon, on the east side of the island. It flourishes with bright, multi-colored buildings on a hillside that reminds you of ocean towns in the Mediterranean.

On the beach of Avalon, you have the port, a number of beachside restaurants and souvenir shops, and a brief 10-minute walk to the historic casino where a lot of big entertainers would play in the early part of the 20th century.

It was a relaxing and casual setting where guys could show up in shorts and a t-shirt, look out the window and see the Pacific Ocean, and with no cell phones at the time, little disruptions.

We took a boat to Avalon, rented the meeting room on the ship, and started to talk about players.

After the boat ride, we met at a quiet motel that was within walking distance to the water and near the restaurants in town. When our meetings would get heated, I would tell the guys to take a walk down to the water and cool off. Overall, we accomplished a lot the two years we met on Catalina.

When we were scheduled to return to Anaheim three days before the draft, we were informed that the boats were not sailing because the sea was too choppy, and we would have to wait one more day. I didn't get too worried because we still had two full days to get back and get ready for the draft. Problem was that the next day, the sea was still angry, and we spent another day on the island.

We were now concerned, because if we didn't get back to Anaheim, I'm not sure what we would have done for the draft. With no cell phone or laptops yet, we were in a bind. Can you imagine a draft being delayed because a scouting staff was stranded on an island? If the ships didn't sail until the next day, I would probably be fired on the spot.

With no change of weather in sight, I decided we should fly back to Long Beach. However, there was no longer any scheduled air service, and we would have to hire a charter plane.

After finding a service that would get to Long Beach a day before the draft for a reasonable price, we took a van up the winding road to get to the Catalina Airport, thinking we were home free upon arrival.

We saw a TWA Express commuter plane at the terminal and thought it was our plane. Well, of course, we figured wrong. Our plane was one that looked like a miniature "Spruce Goose" with a fat front of the plane where the luggage was stored. I heard a lot of groans when the guys found out this was our ride.

The Catalina Airport sits on top of a plateau, and when you take off there is a large drop at the edge of the runway. When everything was loaded in the plane, the pilots started the twin prop engines and this plane shook like a cement mixer, with the best yet to come.

When we took off, we barely got off the ground and as we got to the end of the runway, we dropped down off the plateau for what seemed like thousands of feet before we ever started to gain altitude. Through this, there wasn't a word said by anyone, especially when the co-pilot cranked up the wheels by hand.

After an hour and 26 miles across the sea, the pilot cranked the wheels down and we landed at Long Beach Airport. This was the quietest day of our meetings and one I am sure they wouldn't forget.

We got to the stadium a short time later and started our preparation for the draft, trying to get back to normalcy.

Our first two picks in 1989 were Kyle Abbott, a left-handed pitcher from Long Beach State, and Joe Grahe, a right-handed pitcher from the University of Miami. Both pitched in the majors, with Grahe having a solid seven-year career as a starter, reliever, and closer. The overall draft for us, even though not deep, added to the foundation we were trying to build.

With the strength of the class being the outfielders, we felt we could select one in the third round and get a player of quality. Of the 26 outfielders to be drafted in the first three rounds, we got the one we liked the most.

Tim Salmon of Grand Canyon University was our choice all along, and even though he was having an off year, we felt he had first-round ability and would slide. His subpar year hurt his chances of being a first-rounder, especially when executives from teams that trained in Arizona left after spring training. We began concentrating on him later in the spring when clubs had already observed him early.

He ended up with a three-part approach to hitting that made it difficult to be at his best. A three-part approach used to be taught by some colleges and is where the batter starts his swing by bringing his hands back and beginning his stride forward, stopping his stride, and starting back up again when the hands go forward. I am still amazed he was able to do what he did that year with that approach. Once he got into pro ball and made the needed adjustments, he started to take off, helping make this draft one of our best during my 13 years with the Angels.

Tim Kelly, our scout in Arizona, and Joe Maddon, who scouted in Arizona until spring training started, stayed on top of Salmon the entire year. Grand Canyon also had Chad Curtis, a center fielder, and Paul Swingle, a right-handed pitcher, both of which we would draft and sign that year as well.

Kelly had done a good job, especially on Swingle, as he didn't pitch a lot and was inconsistent. We got Swingle in the 29th round and Curtis in the 45th. All three of our Grand Canyon picks got to the majors with Salmon having an outstanding career and Curtis a solid one. To get three major leaguers from one college team in a season was something I had never heard of.

When it came time to sign Salmon, Kelly was unavailable, and Joe ran the negotiation. They were to meet and have dinner, and Joe was going to make our initial offer.

I waited by the phone for a few hours to hear from Joe and see how it went, when he finally called and said we are close and could probably get it done that night. We got it done for the money we felt was right and what Tim and his wife felt was right. This is how you wish all negotiations would go, where both the player and club felt good starting their relationship.

Joe did a fantastic job and would be involved with Tim for most of his career, working with him in the minors as our minor league coordinator and later in the majors as interim manager and bench coach. Joe would later return to the Angels as full-time manager in 2020 after 16 years managing the Tampa Bay Rays and Chicago Cubs, winning a World Series with Chicago in 2016.

Tim got hit in the face and head twice his first few years in the minors, including breaking his jaw the second time, and was out of action for a while. He was playing for our Palm Spring affiliate in the California League when he made his first appearance after the layoff, leading to a pivotal time. When a player gets hit in the face, it is important to see the first pitch of the first at-bat when they return. One of our minor league coordinators, Eddie Rodriguez, was in Palm Springs when Tim was making that first appearance. I asked Eddie to call me after that first pitch and at-bat to let me know if he showed any fear or flinched at the pitch.

Eddie called and said, "No flinch. No fear."

That is all you need to know. He never had any problems.

Another time while Tim was in the minor leagues, the team president asked me why everyone liked Salmon so much, as was headed towards 160 strikeouts in a season. I was surprised, but when people go just by stats, it is easy to miss on a good player.

"Look at his walks," I told him. "They keep increasing which means he is swinging at better pitches as well as getting on base more often. When the walks get to about half the strikeouts, the hitter is becoming more selective, and making more contact which leads to higher home run totals."

I'm not sure he bought it, but it is true, and Tim had high walk totals, a high on-base percentage, and of course, good home run numbers his whole career. This is why you must stay with a power hitter through tough years in the beginning to get to the successful years.

Tim would go on to have a 14-year career, all with the Angels, and become the face of the organization. He won American League Rookie of the Year honors in 1993 and became a leader on the Angels 2002 World Series championship team. Until the arrival of Mike Trout in the 2010's he led the Angels franchise in most offensive statistics.

He had a great approach as a player, with a background as a person that is a model for young players. He made things happen and made players around him better. From the moment he started his career, he gave a great effort every game.

The year 1990 would prove to be another important one for the Angels. We didn't have a first-round pick after we lost it for signing a major league free agent. Our first pick was in the second round, 57th overall.

When you draft that low you never have an idea of who you may get. One thing we did was compare notes with another team that didn't draft until the second round as well. Between us, we probably had 35-40 names we thought we didn't need to concentrate on, unless we heard something different later. This allowed us to spend more time on players we thought we may have a chance to get instead of wasting days watching players we couldn't. This became a big asset, as we could spend more time deeper into the draft. In the end, the picks we got down the line turned out to be important players in the building of the foundation.

The depth of this draft was uncertain, even though some names at the top were outstanding prospects. Chipper Jones, a high school shortstop from Jacksonville, Florida, went number one in the draft to Atlanta. Other standouts like Alex Fernandez, Mike Mussina, and Dan Wilson also went in the first round.

When you select as deep in the draft like we were, scouts will recommend a large number of players to be considered for your first pick. It is good to have a lot of names, but at some point, you need to narrow things down.

We had a lot of meetings with our crosscheckers, Duane, Paul, Rich, Jon, Tom Davis, and Tony LaCava, to try and make some sense of the direction we needed to pursue. These meetings were important to me, as I lived on conversation over written reports.

By May, we still had not narrowed it down much. On a trip back east, I asked Rich and Duane to meet me at the Big South Conference Tournament to go over things. It was a Sunday with not much going on, so I thought it would be a good spot to meet. I asked Bobby Myrick, our area scout, if there was anyone in the tournament we should look at while we were there. He mentioned a pitcher at Radford University by the name of Phil Leftwich, that he said he had some interest in.

Sometimes, it is better to be lucky than good as this day proved to be important in deciding our first pick. There were maybe two other scouts from opposing teams at this tournament, so we thought that there weren't too many players to see.

Most of Radford's history was as a women's college in the early 20th century, and the school later allowed men to attend classes beginning in 1972. No baseball players had ever been selected in the draft out of Radford.

Leftwich was their top pitcher, and when he took the mound, we were shocked at the good pitcher's build he possessed as well as a smooth delivery and loose, free arm. The ball came out of his hand easily, with good extension and finish on his pitches. He showed a better than average fastball with life and the makings of a good breaking ball.

When we left, we started comparing notes and we all thought we may have found our guy. I called Bobby and asked why there wasn't more interest in this kid, and he said Radford doesn't get seen a lot, but Leftwich had gotten better as the season went on. I told Bobby to stay on this kid and know everything about him.

Bobby did a fine job, as Leftwich ended up our first pick, the first in Radford's history. Leftwich had a solid start to his career and by his second season in the majors, he had elevated himself to our third starter before an injury took him down, derailing his career.

Our final pick of the 1990 draft left a lasting memory for my family. My son, Jimmy, was 10 years old and would come with me to the third day of the draft each year. He liked being around it and seeing all the scouts. This particular year, we were going to draft Bimbo Coles, a star basketball player out of Virginia Tech. As we got about four or five rounds away from selecting him, Bill Bavasi started working with Jimmy on making the selection. He wrote his name and info on a big piece of paper and Jimmy practiced for about an hour. When we got to the 54th round, I told him to get near the phone and get ready.

I had scouts watching at the door to make sure none of our superiors were coming by, so we could abort if necessary. The coast was clear and when our turn came, my 10-year-old son said into the phone, "California selects: Coles, Bimbo, shortstop/point guard from Virginia Tech."

It was read back by the Commissioner's Office and they then said, "next, Kansas City."

It went smooth as silk, and I am going to bet that he may still be the youngest person in any draft to select a player for a team.

Our coverage deep into the draft was about to pay dividends, as we were to get five more players to the majors besides Leftwich. Two would prove to be key players in the long-term success of the Angels and be part of their foundation for many years.

Garret Anderson, an outfielder from Kennedy High School in Granada Hills, California, and Troy Percival, a catcher from UC Riverside, would be our fourth and sixth round selections in this draft.

Duane and Rick had seen Anderson play late in the year and really liked his swing. They called me and said you have to see this kid, so we set up a workout with him and the three of us, along with Rich and Steve, went.

The fluidity and quickness of his swing was outstanding. He kept the bat level through the zone and made solid contact. The bat was obvious, but the thing that impressed me was his aptitude to pick things up.

When we had him throw from the outfield for us, one of our scouts mentioned to him about keeping his elbow higher and getting a better angle on his throws. Sounds easy, but usually this takes a while before a player gets used to it. Garret made the adjustment on the spot and threw each time the way he was asked, and his throws were immediately better. Great aptitude.

Garret was a good basketball player who could have played in college if he wanted, and we figured because of that and his one-speed approach to playing, that he would fall to us where we selected him. He ended up one of the most consistent and reliable players I have seen. He had an inner aggressiveness that many people don't understand. He played hard and wanted to win even though it didn't come across in an outward fashion. A professional in every way.

When he and his mom came to Anaheim Stadium to negotiate his contract, it was as pleasant a negotiation as I had been a part of. His mother was a businessperson who was realistic and asked all the right questions and had all the right concerns. Garret was very respectful, and they knew what they should receive. It didn't take long before he was on his way into professional baseball.

Garret played 17 seasons in the majors, all but his final two with the Angels. He was a three-time All-Star and won the 2003 Home

Run Derby in Chicago. He became the franchise's all-time leader with 2,013 games played, 1,024 runs scored, 2,368 hits, and 1,292 runs batted in. Most importantly, Garret hit a bases-clearing double in Game 7 of the 2002 World Series, which would prove to be the winning hit. Simply, a remarkable career.

Percival was a catcher at UC Riverside for legendary coach Jack Smitheran. He had one of the best arms I have seen from a catcher, and his receiving skills weren't bad but certainly could be helped. His arm could throw out above-average runners like they had cement boots on. The problem was that even though he had some power, he had a long swing that couldn't catch up to a lot of fastballs.

Kelly was the drafting scout and said if he can't catch, we can put him on the mound. I agreed with that, but one game he hit a ball hard for me and I thought if this kid can hit at all, he will catch for a long time in the majors.

After Troy signed, he reported to our Rookie League team in Boise, Idaho to play for probably the best Rookie League manager in the game, Tom Kotchman. He reported as a catcher and did a good job defensively. Only problem was he hit .203.

He went to instructional league that winter and I received a call from Marcel Lachemann, our pitching coach, and Bob Clear, one of our veteran instructors who was well respected in the game. They got on the phone and Marcel said to me, "I think it is time to put this kid on the mound. Besides, he wants to."

"Can't we wait one more year?" I asked. "His catch-and-throw ability is almost impossible to find."

"Fountain, it's time!" I heard Bob yell in the background before Marcel could answer.

Not much I could say, as I deep down knew it would happen and Bavasi and I would talk about it off and on. It was tough to see a catcher with an arm like that give up the position. That said, it was certainly the right move.

Troy went on to pitch 14 years in the majors, 10 with the Angels, as one of the best closers in baseball. He was a four-time All-Star and, in 2004, became the 18th pitcher to reach 300 saves. Above all else, Troy threw the final pitch of the 2002 World Series, clinching the title for the Angels. Truly, one of the greatest closers in the game's history.

Just another reason why you must approach every round in the draft as if it were the most important round. You just never know.

CALIFORNIA YEARS
(1990 – 1994)

The years 1988-1991 would prove key in building the young nucleus of the Angels. Our drafts and development system from these years would produce five starting pitchers, eight everyday regulars, one closer, five relievers, and eight utility players. With this foundation in place, we continued to add over the next eight years and contribute to many years of success for the organization.

By this time, our scouting staff had grown together, and we had one of the strongest minor league staffs in the game. I always said the best staff is the one that can operate on autopilot, because they know what needs to be done and they do it without much direction. We weren't there yet, but we were getting close.

In 1991, our first-round selection came at 17th overall, but we had received a compensation pick in the sandwich round at No. 34. With the two high picks, we hoped to stock up on position players in a good class to do so. Among the position players in the draft class were Dmitri Young, Doug Glanville, Manny Ramirez, Cliff Floyd, and Shawn Green.

We started to focus our attention on two players in Florida: Eduardo Perez and Jorge Fabregas.

We had a split camp on these two players among our scouts. Both players had the type of ability that we thought would fit well with us. Everyone liked both but had a difference of opinion on who they would take first.

Eduardo played first base for Florida State and was the son of Tony Perez, who played with Cincinnati as part of the Big Red Machine. He was a big, strong kid, like his father, and was someone we felt could move to third base. He had enough agility and foot movement to make the switch to the hot corner. His hands were good, and he had plenty of arm to make the hard throws across the diamond. If he couldn't stay there, he could always go back to first base or possibly left field. His bat is what really intrigued us. He had a long and level swing with good bat speed that allowed him to make hard contact and drive the ball to the right side with power.

Jorge was a third baseman at the University of Miami who we were going to make a catcher if we got him. Tom Kotchman and I saw him play a weekday game one evening where he caught and showed everything you would want to see in a young catcher. He moved well behind the plate, had soft hands and incredible receiving skills. He was good at transferring the ball to make the throw to second base and showed a plus arm with good carry to his throws.

When we got to our draft meetings, I asked all the scouts to try and figure out what gave us the best odds to get both players. Kotchman was the scout responsible for both players and he and all the other scouts took the week preceding the draft to try and figure out the order that would give us the best chance. They recommended Perez first, and Fabregas second.

Draft day came and we decided to go with Eduardo with our first pick and waited out our second pick to try and get Jorge. It is a greedy approach to try and get two players instead of one, but we really wanted it to happen. As our second pick came, Jorge was available. We quickly selected him.

It worked out for us and it was confirmed we got it right when we found out a club right behind our first pick would have taken Eduardo if we didn't.

Both players would have long careers in the majors, even if most of the years they weren't regulars. Eduardo spent 13 years in the majors while Jorge played nine, including two where they played together on the Angels in 1994 and 1995.

We also landed four other position players that would get to the majors, including three that would have long and valuable careers at part-time regulars and support players. Mark Sweeney, Orlando Palmeiro, and Chris Turner would contribute to good teams in their careers.

During the 1991 season, Mike Port was relieved of his duties as general manager, and was replaced by his assistant, Danny O'Brien. This was a shock, and I wondered if things would be alright for Bill Bavasi and me. Things in the minor league system were going well, but even though we thought things would be alright, you just never know.

Mike was a great boss and I hated to see him go. He understood what we were doing and delegated responsibilities well.

As things turned out, Danny was outstanding to work for as well. He believed in delegation, and even though the local papers kept speculating that I could get fired, Danny stayed with me.

Rumors of my potential firing came up often. John Young, a longtime scout and former scouting director, once said to me, "If I could have a dime for every time you were rumored to be fired, I'd be rich." John had a great sense of humor and I appreciated it. It is tough, though, when your name is in the paper in a negative way because it can be tough on your kids. It is baseball though, and it comes with the territory.

When 1992 came around, we were to have six picks in the first three rounds. We were usually lucky to have our regular picks, but to have three additional high picks would be a chance to stock up. Our first pick was at eight, with a sandwich pick at 29, three second-round picks, and our standard third round selection. The staff was looking forward to the draft, as it looked as though there would be some good high school players available.

We added some experience to our scouting staff as Bob Harrison, a former special assistant with the Mariners, had joined us in 1991 and Hal Keller, a longtime farm director and scouting director and former general manager for Seattle, had joined us for the 1992 season. The addition of these two men was extremely valuable as they not only added important evaluations but were able to help so many of our staff, including myself, by sharing their experience and knowledge. They would prove to be valuable to me through not just this draft with so many picks, but the next eight years I remained with the Angels.

The expectations were high with the extra picks, and we hoped to get a mixture of college and high school players. Unfortunately, it wouldn't turn out like we hoped.

We scoured the country for high school athletes and hoped to get a couple. As the spring ended, we thought we had two college pitchers that would work as our first and second-round selections and a group of about six high school players to select later.

This draft contained quality players at the top, with Phil Nevin, Derek Jeter, Jeffrey Hammonds, and Jason Kendall. It turned out to be a solid draft, with several good major leaguers and a couple of franchise players.

Whitey Herzog had joined the organization as co-general manager to work with Danny and was active with scouting and the minor league system. He had extensive experience in both scouting and player development with the Cardinals and Mets, as well as a Hall of Fame career as a manager.

When Whitey first joined the Angels, he asked to evaluate our minor league system, as many people were taking shots at us and saying we had no players. After Whitey was done observing the system, he told the powers above to leave it alone, and that there were good players in the system.

Whitey helped preserve a system that had Tim Salmon, Garret Anderson, Jim Edmonds, Damion Easley, Chad Curtis, Gary Disarcina, Troy Percival, Eduardo Perez, Jorge Fabregas, and others who would go on to have solid major league careers. I will always be grateful to Whitey for standing up for the scouting and player development departments.

During that spring, I had a proud moment while getting a look at a player. Eddie Pearson, an infielder from Bishop State Community College in Alabama, was a prominent name for the draft. I hadn't seen him play yet and Kotchman told me to call to find out if they had any playoff games or if I could work him out.

When I called, Eddie told me he didn't have any more games to play in and couldn't do a workout because Seattle was working him out that day. I told him I was sorry it didn't work out but did get out of the conversation when and where his workout with Seattle would be.

It is an unwritten rule that you don't go uninvited to another team's workout unless you can do it and not get caught. That day, I was determined not to get caught.

I arrived at the site about 15 minutes after it was scheduled to start, so as not to be seen. Parking out of view of the ballpark, I snuck down the right field line. It was a good place to hide as there were big trees down the line I could stand behind. I found one that barely hid my body and would just turn my head around the tree to see inside the park. Everything was going well, as I got to see him run and throw before he started to take batting practice.

Eddie had a good line drive swing and made hard, solid contact. From the right side, he was pulling most everything to left field, making it much harder for anyone to see where I was. Then, something happened that I hadn't expected. He switched to the left side.

I had no idea he was a switch-hitter, and now he was pulling balls to right field and many were landing foul right by where I was standing. I didn't move, as everyone was now looking in the direction of where I was hiding. As soon as he stopped hitting, I took the strategic route behind the trees to get out of there, as I knew any minute, they would be coming to get the baseballs that were hit my direction.

When I got to the car, I was sure no one had seen me and was quite pleased. I had seen a workout that I needed to see and one that I wasn't supposed to see. Most veteran scouts would do the same thing if they didn't get caught. It was a good day.

As the spring went on, we had high hopes that Phil Nevin would slide to us. We had known about Phil since high school, he just kept getting better. Phil was a power-hitting third baseman at Cal State Fullerton who could play outstanding defense and had the ability to change a game quickly. If he didn't go first overall, we thought he may get to us.

We anticipated the names that went before us and started to concentrate on two local pitchers: Pete Janicki of UCLA and Derek Wallace of Pepperdine, both right-handed pitchers. In the end, we thought Janicki may have a better chance to move quickly and stay a starter.

We selected Janicki with the eighth pick, and about a week after the draft, he broke his arm with a stress fracture. He had pitched several innings in a college regional before the draft that many people thought may have caused the break, but there was no way to know for sure.

After a long summer of trying to negotiate a contract with a player involved with an injury, Danny got it done and Janicki started the next year in Palm Springs with our California League affiliate. He had moments where he would show his plus fastball and quick breaking curveball and was promoted to Triple-A within two years. Unfortunately, his arm broke again and he didn't make it the majors. He had a fine arm, and if he hadn't gotten hurt, I think he would have had a good career.

We decided on Jeff Schmidt, a right-handed pitcher out of the University of Minnesota, for our sandwich round selection. Jeff was a tall, slender pitcher, with a loose arm and good delivery. His fastball was better than average and even though he was 21, he was a kid you could easily project getting better. When he signed, I thought he had a good chance to be a starter in the big leagues.

He ended up having an inconsistent minor league career but did make it the majors for a portion of 1996 as a reliever.

When we got to the second round, we thought we struck gold selecting two high upside high school players that we didn't think would get to us: DeShawn Warren, a left-handed pitcher from Alabama, and Chris Smith, an infielder from California. Warren was an exceptional athlete with a loose, live arm, who also was probably the fastest runner in our system. Smith was an athletic infielder who had a good arm and bat potential with good speed. As promising as both kids were, neither made it to the majors.

Overall, we ended up drafting four players who made it the majors with Bill Simas, a reliever from Fresno City College we took in the eighth round, having a very productive six-year career.

Anthony Chavez, our final pick in the 50th round, made it to the majors. For me, that is good scouting when you get someone in the final round and he makes it to the majors. It shows the perseverance of an area scout and why every round is important and requires serious attention.

The 1992 draft was looked upon shortly after by many publications and media as an exceptionally good draft for us. It turned out to be the least productive of any draft I have been associated with as a scouting director. It is a perfect illustration of why you cannot evaluate something like a draft that takes five years to know the results immediately after the selections are made. I still wish we could it all over again.

As the summer progressed there was a proposed in-house move to transfer me from scouting director to strictly a scouting position. There was some thought that I would like to get away from the administrative and decision-making parts of the job. That was far from the way I felt and when Danny asked me if I wanted to move out of the job, I said, "No."

"Okay," Danny replied. "I will take care of it."

He did.

People were just trying to help me, but no one really asked me until Danny. I will always be grateful to him for saving me and allowing me to work in that position another seven years.

The 1993 draft was one where we would select third overall. It was the year of Álex Rodríguez and Darren Dreifort, two of the most publicized players in draft history. Out of high school in Miami, Rodríguez was an immensely talented kid who could play shortstop with a strong arm and had a quick bat with well above-average power potential. His name and Dreifort, a right-handed pitcher from Wichita State who could get the majors in a hurry, were rumored all spring to be the first two players selected in whichever order. Seattle obviously took Rodríguez first overall, and the Dodgers took Dreifort second.

With our hopes of getting a college pitcher, it basically came down to two: Brian Anderson of Wright State and Jeff Granger of Texas A&M, both left-handers. Anderson was a control pitcher with a great feel for pitching, and Granger was a hard-throwing lefty who we envisioned as possibly being a reliever if he couldn't start.

We started the year concentrating on Anderson, Granger, and Wayne Gomes, a hard-throwing right-hander from Old Dominion. We felt that unless something happened with Rodríguez or Dreifort falling, we would have our pick of these three arms. A short time into the process, we decided it would come down to Anderson or Granger. Gomes threw hard but had some effort to his delivery and fit only as a reliever for us, and we wanted a starter.

We saw both Anderson and Granger throw many times and had a split camp on them. Granger had power to his arm and could throw his fastball by hitters. I saw him dominate some games, but I must admit, I had reservations about his long-term ability to start and saw him more as a reliever.

Anderson was intriguing in that he was *truly* a pitcher. He repeated his delivery with three *right now* average pitches. Tony LaCava, our crosschecker, really liked this kid and his pitchability. He developed a close relationship with Brian and his family, and it proved to be extremely helpful later.

I saw Brian pitch three times and he threw 19 innings in those games before he ever got a three-ball count on a hitter. He had more wins (10) than walks allowed (6) that season, which is an incredible feat, and is still hard to believe. His control and command in the strike zone was, and still is, the best I ever saw from a young pitcher.

One of the three occasions I saw Brian pitch, I sat with Tony. In the fifth inning, while Brian was still pitching and had one out, I told Tony, "Let's go and let the scouts talk."

We walked out in the middle of an inning while he was pitching and the scouts all watched us, probably not believing it. We didn't actually leave, as we hid behind a car in the left field parking lot and watched the rest of his outing out of sight.

Hopefully, what we did was have clubs think they might have a chance of getting him if it looked like we were going to pass. We liked to have teams waste days going to see players who we already decided we were going to take. At this point, we knew we were going his direction unless something unforeseen occurred.

Four days before arriving in Anaheim to put our draft list together, we held a draft meeting in San Diego. This was going to be a particularly important meeting for us, as we had a limited signing bonus budget and had to have a plan to get players we selected to stay within it. We worked hard to get everything done a day and a half early, and then sent our supervisors, Tony, Paul Robinson, and Tom Davis back home so they would be in position to help with signings immediately.

With no way to follow the draft online yet, I had every scout buy a speaker phone and hook it up in their homes so they could hear the draft from our draft room. This way we could ask them questions if needed, but primarily so they would know the moment we selected one of their players and they could call right then to make an appointment to meet with the player that night or the following day.

By doing this, the scouts could get into the house before the player or his family could be contacted by any outside influence that could cause them to change from the signing figure they told us before the draft to a higher one that we couldn't pay. We had little extra money to operate with this year, and we had to operate this way.

Our plan to meet with players right away worked well, and we signed nine of the first 10 we selected quickly. Only one held out, and of course, that was our first pick.

When it got to draft day, I will admit, I was sure Anderson was the guy, but I did give last minute thought to Granger as above-average fastballs from left-handed pitchers are tough to find. Ultimately, when it got to our pick, it was Anderson.

I kept thinking about Randy Jones when I was in San Diego and how he mowed down hitters, throwing well below-average fastballs but with great control low in the zone. Brian threw much harder but had that same great low zone control. He could also be on the fast track to the majors, which made him even more attractive to us.

It took a few months to get Brian signed, as Tony did such a great job staying with it. Tony and I had a couple of meetings with Brian and his family, and you could see their respect for Tony. It made our meetings, while at times difficult, always cordial.

Danny finally entered the negotiation and signed Brian with the stipulation of pitching in the majors in September. This is something you never like to do, but if any kid could hold his own because of command of the strike zone, it was Brian.

Brian ended up pitching four games with the big-league club that September, with an ERA under four in just over 11 innings. He held his own just fine.

Brian went on to have a solid 13-year career, throwing over 1,500 innings with an 82-83 lifetime record and pitching in two World Series, including winning one with Arizona in 2001.

We ended up getting eight players out of this draft that played in the majors, including our first four, and six of our first 10. The most prominent was Anderson, but Matt Perisho, a high school left-handed pitcher from Arizona, and Andy Lorraine, a left-handed pitcher from Stanford, spent a lot of time in the big leagues.

This was the year we began putting effort into converting players to become catchers. We drafted both Jamie Burke, a third baseman from Oregon State, and Todd Greene, an outfielder from Georgia Southern, with the idea of converting them to catching. Jack Uhey, Tom Kotchman, and Bobby Myrick did great jobs understanding those players' versatility and makeup to know they could possibly handle the switch.

The first thing that is important when you try to convert a player to another position is the player has to want and believe he can do it. They usually are a bit apprehensive until you tell them that it could get them to the majors quicker. Both Burke and Greene bought into it, and even though it took a lot of work and passed balls, they both made it to the majors and had nice careers. Jamie caught as a backup and played parts of eight seasons, while Todd played 11 years in the majors and was an aggressive hitter who showed power when he played.

Most of the catchers that we developed were converted players that John McNamara and Bill Lachemann did a great job of helping to develop. It's not easy, as it takes much patience and time, but this staff was excellent at it.

In the 43rd round of the draft we selected Marshall Faulk, the star running back from San Diego State. He never played baseball in college but was obviously a superb athlete. Jim Dietz, the longtime successful baseball coach for the Aztecs who I had known for years, told me he saw him work out and that he thought he could play baseball. That's all I needed to hear, and we selected him as an outfielder.

When it was time to talk with Marshall, I met him at an office building in San Diego where he was working in the summer as an intern, and we had a great conversation. A truly impressive young man, who seemed to have some interest in baseball, but worried that not having played he would be behind other players in his ability to compete at the level he would expect. I tried to tell him that he would excel at baseball if he gave it a chance and I believe it to this day. To be that athletic and intelligent, there is a great chance he would have been a fine baseball player. He said he would talk to his representative.

Danny took over the negotiation and told his representative that we were serious, but the overall concern of possibly getting hurt and damaging his football career was an obvious stumbling block on Marshall's end. We never got close to signing him.

I would say it turned out to be the right move as he was the second overall pick in the 1994 NFL Draft, the NFL's Most Valuable Player in 2000, a seven-time Pro Bowl selection, a Super Bowl champion, and Hall of Famer.

We selected many players from other sports during my years with the Angels like O.J. McDuffie, a wide receiver at Penn State, Todd Marinovich, a quarterback at USC, Tony Rice, a quarterback at Notre Dame, and Bimbo Coles, a point guard at Virginia Tech. Even though we didn't sign any of these top players in other sports, we gave them a chance to think about baseball and gave coaches something to worry about. Football and basketball had been getting many kids from baseball through the years, and we wanted them to know we were looking at their players as well.

As we headed into 1994, we were drafting sixth overall in the first round. It was also the first year that Bill Bavasi would be the general manager of the club. Danny left the year before and Whitey left not long before the start of spring training. When Whitey had been hired as general manager, Bill had become his assistant and Ken Forsch was hired to become the minor league farm director. Tim Mead had become the new assistant general manager, moving over from the media relations department. Working with those men, along with Jeff Parker, who was the assistant minor league and scouting director, was the best environment I ever worked in.

The 1994 draft would prove to be one of the weakest ones in baseball history, but it did produce solid talents such as Nomar Garciaparra, Paul Konerko, and Jason Varitek. Everyone had us projected to take a pitcher, especially Cade Gaspar, a right-handed pitcher out of Pepperdine. We did have interest and considered him until the end, but there was a young outfielder in Fresno that made us do something that messed up other clubs' draft boards for most of the first round.

McKay Christenson, and outfielder from Clovis West High School, was a star football and baseball player. He was a sought-after college recruit in two sports but was going to start a church mission right after high school for two years. He was one of the most gifted athletes in baseball I had seen. He was a well above-average runner with an extremely quick first step and could steal bases easily. He had a solid arm and was a good defender. He made hard contact with a quick line drive swing and had enough strength to hit a ball out of the yard. He wasn't a big kid but had all the ability to be a quality major league player.

With him leaving after high school for his mission, most clubs weren't considering him in the early rounds, but as we kept looking at players we may take, I couldn't get McKay out of my mind. Tom Davis, who knew McKay and his family well, kept talking about him and it was getting tough to not find a way to take this kid who could be a complete, five-tool player.

Our staff liked McKay, but the concern became what would he be like with a two-year layoff? It was a valid point.

I decided that if we were all in agreement, that at 18 years old, I thought he could bounce back from two years off. The next step was to talk to our new general manager, who was in the process of watching our big-league club finish in last place.

I met with Bill and talked about the possibilities that were obvious for our first pick, then hit him with McKay Christenson, and told him all about his ability.

Bill sounded excited and said he sounded like a good pick if we could get him. Then I told him, "A slight problem, he is going on a church mission after the summer to Japan for two years."

There was some silence before Bill responded.

"I am the new general manager, we are in last place, and you want us to take a high school kid who is going on a mission for two years?"

"Yeah," I said. "That's about right."

"Ok."

It took a lot of guts for Bill to approve, but he was a player development and scouting guy who knows you sometimes must take a chance. It made my job a lot easier.

The morning of the draft, all the newspapers had us taking Gaspar and not a mention of Christenson. In fact, after the draft, a writer got mad at me for not telling him because he said we were taking the Pepperdine pitcher. I was rather good at keeping secrets and that is why a lot of baseball publications didn't like me. I always felt the club was paying me for the information and giving anything out as an unnamed source was still giving away the information.

After we selected Christenson eighth overall, every club that selected for about the next 20 picks asked for more time, as us not taking one of the apparent top names meant there was another player for teams to consider that they never thought would be there. I kind of enjoyed that, knowing we caused disruption to the other clubs. The hope is that they will make a mistake, and another player you want may slip to you in the second round that *you* didn't expect.

Davis and I met with the Christenson's frequently over the summer to try and figure something out with our plan. We had met with them before the draft to see if they would be interested in signing and they said they would be open to it, but only if McKay would go on the mission. We did try to get him to at least play the summer before he left, but it didn't work. We even tried to see if he could work out with a Japanese team while he was there, but there wasn't enough time in his schedule. We finally got to an agreement and would see him in two years.

McKay left for Japan, but only one year later and without playing a single inning in the Angels organization, he was traded with Bill Simas, who we had drafted in the sixth round of 1992, to the White Sox in a deal that brought Jim Abbott back to us.

Christenson played a couple of years in the Majors, but never quite ended up the player that we projected. I always thought he didn't utilize his speed enough and tried to hit too much for power instead of contact and using his speed. Regardless, McKay was a great talent and wonderful kid who did reach the majors even after a two-year layoff.

We only got four players from this draft to the majors, but two of them had good careers. Jason Dickson, a right-handed pitcher from Canada who became helpful to me later, became a starter for many years and made the 1997 All-Star team. Mike Holtz, a left-handed pitcher from Clemson, had an eight-year career as a relief pitcher. These two pitchers were a solid part of that young Angels foundation.

The year 1994 was also when Major League Baseball went on strike, beginning August 12, leading to the eventual cancellation of the World Series. We were in last place at the time but were able to let several young players get some needed experience. We thought we were getting better and were looking forward to the next year.

CALIFORNIA YEARS
(1995 – 1999)

The 1995 season would prove to be interesting, as we had two spring trainings. With the strike carrying over to 1995, we had to prepare with replacement players because it looked as though we may start the season that way. But when the strike ended right before we were set to open the season, we went back to Tempe to have an abbreviated spring training with our regular major league team. It was an adventure to say the least.

We knew we were young when the season started but were getting better and more experienced. Bill Bavasi had added some pieces to the team, and we thought we could compete much better.

By August 1, we were 11 games up in the division and exceeding everyone's expectations. It was a fun year until we started to flounder near the end and tied with Seattle for the division title. We were forced to play a one game playoff and unfortunately, came up short. Despite that, it was a great year for our young players and a real future to build on. It was a fun year with the success of the major league club, and because of our last-place finish in 1994, we had the first overall pick in the draft.

I had never been involved with the first pick before, and normally it just means that your big-league team is brutal, but this year with us winning and having the first pick, it was a little less stressful. We were the focus of the draft, and I had a blast with it.

Darin Erstad, a center fielder from Nebraska, was one of the most touted amateur players going into the year along with Ben Davis, a high school catcher from Pennsylvania; Jose Cruz, an outfielder from Rice; and Kerry Wood, a high school right-handed pitcher from Texas. This draft would produce several top major league players in Erstad, Wood, Cruz, Roy Halladay, Geoff Jenkins, and Matt Morris. It was a great year to have the number one pick.

We didn't get many of our selections to the majors, but we got quality and a solid contribution to that young foundation. The best part of what I believed we did was to get into position to get a dominant second-round selection. With our crosschecking manpower and the direction we were going, I believe we were in a better position than most clubs.

The University of Nebraska was playing in San Diego in an early season tournament. Because it was before spring training, I told Bill that we would go together to see Erstad play. All our scouts who had seen him before liked this kid and I knew he would certainly be in the mix. After Bill and I saw him that day, we knew.

He hit a couple of balls hard with his short, quick swing, ran hard and effective, and played solid defense with a good arm. Bill and I didn't sit together during the game as I sit way down the line, but after the game we just looked at each other and I said, "I guess it's time to look for the second-rounder."

"I agree," Bill said.

Case closed. In early February, we were looking for number two.

With the Angels in those days, everyone figured that money would decide who we took. Even though it didn't, I wanted teams to think it would. I did my best to let people think we weren't sure. I always believed if you had the first pick, you had to take who you thought was the best guy because history shows that you have well over a 90 percent chance of signing him. Plus, how do you live with yourself if you pass and someone down the line gets the best player in the draft and you don't? At least if you draft the player and don't sign him, no one else will get him either.

With us telling clubs that we were unsure of our pick, they would send their scouts to see Erstad, and I loved it as they were wasting a good day with their scouts when they could be elsewhere. Other clubs thought we had interest in Davis and Cruz, and especially Ariel Prieto when he burst on the scene as he was going to be quick to the majors.

Prieto had defected from Cuba and was pitching for Palm Springs in an independent league. He was older but was an accomplished pitcher who could help right away, which he did, going right to the majors when he signed with Oakland.

Again, we just made noise because we had been working hard on our second-round pick.

We had Hal Keller, Bob Harrison, Rick Schlenker, Rick Ingalls, Tom Romenesko, and Tony LaCava spend a lot of time focusing on potential second-round players. One pitcher that proved to be of real interest was Jarrod Washburn, a left-handed pitcher from the University of Wisconsin-Oshkosh. Because he came from a small college and had bad weather for much of the season, he was tough for clubs to get a good feel for. We had the manpower and availability to sit on him and get all the looks needed to know he was the guy we wanted.

Before we had our draft meetings, Tim Mead, our assistant general manager, and I went to Jamestown, North Dakota to meet with Darin and his family. I called Darin's agent, Jeff Moorad, and told him that Tim and I were going up to meet with and get to know Darin, and that we weren't trying to go behind his back. I think Jeff appreciated the fact that we contacted him first. I always got along with him well, as did Bill and Tim, and it turned out we had a good negotiation with Darin and Jeff.

It was a long trip to Jamestown, and Tim and I had time to decide how to best present things. Tim was great with the family, and there is no one better to represent your organization than Tim.

My input was basic.

"Darin, we are not here to negotiate, but with that said, we are going to take you first. Now we think you can stay in center field. What do you think?"

He reacted with total enthusiasm to Tim and I, and we talked baseball the entire time. His parents were great, and it was a terrific meeting.

On the way back to Fargo where we were going to catch a plane the next day, Tim and I stopped at a casino and talked about our meeting at the blackjack table. We both agreed that these were great people and that we would get it done.

As the draft approached, we had our usual meeting away from Anaheim, this year in San Diego. We had a nice and relaxing meeting at the San Diego Marina that got everyone prepared before we went to Anaheim. When the first pick stands out like Erstad did, it is fortunate and makes you more relaxed as you try to get the rest of the draft in place.

Our meetings were relatively quiet, as we felt comfortable that after Erstad, we would get Washburn, and then things would fall in place nicely.

Tom Osowski, the drafting scout of Erstad, did a good job staying on top of how Darin was doing and his health status. Tom had been an assistant farm director and was aware of what was needed, leading to one of the most relaxed and productive meetings we ever had.

I had started the process a few years earlier, which I wish I had done every year I was scouting director. We started our master preferential list from the bottom up. I have always believed in the importance of lower draft picks, draft and follows, and college senior selections, and this process keeps everyone focused. Most emotion and conflicts of opinion are on the top round. Because of the hard work involved and scouts opinions of what is best for the club, it is expected. By getting the list done before you got to the top players and after all the emotion and fighting of the first-round players was completed, the list was in order, and you were done. This doesn't disrupt the process for the other rounds. It worked great.

We kept up the facade until the last days before the draft that we were still considering players other than Erstad. When we showed up in Palm Springs to see Prieto pitch in late May, the buzz was we were going to take him, save money, and put him right in the majors. Then we heard that people said we were going to take Davis, the fine hitting young catcher, or Cruz, the outfielder from

Rice. We finally let other clubs know right before the draft that Erstad was our guy.

I received calls from writers all spring from across the country about who we would take first. Most writers and publications thought we would go for the cheaper sign and pass on Darin, but like I said, Bill and I decided he was the kid and we thought history was on our side allowing us to sign him.

When the draft started, we made the selection of Erstad.

As soon as it was done, I went to meet with the press before we got to the second round. It is a common practice, but because we were the first pick in the draft and the Angels had only had one before in 1975, there was more interest than normal. When I went in the room, I was met with the expected questions.

"Do you think you can sign him? When do you think he will be in the majors? How do you feel about getting him?"

I told the writers without missing a stride and very seriously, "I am surprised he got to us."

Most of the people in the room just snickered, but someone actually printed it. I still can't believe he printed it.

Jarrod Washburn became our second-round selection, and from there, we got two other draftees to the majors: Brian Cooper, a right-handed pitcher from USC, and Justin Baughman, a middle infielder out of Lewis & Clark College.

Cooper, our fourth-round pick, spent parts of six seasons in the majors. Baughman, our fifth-round pick, played parts of two seasons, but if not for an injury in the Mexican Winter League, he may have been our second baseman for years. He could really run and was a good defensive infielder with a solid arm. He understood his role as a hitter and concentrated on making contact to utilize his speed and steal bases. He broke his leg and was not able to bounce back to the player he was. He had great potential and was a quality kid.

It took a little time to sign both Erstad and Washburn, but they both signed in time to play during the 1995 season in the minor leagues. It helped both to accelerate their development. Erstad was in the majors the year after and Washburn came in 1998. In present times, the first player chosen and a few other high picks don't sign and start their pro careers that same summer. Both these kids wanted to get started.

Although we didn't sign many major league players out of the 1995 draft, Erstad and Washburn would be key members of the Angels for years.

Washburn pitched for 12 years in the majors, eight with the Angels. He was a part of the Angels 2002 World Championship rotation and is recognized as one of the better starting pitchers in franchise history.

Erstad is one of the most hard-nosed and dedicated players I have ever been involved with signing. He didn't just want to do good, he wanted to win. He played hard every game and had the type of makeup you always hope to get in a player. He played 14 years in the majors and 11 with the Angels, including the 2002 World Series championship club. He won three Gold Glove awards, was named an All-Star twice, and ranks in the top five in games played, runs scored, and hits in Angels franchise history.

As productive of a year that we enjoyed at the big-league level in 1995 and with so many of our young players starting to come into their own, we did have some unavoidable distractions. Mr. Autry sold a quarter share of the Angels franchise to Disney, and there were some incoming changes that would cause some stress. This is also the period where Disney changed the team's name from California Angels to Anaheim Angels.

Disney would take over soon and we each had to be interviewed for the job we presently held. During the season, I had to put together a resume and go through the process. It was completely understandable and a required procedure during a sale, but it did seem a little strange with us doing well and getting Erstad and Washburn in the draft.

What was tough, though, was with the sale not completed in late August, we couldn't yet offer our scouts contracts. I told them I was sure they would be coming back, but they had permission to look elsewhere if they wished because they had to look after their families. It was tough to do, but luckily, they all stayed, and we got them under contract soon after.

The sale of the club from Autry was in place, and we were now being directed by Walt Disney Company with many changes as we entered a more business-like atmosphere and approach.

Tim Mead was heading back to the public relations department as the vice president to oversee not just the Angels, but the NHL's Mighty Ducks of Anaheim as well. Ken Forsch was to become the new assistant general manager to Bill Bavasi and Jeff Parker was the new minor league farm director.

Tony Reagins became an assistant to Jeff and myself. Tony would fit in perfectly with our operation and would later become not only the Angels minor league farm director, but their general manager from 2007-2011.

Many people in the business portion of our front office lost their jobs, as the Angels were incorporated with the Mighty Ducks, who were owned by Disney as well. Many people were working for both teams and this eliminated many positions. We were asked to resign from Golden West Baseball, which owned the radio stations and the team for Autry. Everyone who stayed with the Angels signed a paper resigning from Golden West and was then hired by the Walt Disney Company.

I was on the road at the time of all this change, and when I found out that there was a chance we may lose some seniority by resigning, I didn't sign the paper. No one ever followed up or asked for it, so I guess technically, I still worked for Golden West Baseball.

Because of our good results in 1995, we had a low draft pick, and because we signed a major league free agent, we lost our first-round pick in 1996. Just the opposite of where we had a productive season and the number one overall pick, the major league club had a bad season in 1996 and we didn't have a first-round pick. Our first pick would be 55th overall.

This didn't appear to be a deep draft and even though there were some good players that came from it, it was nothing like the year before. Because of this, we had no idea who or what position we would get when we selected. Mark Kotsay, Eric Chavez, R.A. Dickey, and Jimmy Rollins were the best of the overall group.

We settled on a shortstop from Austin Peay University by the name of Chuck Abbott. He had good tools across the board, but nothing that showed plus. He played shortstop in college, but we saw defensive versatility and felt he could play second base or become a good utility player. I thought he would become a good line drive hitter, but he never hit enough to reach the majors. Although he wasn't a first-round pick, it always hurts when the first player you select in a draft doesn't make it to the Show, no matter where he is selected.

We only got three players to the majors from this draft, but all three would play for at least parts of four years, with one being an important member of the Angels foundation.

Scott Schoeneweis, a left-handed pitcher out of Duke, was our third-round selection, went on to a 12-year major league career. He began his career as a starting pitcher, but ended up having big years as a reliever, including a strong World Series performance in 2002. Scott was a tough-nosed kid who challenged hitters.

Jarrod Riggan, a right-handed pitcher from San Diego State, and Greg Jones, a converted right-handed pitcher from catcher out of Pasco-Hernando Community College in Florida, both spent parts of four years in the majors as relievers.

Though the draft didn't reap much, it was no comparison for a scouting trip to North and East that spring that fit perfectly with the way the year went and proved memorable for non-baseball reasons.

I was on a redeye flight from Ontario, California to Chicago, connecting to a flight to Hartford, Connecticut. Somewhere halfway to Chicago, a big, husky woman with an accent walked to the door at the front of the plane. She grabbed the door handle and announced that she wanted to get off the plane, *now*. I had been upgraded for this flight and was half asleep but not far away when she made her declaration.

"Sh*t! She's gonna jump!" a man yelled.

When you're half asleep and something like this happens, you aren't thinking clearly right away, knowing that she can't open it because of the pressure at that altitude, but until you get to that point it is a little unnerving. Besides, she looked strong enough to do it.

After the flight attendant and co-pilot – armed with a large flashlight that he held in the air ready to strike – were able to reason with her and get her to return to her seat, all passengers in the first-class aisle seats were instructed to get in the walkway to block the woman's route if she attempted again.

It was the quickest landing into O'Hare Airport that I ever had. The FBI had a greeting party waiting for the woman at the gate.

That was just the start of the trip.

When I arrived in Hartford later that day, I was driving through a rough part of town when I was suddenly stopped in traffic in front of an apartment building. I didn't think much of it until a police officer jumped in front of my car, pointing a gun up towards the building. Apparently, a slight difference of opinion between someone in the building and the police required guns. I made a quick right onto the sidewalk and motored away.

A few days later, I was down in Florida for the last segment of this trip in the Orlando area. Jon Neiderer and I were going to a high school game one evening and on our way to the ballpark we were stopped at a stoplight on a corner where there was a Denny's restaurant. We stopped in front of the driveway into the Denny's when suddenly, we heard tires screeching and the sound, *pop, pop, pop.*

We looked to our right and three officers were shooting into a car that was trying to get away and was heading right towards us. We had nowhere to go so we ducked, waiting for a collision. The gunshots continued, but as we waited, there was no collision. We looked up and saw the car made a late move to avoid us and turned, departing from the back of the parking lot. We found out later it was a sting operation, and they caught the guy a few miles away.

The trip was fitting for the year.

After the poor major league season in 1996, we were again drafting high in the first round in 1997. We had the third overall pick and it looked like it would be another solid draft. We focused on college bats with power potential. There were also some good young arms, both at the high school and college levels, leaving us plenty of options. There would be several good major league players to come out of the 1997 draft, with Troy Glaus, J.D. Drew, Vernon Wells, Michael Cuddyer, Jon Garland, Lance Berkman, Jason Grilli, and others.

The top two college hitters this year were Drew, an outfielder from Florida State, and Glaus, a shortstop from UCLA. Both had power, with Glaus having more, but Drew being the better runner. Drew was the most famous of the two and probably had more clubs leaning his way. Glaus had been followed for years since his high school days in San Diego and was well known. Both were good choices, and we learned that Philadelphia, picking in front of us, was also leaning towards a college bat. The biggest worry we had was who Detroit would draft with the first overall pick.

Matt Anderson, a right-handed relief pitcher from Rice, was topping out at 100 miles-per-hour and starting to draw a lot of attention because of his velocity and that he may be close to the majors. As the spring went on, it looked more and more like he would go to Detroit.

Berkman was also at Rice and getting a lot of exposure himself, giving us another college power-hitting option. We tried to let people know that we had real interest in Drew first, when actually, we had Glaus in front of him.

Glaus played shortstop at UCLA and was big for the position but was able to cover enough ground to play the spot. He had good hands and a powerful arm that could make the throw easily from the hole.

Early in the year, Darrell Miller, the scout who covered UCLA and had a good read on the kid, attended UCLA's alumni game with me. I always like alumni games at good baseball schools because you could learn a lot about a college player or pitcher. Schools like this have several alumni that are present or former professional players that know how to adjust and do the things you need to do in a professional game. Often, the college team will use a wood bat which gives you more insight into that adjustment from aluminum, the regulation bat for college players.

This alumni game gave us insight on how Glaus would adjust to professional pitching. The UCLA alumni team featured several current professional pitchers who, despite not being in midseason form, knew how to pitch and set up hitters. They tried to set him up inside and then away, but he handled everything well, and had good swings. This was a big asset to see how he reacted and helped to set him apart from the others.

We held a meeting with our crosscheckers in Anaheim early in the spring. At the conclusion of the meeting, it was decided that Tony LaCava, Jon Neiderer, and Paul Robinson would take a quick side trip to see Glaus play in Las Vegas. They came away impressed with the strength of his bat, and with Rick Ingalls and Rick Schlenker already comfortable with what he could do, we had to have somebody really come on strong to change the way we were thinking.

As we got closer to the draft, we were getting a bit concerned that Philadelphia may change their thinking and go with Glaus instead of Drew. Had that happened, although we liked Drew, we were starting to gain interest in Jon Garland.

Garland, a right-handed pitcher, had one of the finest deliveries I have seen in a high school pitcher. It was a straight up, smooth delivery, with a free and quick arm from an overhand slot. He had a solid fastball and a quick, long-breaking curve. Bob Harrison stayed on him all spring and had great interest in him, and with Bob's background and reference, that meant a lot. Had Glaus been taken in front of us, we would have gone with Garland.

When draft day arrived, Detroit took Anderson, Philadelphia took Drew, and we got Glaus. The day started like we hoped.

We didn't have a second-round pick this year and didn't get another player to the majors after Glaus until the sixth round. We ended up with six players from this draft reaching the majors, with two of the pitchers having good careers out of the bullpen: Matt Wise and Scot Shields.

Wise, our sixth-round pick and a right-handed pitcher from Cal State Fullerton, pitched against us in spring training while with the Titans and showed average stuff that kept us in check for quite a few innings. (That was a glowing report that led to us drafting him). He was tall and created a good downward angle to the plate, along with pitching inside. He took that approach to a successful eight-year major league career. He returned to the Angels organization in the 2010's as a minor league coach and was named the big league pitching coach in 2021.

Shields, our 38th-round pick, was one of the steals of the draft and had a 10-year major league career, all with the Angels as a top setup man. A senior sign out of Lincoln Memorial University in Tennessee, he was worked out right before the draft by Tom Kotchman, who had his name recommended to him. Tom liked what he saw and turned his name in at the end. Another productive late round sign from Tom.

"*Kotch*" came out to the draft almost every year I was there. He was invited as the manager of our Rookie League team and may be the best scout I have ever been around on players selected low in the draft.

He had a great information network and feel for late picks. He signed, or was instrumental, in so many senior sign or low draft picks over the years. Players like Shields, Todd Greene, Orlando Palmeiro, Alfredo Amezaga, and Greg Jones, just to mention a few. This doesn't count the many players who reached Double-A and Triple-A and were good organizational players who helped expedite the development of our prospects.

We stressed the importance of the low draft picks and college senior signs. I was always taught that a baseball team is like a Broadway play. If you have a good supporting cast, the stars will shine brighter. I never forgot it, and it is true. The better the support players at any level, the better the good players will become.

The biggest task after the draft concluded was to try and get Glaus signed and on his way to professional baseball. We felt his bat could be in the majors soon and wanted his power in our lineup. Although I personally believe he could have made it to the majors as a shortstop, our immediate need was at third base, and it could get him up in a hurry.

I always believed if you have a player who is playing a position such as shortstop, center field, or the outfield, but you know they are probably going to be moved at some point, it is best to leave them at their natural position as long as possible. It helps to keep them more active and prepares them better for the position they will end up at. I think if Glaus would have gotten to the majors as a shortstop, it would have allowed him to have more range at third base, even though he was an outstanding defensive third baseman. Challenging a player is a good thing.

The negotiations were very constructive, as he was represented by Doug DeCinces, the former Angels third baseman. Something useful when dealing with a representative or agent who has played the game is that they can prepare their client for what is ahead. Doug was a long-time player and when Troy eventually went out the next spring, he took to it like he had been playing for years. Doug must be commended for a lot of that.

It took most of the summer to come to an agreement. At one session, it was Doug, Bill, and I at dinner and we talked about the contract for a while but got to the subject of Troy the player and were able to be on the same page about where he should start and what he needed to do when he began. He signed and went to Instructional League in Mesa in September and would be ready in 1998.

Troy started his professional career off well in 1998 in Double-A and Triple-A. He was moved defensively to third base, as we had Gary Disarcina at shortstop and needed someone at third base with power. As much as I would have liked to see him stay at shortstop, this was the right move for the team, and for Troy, it got him to the majors when he was ready. He played just four months in Double-A and Triple-A before he was called up to the big leagues.

When Troy arrived in Anaheim, he played almost every day until the end of the season. He didn't have a great batting average, but certainly was not overmatched. What surprised some people was that he had only one home run in 165 at-bats. This is not uncommon, as it takes a power hitter longer to get comfortable at the plate more often than a contact hitter. I thought he did fine, as he had a good approach to everything he did. The next year, he hit 29 home runs.

Troy had the ability to drive the ball hard with power to all fields, and when he was hitting balls to the right side, you knew he was zoned in not only to hit the long ball there, but to turn on a pitch and pull it deep into left field. He had some length to his swing but had a quick load and start to his bat with strong hands and a quick path to the ball. He could hit a ball extremely hard.

Troy had a strong 13-year career in the majors. He hit 320 career home runs and was a four-time All-Star, American League home run champion in 2000, and the World Series Most Valuable Player in 2002. He was a key in the Angels foundation for many years and was the type of player we hoped for when we drafted him.

The 1998 draft would be a year that we didn't get much after our first selection. We had a good year at the major league level in 1997, finishing in second place behind Seattle. We had bounced back from the poor showing in 1996, and our young players were getting more established. With this finish, it placed us with the 18th selection in the first round.

The draft had some good players, and although I wouldn't call it a strong draft, it was a productive one for many clubs. Pat Burrell, a third baseman from Miami, was the first player taken, and such players as Mark Mulder, J.D. Drew (who didn't sign with Philadelphia the year before), Austin Kearns, Carlos Peña, Brad Lidge and C.C. Sabathia were all taken in the first round.

We saw that there was some depth to the draft with pitching and were looking for a starting pitcher if possible. As the spring went on, we really thought we had a good chance at Lidge from Notre Dame. College pitchers from cold weather parts of the country have always been of interest to me. With the shortness of their season and poor weather, they don't seem to get the overuse that pitchers sometimes get from the warm weather areas. Even though Lidge would become a quality major league closer, we felt he could be a starter when he was in college.

As we got closer to draft day, we had Lidge and Seth Etherton, a right-handed pitcher from USC, as the two pitchers we thought we could get. Our scouts talked with clubs drafting all around us to see where they were leaning and by all indications, it looked as though Lidge would get to us. The only club that wouldn't tell us anything was Houston, who drafted the pick ahead of us. Usually, you will give info to the team behind you, but they didn't, and I can't blame them. I probably wouldn't have either.

Houston took Lidge, right in front of us.

With our pick, we took Etherton and were happy to get him. He didn't have overpowering stuff, but he had a good repeatable delivery that brought a lot of strikes, and he knew how to pitch to utilize his talents. He had an average fastball, good breaking ball, and good changeup, but it was his ability to spot the ball where he wanted that could make him effective.

Etherton was in the majors by 2000 and started off strong with a 5-1 record in 11 starts. It looked like he would in our rotation for a while, but he had shoulder problems late in the season. He was traded at the end of 2000 and missed the entire 2001 season. He spent some time with Cincinnati, Oakland, and Kansas City, but didn't pitch in the majors beyond 2006.

Our team had a good year in 1998 and was in the division title hunt until three days before the end of the season. Our young players were getting experience in the major leagues and with a few more pieces, it looked as though we were close.

In the offseason, Bill made a strong effort to sign Mo Vaughn in free agency. Vaughn was coming off four straight seasons of 35 or more home runs and was the AL MVP in 1995. His bat, power, and veteran presence could really help our young players.

Bill's efforts to sign Vaughn were successful and we appeared to be a strong contender for the division if we stayed healthy, which unfortunately, we didn't.

In the first inning of the first game of 1999, Vaughn went to try and catch a popup near the dugout and he slipped and hurt his ankle. Even though he played 139 games that year, it wasn't quite the same, and everything seemed to go south from there.

Tim Salmon was out for more than a third of the season, Jim Edmonds was out for two-thirds of the season, and Gary Disarcina missed half the season.

When you only have partial seasons from four of your key players, it is tough to compete. We were told that injuries are no excuse. I agree that everyone experiences injuries, but when it affects that many key players, it is not an excuse. It is a reason.

We knew we were losing our first pick in the 1999 draft due to signing Vaughn, so, to ownership's credit, we were told to make a splash internationally. We had never had any money to speak of internationally over the 12 years I had previously worked with the club.

This was something I looked forward to because, as Disney understood, if you are competitive with bonus money internationally, agents will bring players to you.

With the new allowance in place, we started looking at better international players, knowing we could be involved. We looked at all the obvious players in the fall and winter of 1998, but there was a young right-handed pitcher from Venezuela that caught our attention.

Francisco "Frankie" Rodríguez had been seen in different events by our international supervisor George Lauzerique, Tom Kotchman, and Rick Ingalls. After talking with them, I planned on attending a workout that Frankie's agent had scheduled in Florida.

I got to Miami the night before the workout, and of course, it rained all night and morning. When I showed up at the field the next day, there was Frankie, his agent, and one other club. All the other clubs that were supposed to attend probably thought there was no way he would work out today. To the agent's credit, we found another park that had a field, and the mound was playable, so we were able to see him throw.

Frankie was a nice 16-year-old kid who had a big smile on his face. As soon as he started warming up, you could see the looseness in his arm. Although he needed work with this delivery, his arm was very quick, and the ball came out of his hand extremely well. The fastball he threw had a late, hard finish, and you projected it getting even better. He didn't show that great slider or changeup that he would develop, but he showed the ability to spin a breaking ball that let you know he had a strong wrist that would allow improvement to those pitches. It was a good workout, and I knew we had to move fast to try and get him signed.

We contacted his representative and started the negotiating process. I felt there were probably about six clubs or so involved with strong interest, and with time, when we got to around $500,000 in the negotiation, I thought it was between us and St Louis.

I felt the negotiation was headed upwards of $750,000 or more to get it done. With that direction, I had to make a splash.

I contacted his agent and said, "If we can get a deal done *right now*, we will offer $900,000."

We had a deal later that day.

Rodríguez started his professional career in 1999 with our Rookie League affiliate, and outside of some growing pains young kids face when they sign so young, he did well and progressed to the majors by 2002. Although he pitched as a starter in the minors, he was moved to the bullpen in 2002 before being called up.

The start of his major league career was historic, as he arrived in the majors as a 20-year-old just 11 days before the end of the season. He did not allow a run during five appearances in the regular season and was placed on the playoff roster, where he made a real name for himself. Frankie, or "K-Rod" as some called him, struck out 28 batters in 18 2/3 innings that postseason, proving himself a key figure to the Angels World Series Championship.

In 2008 when I was with the Mariners, I attended a game we played against the Angels on September 13. That was the night Frankie recorded his 58th save of the season, setting a new single-season record. I kept thinking back to that soaked field where we had a makeshift workout when he was 16, and now he was setting a major league record. He would go on to record 62 saves in 2008, which remains the record to this day.

With the signing of Frankie in the winter leading up to the 1999 draft, we were off to a good start. We still had the draft ahead though, and with this not being one of the stronger overall draft classes, it only made it a more difficult task that our first pick would be 68th overall.

The first round had just under half the players reach the majors, with Josh Hamilton, Josh Beckett, Barry Zito, and Ben Sheets being the most notable.

We started the spring by eliminating as many names as possible we were sure wouldn't get to us, and put together a list of potential players who may be around at pick 68.

As the spring went on, we felt that the best chance we had was with a pitcher. There were some interesting young arms that we were focusing on, and with our large crosschecking staff, we could get a lot of looks. We started to narrow the names down and finished with John Lackey from Grayson Junior College and Jon Rauch of Morehead State, both right-handed pitchers.

Lackey and Rauch were both tall pitchers, which we really liked. I learned through the years that the angle a tall pitcher can create can help him to be successful, even on days when he doesn't have his best stuff.

Kris Kline, who scouted in Texas for us, and Paul Robinson really liked Lackey. He had been at Texas-Arlington and was a big, strong kid who until recently had been a position player. He had played first base with an occasional relief appearance, but it wasn't until the summer in the Jayhawk Collegiate League that he took pitching more seriously. He transferred to Grayson as a sophomore where he would pitch and play first base.

Kris had seen Lackey early and liked his arm, and when Paul saw him, they were both on board that he could get to us because of his limited time pitching and that junior colleges were not seen as often. We got looks at him and were comfortable that even though he was crude as a pitcher, he had a fine arm and aggressive makeup.

It was a windy day when I went with Kris and Paul to see John pitch out west in Ranger, Texas. We got to Ranger early and there wasn't much to do, leaving time on our hands, which led us to a great waffle house off the freeway before heading into town. It was a doubleheader where Lackey played first base in the first game. He was having a good year with the bat and was hitting some home runs. He was scheduled to pitch the second game of the doubleheader, and it started to get colder and windier.

It seems I attract bad weather more than anyone. I once saw a game at Baylor where they played in the snow in 25-degree weather. It snows maybe once every few years in Waco. This happened to me often, and it always seemed to be a pitcher I was seeing.

As soon as John started with his first pitch, it was apparent how aggressive he was, challenging each hitter from the first pitch on. He had a quick arm with the ball jumping out of his hand, and the delivery wasn't bad. His fastball had that late life you like on the ball and he had above-average velocity. His breaking ball was just fair, but he could spin the ball and you could see where some adjustments might help him in a hurry. With his stuff, aggression, and potential to improve quickly, he was definitely in the mix for our first pick.

On the way back to Dallas after the game to catch my flight, Paul's car broke down. It was an older Mercedes whose odometer and speedometer didn't work. It was a diesel and Paul said it would run for a few hundred thousand miles more. Well, not this day.

Luckily, Kris had driven as well and was able to get me to the airport in time to catch my flight. Paul said he could get it fixed and I guess he did, as he ended up only about an hour behind us getting back.

The next stop was to see Rauch pitch for Morehead State. I saw them pitch on the road and once again, it was cold, windy, and miserable. One thing the weather couldn't take away was seeing a tall, 6-foot-11, right-handed pitcher, who had a great angle to the plate.

When the game started, Rauch had a good fastball with that downward angle that can be so tough on a hitter. He had a short breaking ball that would get better. At his size, he was still trying to develop consistency, getting his entire 6-foot-11 body into sync to throw more strikes.

Rauch was inconsistent with his control and didn't last long into the game, but I liked what I saw and could see the potential to just keep getting better. I was glad so many opposing crosscheckers saw this outing, because several clubs like good performances to go along with ability before selecting a player high. I was a bit worried though that Duane Shaffer, who had moved to the White Sox as scouting director, was there because I knew how he scouted pitchers and I knew he would like this kid.

As we approached our pre-draft meetings in San Diego, I told the staff that we must figure out a way to get both Lackey and Rauch. Our guys were the best at getting information, especially right before the draft, and I knew we would have the best information we could get.

Even though we didn't have a first-round pick, the staff was excited, because it looked like we would have extra money to take chances on more high school players or college players that were more difficult signs. We felt that we could get some players in rounds where their ability was better than the spot selected. This would not be the case.

A few days before the draft, Bill and I were informed that because we spent $900,000 on Frankie, it would come out of our draft bonus budget.

"We were told to make a splash internationally and we did," I said disappointed, "but no one said it would come out of this budget."

Again, I was wrong, and we were told that is the way it is. Bill and I were shocked but had to figure out a plan as we were losing almost half of our entire budget. Talk about feeling like you got hit in the stomach and having the wind taken out of you, this was it.

We decided that we would draft the first two picks like normal, but instead of taking chances on players that would cost more, we would have to take players we knew we could sign and hopefully at a reasonable rate.

When I went back to the draft room to tell the guys, I got inside and listened to the enthusiasm they had. I just couldn't tell them then and crush their spirits. I decided I would face it later.

When draft day arrived, there was a nervous tension with the club not playing well and the feeling we may be in trouble as a group if the year didn't get better. Even though everyone felt the organization was strong with players both at the major league and minor league levels, there were many on the national media scale that thought we were in bad shape. Despite Disney operating the club for the last four years, a lot of us knew we weren't their choice, but if we were doing well, it would be ok. It was more important than usual that we do well in this draft.

The feeling among our staff was that the only chance we had to get both Lackey and Rauch was to take them in that order. I really wanted to get both pitchers and wanted to have the best chance possible to get both.

It seemed to take forever to get to our first selection at 68, but when we did get there, Lackey was still available. We took him.

Now the waiting game started for our second pick, 33 picks away. As we got to within 10 picks of our third-round selection, I was fairly sure we would get Rauch unless the White Sox, who were two picks ahead of us, took him. As I started to think they may take him right before us, his name was called. Jon Rauch, 99th overall, Chicago White Sox. I was so ticked off, even though there was nothing that could be done.

As soon as the draft ended, I found out that if we had not taken Lackey first, he would have been taken soon after, leaving us no chance to get both pitchers. Regardless, our guys did a great job getting us in position to at least have a chance.

As the draft went on and the guys were pushing for players that were harder signs but who we thought had better ability than the round, I started taking players we knew we could sign, and in many cases, at reasonable costs. I started getting funny looks from the guys and after a while, they were getting upset with me. I couldn't blame them, but I didn't want to tell them why because we needed to get some good lower-round picks.

I didn't tell any of the scouts about the change in our budget at the last minute until years later. I remember one of them saying to me,

"I knew something had to have happened as it wasn't like you to do that. I was mad."

I couldn't blame any of them for being mad.

A day or so after the draft finished, Kris and Paul went to Abilene, Texas to meet with John and his family to try and sign him. Kris and Paul were excellent in the house and were good negotiators that made players and their families feel good about the process.

Paul was so good that he almost once signed a player for a pair of boots.

"Bob," Paul said over the phone when trying to sign the player, "if we can get the father a pair of Mr. Autry's boots autographed, I think we can get it done."

Mr. Autry agreed to do it, but as it turned out, Paul had the player signed before we even got to that point.

Sometime during the meeting with John, Paul called me to tell me he thought they could get John signed. I was surprised because it hadn't been going well to that point. I got a call from Kris that same night as the call from Paul, and he said, "We got it done, John is ready to go. Do you want to say hello to him?"

Of course I did! The job that Kris, Paul, and John did is what you want out of a negotiation. Quick, fair, and get out and start playing.

John made it to the majors just over three years after the day he was drafted. He arrived with the Angels in the championship year of 2002 and went on to pitch in Game 7 of the World Series, helping clinch the title for the Angels. He was only the second rookie, and first in 97 years, to start and win Game 7 of the World Series.

John would go on to win two more World Series, one with the Red Sox in 2013 and another with the Cubs in 2016.

He spent 15 years in the majors, including eight with the Angels where he established himself as one of the best starting pitchers in franchise history. In 2007, he was named an All-Star and won the American League ERA title. A true professional pitcher.

Though we may not have expected it, we drafted and signed six players in the 1999 draft that got to the majors. Robb Quinlan (10th round) and Alfredo Amezaga (13th round) were two players that had a few years in the majors as good utility players. Considering we didn't have the money we thought we had, to get John, Robb, and Alfredo from the draft and Frankie in the winter made it a successful year nonetheless.

Not long after the draft ended towards the end of the summer, Bill Bavasi resigned as general manager. The team was in one of those bad spells with injuries and poor offseasons with key players. Usually, if you are healthy and make a few adjustments over the winter, the club comes back and plays like they are capable of doing.

The Angels did play much better in 2000 and continued to play high-caliber baseball for the next 15 years. Unfortunately for Bill, myself, and many others, we would experience the success of the young Angels foundation as spectators.

Bill had done a great job of keeping the club in contention and allowing the scouting and player development departments to operate the same, no matter what the direction of the big-league team was. Bill is at his best when there are problems or adversity to deal with, and we had our share of both. His even temperament carried over to the whole staff. He treated everyone the same and it is something you don't see enough of, especially in sports.

Not long after Bill left, our manager, Terry Collins, left. Terry had been our manager for the last three years and had been so supportive of our young players. Even with the pressure we were under to win, Terry would go with a young player even if it appeared more of a risk. He made the scouting and minor league staff feel like all their work was appreciated.

Joe Maddon took over as interim manager and would stay with the Angels for another six years before starting his own incredible managerial career. He led the turnaround of the Tampa Bay Rays organization, taking them to their first World Series appearance in 2008, and was at the helm when the Chicago Cubs snapped their 108-year World Series championship drought in 2016.

Joe, with his relationships with the young players, would prove to be very instrumental in the Angels success in the years to follow.

When all these things were coming down, I was told that I would have to wait until a new general manager was hired to know my fate as far as what I would be doing. I was told I would be brought back in some capacity the next year. As the process to find a general manager was getting into September, I asked if I could renew the scouts and was told no, but that I needed to be prepared to tell the new general manager about everyone to get his approval.

For the next month, I had to keep telling our staff that I didn't know what was going to happen, and we needed to wait. Waiting is a hard thing for a scout to do, especially when you get close to October as jobs get filled and there are very few openings the rest of the year.

We lost Tony LaCava, who went to Atlanta, and I think he would have had an opportunity at a bigger job with the Angels. It was hard because deep down, I knew I would be irrelevant in any decisions and couldn't do much to help.

As we got into mid-October, we still didn't have a general manager and scouts' contracts were up October 31. Finally, we were given the go ahead to send out contracts to all but nine scouts. Three days before contracts were up, I was told to let those nine scouts go and if I didn't feel I could do it, then someone with Human Resources would.

I knew I couldn't let someone else do it after all we had been through and they deserved to hear it from me even though they knew it wasn't my decision. Even though they knew it wasn't direct from me, the messenger is usually blamed and as I found out, that is the natural response.

The hardest day in my life was making those nine phone calls.

I knew while this was going on that I was going to leave, but I wanted to meet with the new general manager before I did anything. Around the start of November, Bill Stoneman was hired as the new general manager.

Stoneman was a former quality major league pitcher who had been an executive with the Montreal Expos. I worked with Stoneman in Montreal and he was an excellent baseball man who could be tough but fair. I thought it was a good hire.

I met with Stoneman a few days after he was hired. He said to me right away that I was going to be reassigned and that a new scouting director would be hired. He said he didn't know why but the perception of people was that we didn't have many solid players from our farm system. I just said, "Bill, we have kids and our people have done a great job."

He said he looked forward to seeing what we had.

I did ask where I was being reassigned and he said he didn't know yet. That was a big clue. When re-assigned to nowhere, you better leave.

During my time with the Angels, many people labeled me a college scout or safety scout. The thinking among many people in the game was that if you draft high school players, you are drafting high-risk, high-ceiling players. If you draft college players, you are drafting safely. I never understood the rationale, as ability is ability. Ability knows no age. Besides, you can't be a star in the majors if you don't get there in the first place.

For me, college draftees are the higher risk because when you draft them, the clock starts. People are expecting them in the majors quickly and watching closely. High school players, on the other hand, are the safe route, because people expect them to take four to five years to reach the majors, and after three years, if they can't play, no one seems to notice as much.

We got players such as Garret Anderson and Jim Edmonds and others out of high school to the majors, and if taking college players such as Jim Abbott, Tim Salmon, Darin Erstad, Troy Percival, Jarrod Washburn, Troy Glaus, John Lackey and others is safety, then I guess I was a safety scouting director.

I knew that they probably had my replacement in mind for a couple of weeks and I'm sure Stoneman didn't want me hanging around. I was just worried about our staff and like so many transitions, a number of our people moved on.

The 13 years with the Angels are probably the most satisfying years I have spent in baseball, with so many of the best people you could work with and become friends with.

I went into the office the next day and resigned. It was difficult to leave, but it was the right time.

I had agreed to go work for Duane Shaffer with the White Sox as a crosschecker and was ready to move on.

I told Stoneman, and he understood. He would go on the next few years to really evaluate what he had before he made player moves. Outside of a key move trading Jim Edmonds to St. Louis for Adam Kennedy and Kent Bottenfield, and some good free agent additions, he gave the young players a chance. With that approach, and Mike Scioscia hired as manager, they went on to become World Champions in 2002.

Stoneman was gracious enough to invite Bill and his wife, Tracy, as well as me and my wife, Karen, to attend the first game of the World Series. It was great to see the people we knew and the excitement they were enjoying. We enjoyed that game, but it was certainly time to leave right after. As gracious as Stoneman was to bring us both, Bill and I felt a little awkward because it was their time, not ours.

When the Angels played Game 7 against the San Francisco Giants, I was on a flight from Chicago to Sacramento. The pilot was giving regular updates on the score and with about 10 minutes left in the flight, he said the Angels were ahead in the eighth inning. When we landed, I didn't know the outcome of the game.

When I got off the plane, I called Karen and all she said was, "4-1, final."

It was a great feeling after all those years there and for all the people that helped build that team, but unfortunately, those brief moments of reflection are all you get.

The 13 years I spent with the Angels saw staffs that worked to develop and solidify a strong, young foundation that would create a nucleus that would last for a long time.

The following is a list of top players signed and developed by the scouting and minor league staffs:

RIGHT-HANDED PITCHERS

- Jason Dickson
- Joe Grahe
- John Lackey
- Phil Leftwich
- Ramón Ortiz
- Troy Percival
- Francisco Rodríguez
- Scot Shields
- Bill Simas
- John Snyder
- Matt Wise

LEFT-HANDED PITCHERS

- Jim Abbott
- Brian Anderson
- Mike Holtz
- Mark Holzemer
- Andrew Lorraine
- Matt Perisho
- Scott Schoeneweis
- Jarrod Washburn

CATCHERS

- Jamie Burke
- Jorge Fabregas
- Todd Greene
- John Orton
- Chris Turner

INFIELDERS

- Alfredo Amezaga
- Gary Disarcina
- Damion Easley
- Troy Glaus
- Eduardo Perez
- Robb Quinlan

OUTFIELDERS

- Ruben Amaro
- Garret Anderson
- Chad Curtis
- Jim Edmonds
- Darin Erstad
- Orlando Palmeiro
- Tim Salmon
- Mark Sweeney

The Angels, to their credit, kept adding to the foundation, and as players left, they had young replacements for them. With Bill Stoneman and Tony Reagins after him, they continued to emphasize the draft. Eddie Bane, who came to the Angels later, went on to have some quality drafts for many years and the Angels kept moving forward in a development direction. It was fun, sad, and extremely rewarding to be a part of that time.

CALIFORNIA YEARS – JIM ABBOTT

"Jim was in the right place. He had the support system. He had Bobby Fontaine and the scouts. He had Bobby's blessing and that's what counted, and Bobby had the trust of Mike Port and Gene Autry. To make that move with a first-round selection was big. I don't think you can underscore how important that was – that Jimmy knew from day one how much the Angels believed in him. Then this guy comes along named Marcel Lachemann who just solidified – basically became a father figure on the West Coast. Jim Abbott belonged with the Angels and the Angels needed to be with Jim Abbott. That relationship, that family relationship, was signed, sealed, and delivered by Bobby Fontaine." – Tim Mead, President of the National Baseball Hall of Fame (2019 – 2021)

Going into the 1988 draft, we were hoping to get a solid left-handed starting pitcher. There were a few possibilities going into the spring that were interesting, but none were as alluring as Jim Abbott at the University of Michigan.

Abbott was a talented pitcher with little doubt about his ability, but there was an issue that concerned most people: Jim was born without a right hand.

Because of this, many thought he would not be able to stay with the tempo of the game as he advanced in professional baseball. History would reveal that of all the challenges in baseball he would face, that turned out to be the least of his problems.

Jim was a star two-sport athlete for Central High School in Flint, Michigan. He played quarterback, leading his team to the playoffs, and was a member of the school's baseball team. He was strong enough as a pitcher to be drafted by the Toronto Blue Jays in the 36th round of the 1985 draft. He declined to sign and instead attended Michigan, where started in their rotation through his junior year.

Over those three spring seasons with the Wolverines, he made a big name for himself. Not only as a college standout, but as a member of USA Baseball's National Team, making him one of the best college players in the country.

Eleven months prior to the draft and just after his sophomore season at Michigan, Jim pitched for Team USA against the best amateur baseball team in the world, the Cuban National Team, in Havana, Cuba, during the Pan-American Games. No American team had beaten the Cubans in Cuba since 1960.

The United States roster was made up of college kids, while the Cuban team had players aged 18-40, with some playing for nearly a decade together. Though they were officially an "amateur" club, they had professionals from Cuba's major league, Serie Nacional, on their roster and many of the players' families received support from the Cuban government year-round.

At that time, Cuba had all their best players, and they were good. They had Omar Linares at third base, a young, good-looking player. He ended up playing in Japan in his late 30's because of strong relations between Cuba and Japan and was quite a talent.

This same Cuban team showed its prowess more than a decade later when it beat the Baltimore Orioles, 12-6, in 1999.

That day in Havana though, Jim went out as a 20-year-old with no professional experience and pitched five scoreless innings against the Cubans, permitting just three hits. As Jim left the mound, the local supporters rose to their feet and applauded, giving a foreign college kid a standing ovation. It was such an impressive feat that Cuba's President Fidel Castro asked to meet Jim following the game. Jim had developed into a fan favorite in Cuba, not only because of the accomplishment of beating their beloved team, but the way he competed.

To that point, I had not seen Jim in person. I was leery myself about how he would handle throwing a baseball, transferring his glove to his left hand, finishing properly, and doing it all in one continuous motion.

Over the winter of 1987-88, I went back to watch video of him pitching against Cuba. Not because he beat them on their home turf, but I wanted to see if my concerns were reasonable. Could he make the transfer and transitions quickly enough to keep up with the tempo of professional baseball? How would he handle teams regularly bunting against him and put pressure on his defensive skills?

After realizing what immense potential he had as a pitcher, the next thing you see is the transition and when you see it, it looks like it's not really a problem. However, you still have to see it in person.

I went to one of Michigan's first games of Jim's junior season to get an eyewitness account. Michigan was visiting the University of Texas in Austin for their first trip south. It was a cold mid-March afternoon, with temperatures in the mid-40's and a steady wind blowing. This can be a hindrance to a pitcher no matter what time of year. Cold weather makes it harder to get loose and more difficult to throw.

I stood on the side, as always, because I didn't want a lot of people to know I was there yet. Early in the year a lot of people don't go to see the northern teams right out of the shoot because they're still stale from the winter. Even though we were drafting eighth, why would you want to alert anybody that you have interest by showing up to a player's first game?

Jim really intrigued me with the way he went about his business and after about three pitches, you don't even notice he's missing his right hand. He's that fast with the transition. He'd throw and move his glove from his right arm to his left hand extremely quickly, to the point that it almost looked natural.

"1988, Ticket stub from Jim Abbott's start against Texas"

He showed no fear and did the transition quickly. He was even better defensively than a lot of other pitchers. Not only was the bunt play not a problem, but he also turned out to be one of the best defending against the bunt I had seen from a young pitcher. He fielded his position well and his strong athletic ability allowed him to get off the mound so quickly that he was in good position to handle plays in front of him. As the game continued, I answered the biggest question I had. Could he field his position well enough to pitch in professional baseball? The answer: absolutely!

He was such a good athlete that you figured the more repetitions, the quicker he would be and adjust accordingly, and he did. Playing two sports in his youth, he would figure a way to do it because he'd been figuring out how to do it his entire life.

Outside of the questions surrounding his ability to make the transfer, you saw premier stuff from a college left-hander. Nobody questioned his ability. Everybody liked his ability. You couldn't help but like it.

His fastball had power and the cutting movement added to its dominance that tied hitters up. It would end up being his premier pitch. Northern pitchers, whether it was Bob Welch, Steve Howe or Jim, tend to throw harder. I didn't have a radar gun reading that evening, but I didn't need one. You knew he was throwing with better than average velocity.

You can project a fastball and you can certainly project more on the finish of a breaking ball. The one thing Jim didn't really have that night was a curveball or changeup of any kind. Those were areas where you projected if he could get a usable third pitch, it would enhance everything else.

He had an assertive presence on the mound that made everyone behind him better. Jim and his teammates were rusty, having come from the north a few days earlier, but the defenders played so well behind him because they knew he was a competitor and made no excuses. He just went out and did his job.

He didn't have a great night statistically, but he had a professional delivery with a well above-average fastball and swing-and-miss cutter. He had so much present ability and easy projection in the future, and his great presence on the field was so rare to see from a young pitcher.

There are few times in a scout's career where you have an immediate impulse or sense the first time you see a player and it turns out well. I have been fortunate to have that happen on three occasions, and Jim was one of those players.

When I left the ballpark that first night in Texas, I knew that barring any unforeseen issues, this was our pitcher. I wanted him to be our guy.

After the game I drove up to Dallas to catch a plane to Florida. I got on the shuttle bus to head to the terminal and the first person I saw as I got on was Duane Shaffer, now a national crosschecker for the Oakland Athletics. Duane and I had worked together earlier with Chicago and knew each other well. Oakland drafted eight picks after us that year.

Duane looked at me square and smiled, "You went down to see Abbott, didn't you?"

"Yeah," I laughed.

I liked to have our draft meetings at a location away from the ballpark. It allowed everyone to get away from disruptions and distractions. No one could ask to go watch batting practice or visit the team store, and you wouldn't have others coming from down the hall walking into the room asking, "Hey, how are you guys doing? Any idea on who you're going to take?"

In 1988, a week before the draft, we had our staff go out to Catalina Island and the casino venue in Avalon. It was a relaxing place where we spent four days. However, things could get heated.

You have a bunch of guys in these meeting rooms, and everyone could vent their opinions and frustrations. You wanted people to express their true feelings and at times, there would be verbal battles and arguments. Catalina would lend me a hand with its natural setting.

When a guy would get heated or upset, I'd simply tell him, "Hey, go take a stroll on the beach for a few minutes and come back when you feel ready."

After we'd finish our meetings, we would go out to one of the oceanfront restaurants and have a meal and drink, and to no surprise, the conversation always came back to baseball and the draft.

During those four days, the staff continued to be split about Jim. When I say split, that doesn't mean people didn't like him. Everybody liked him. They were split on if we should take him first. Up to the very end, it continued to be a split decision.

Before I gave everybody our decision, I asked the group, "Who in this room doesn't think he can field his position in the major leagues?"

There was some mental stirring, but it didn't take long to realize that not a single hand in the room rose. Not one person thought he couldn't defend himself on the mound.

I said, "Guys, you all like him. I realize you wouldn't all take him first, but the one question everybody has, you all agree on. He can field his position and we're going with Jim."

After four days in a relaxed setting, we left Catalina Island and headed for Anaheim. We had made our decision but needed to finalize some things, including informing others of our decision.

The first item was to inform our Mike Port and Bill Bavasi. They both knew of our strong interest in Jim, but Mike still had final approval. Mike and Bill knew all along which way we were leaning. There was no surprise because we wanted a college left-hander. Mike was behind it 100%, and said, "If that's the guy, that's the guy."

Bill, of course, was excited to get that kind of arm in the system. However, there were still two more people we had to make aware and get on board with our decision. The Angels were in last place at the time and with the controversy selecting a one-handed pitcher might bring, we needed approval from the owners, Gene Autry and his wife, Jackie. You want your owners to be on board and not hear about these kinds of things on the radio.

We met with Mr. and Mrs. Autry the following day and Mike explained to them our reasons for wanting to select Jim. We had to add that Jim was a pitcher, but only had one hand.

Mrs. Autry went on to ask about some of his statistics. She was always up on the numbers and always asked good questions about that side of the game.

"How many does he walk? How many strikeouts did he accumulate?"

After telling her about his success not only in the college ranks but also his international success. She seemed satisfied.

Mr. Autry sat, quietly listening, and when we looked to him for any questions, he asked, "Is his situation from birth or from an accident?"

"Birth," I said.

Without hesitation, Mr. Autry approved and looked to Mike asking, "Do you have any other items?"

As draft day approached, our lone concern was whether any club was thinking like us. To our knowledge, we weren't aware of any team ahead of us potentially selecting him because of the uncertainty about how it would be received.

Jim was rumored to go in the late first round or early second round, and that left us wary of the Detroit Tigers, who picked 26th. They had a good knowledge of him, being a local product of Michigan, and they were one of the few teams who had access to Jim and his family.

Personal visits were made challenging as his coach at Michigan, Bud Middaugh, and advisor, Scott Boras, made it tough to meet and feel good about him signing. Taking him in the second round wasn't an option. It was there that we had an in, and it turned out to be big in our conclusion that we would be able to sign him.

George Bradley was a long-time scout who was elevated to scouting director with the Detroit Tigers in the 80's, then was with the White Sox before I brought him with me to Anaheim, where he was one of our top scouts. A few years later, George became a top-level executive with the New York Yankees.

George had ties to the program at Michigan due to his years with the Tigers and was able to secure a meeting with Jim and his parents with Middaugh's permission. Outside of Detroit's front office, George may have been the only other person to get a meeting like this.

George went to Flint, Michigan, to meet with Jim and his family the week of the draft. The meeting went well, and George promptly flew back to Anaheim but not before calling me to say, "Bob, he wants to and will sign. It will take some time and will cost top dollar for the spot selected, but he is a great kid to go along with what we know about him as a pitcher."

George turned out to be as accurate as you could be.

The day before the draft, I had our group in a meeting room. When we started the scouting season, I asked our scouts to view Jim objectively and not get caught up in the negatives they would hear. We had great scouts who did as such with George, Rich Schlenker, Nick Kamzic, Cliff Ditto, Paul Robinson, and others.

I asked our staff about their feelings once again, and the room continued to be split. Fifty-fifty. Four to four.

The same concerns were mentioned, but I knew this was our guy. I told them, "I know not all of you would take him first and half of you would, but I know you all like him. That makes you part of the success that comes with him."

I felt he was the best player for us to take. I thought he was the right guy at the right time for us, and many others in the organization did as well.

The only time a scouting director wants to make a decision like this is when it's not unanimous or a large majority in the room. Even then, you sometimes go against what happens, but not that often. This was a perfect case where a decision had to be made.

When the draft rolled around, we waited patiently, hoping Jim would be available when we selected eighth. We continued to wait pick after pick, and suddenly, it was our selection and Jim was on the board. We happily picked the left-hander from Michigan.

Duane, who I had bumped into at the airport earlier in the spring told me later, "I knew that night that's who you were going to take."

The room was relieved and excited about the pick. Although the selection wasn't unanimous by our staff, all our scouts liked his ability, and everyone left the room eager. When it was all over, our entire staff came together. Even the guys who deep down didn't agree with me came out united and I was proud of our staff.

"We're with you, Bob," they said.

I know for myself, this selection felt different than any other I had made. We took somebody that a lot of people believed we shouldn't have. You knew we were going to open the door to criticism, but you must do what's best for the club because you think all those critics are wrong. You could feel that not only would his ability bring a lot to our club, but his obvious desire to want to play baseball would as well. I have never been so sure in my baseball career about the makeup and love for the game that a player possesses more than with Jim.

Shortly after making the selection, buzz started not only with the media but in the halls of our offices. People would question you, which is fine, but they would never question you to your face. A lot of people took special interest in the pick, both good and bad.

"This is a gamble."

"What a surprise!"

"Why would they do this?"

Even in our own organization, people didn't share the same excitement as the baseball operations staff. Some people within our offices saw it as a media stunt and we took Jim for publicity. Jokes were made about how we didn't know what we were doing and that we were becoming a circus. Our own people were laughing at us.

You think we took the eighth player in the country for publicity? Really? I was pissed.

It got to a point where once the draft concluded, Mike had everyone in the organization from switchboard operators to the vice presidents assemble in a conference room behind the home plate press box where he addressed the group. He told them that we were fortunate to draft Jim and that his talent was what we were looking for and a lot of thought, preparation, and discussion went into this selection.

Mike said he didn't want to hear anything more against the selection. We were looking for this type of pitcher and just because he had one hand didn't mean he wasn't the one the baseball operations department felt was best.

He told the group that most in the room had never seen Jim pitch. He took one of our VHS tapes and placed it on the television screen for all to see.

When people heard of Jim Abbott, they thought of Pete Grey, who was a former player who had lost his right arm due to a childhood accident. They had those kinds of thoughts in their mind, but as they watched the video, their mindsets changed.

Outside of an occasional, "Woah," from those who had never seen Jim pitch before, you could hear a pin drop from the silence.

Once the tape concluded, Mike asked, "Are there any questions?"

None were asked.

Because 1988 was an Olympic year, the players on the National Team who were drafted were in no hurry to sign contracts because they couldn't report until the following spring training. There was an agreement with the Olympic Committee that players could sign contracts if they didn't receive any money until after the Olympics. This happened every four years and would always cause longer negotiations and a spike in bonuses. You had until the players' first class in the fall to sign them, and this gave players more leverage because as it got closer to the school year, they had more bargaining power.

Bob Gardner, who was Jim's drafting scout, and I went to Flint to meet with Jim and his parents, Kathy and Mike. There was something about the way they raised Jim and his brother that we immediately noticed and aided our belief in Jim's makeup and love for the game. They were great people who were down to earth but were well-informed about the process.

Mike was a businessman and Kathy was an attorney. They had Scott Boras, who is now one of the game's best agents, as an advisor. All were well-prepared for a tough negotiation and were in no hurry to sign.

During that first meeting, we learned that the Abbotts wanted to wait and see what would happen with Andy Benes, who was selected first overall by the Padres, and wouldn't give us a figure until they saw what occurred with Andy's situation.

This meeting was important. It was our first meeting, but Jim would soon be headed out to the Olympics with Team USA and so much of the negotiations would be done with his parents. It was important that all of us were present. Gardner and I made an offer that was kindly refused. I still left the meeting feeling that we would get a deal done.

We continued to meet on-and-off for a few weeks after that first meeting. We came to a stalemate after realizing we couldn't get a figure from them to negotiate with.

The NCAA had strict guidelines on players discussing money, so it was often a tougher process than it should be. The lack of urgency from the players knowing they couldn't do anything until after the Olympics made it more challenging to have serious dialogue. I always felt this was more of a stall tactic by the agents to see what other players would get first and see if they could get more for their clients. I would probably do the same.

During one of our meetings at a Hilton in downtown Flint, I was able to get a bonus range from Jim's parents. Jim was off with Team USA right before heading to South Korea for the Olympics. Since Boras was technically an advisor, he couldn't attend the meetings. It was just Jim's parents handling things. Kathy was very businesslike while Mike was a bit more casual. As we chatted during that negotiation, it got across to me that $200,000 would be the amount acceptable for Jim to sign.

I spoke with Mike Port and Bill Bavasi after and we decided that although it was higher than we wanted to go, it was reasonable, and we should do it. You could always budget in a non-Olympic year and be close, but with the Olympics approaching you don't know what you're going to do. Jim had notoriety all over the country. He had something to bargain with.

I called and set up a meeting with Jim, who would be home for a few days before leaving for Seoul, his parents, Gardner, and myself.

We all met at his home in Flint. I sat in a chair across from the Abbotts. After chatting about the team and baseball in general, I looked at the young man across from me.

"Jim, would $200,000 make you a California Angel?"

"Yes."

"Congratulations, you are now a professional."

The Abbotts hugged. We shook hands. Both sides were happy with the negotiation.

We could have tried to get a deal done for a little less money, but I don't feel that would have been right. Jim, his parents, his advisor, and our club had concluded a hard, fair, and successful negotiation. Mike never hesitated throughout the draft and negotiation to get the kid we wanted signed. It took time to complete, but I think both sides felt that was a good place to be.

It was what negotiations are supposed to be. Give a little on each end where neither side is completely where they want, but in the area where they're comfortable. I think everybody felt good that this was his starting point. Jim Abbott was a member of the California Angels.

Jim pitched for the United States in the Olympics that summer in the grandest fashion, throwing a complete game in the final against Japan, clinching a gold medal for the United States. The Japanese team honored Jim by lining up to congratulate him on the feat.

I was on the road back east the day after that gold medal game, but Mike called me to inform me of Jim's triumph.

"Bob, it's all over the papers here. 'Abbott wins for U.S. gold.'"

Later that year he received the Sullivan Award, presented to the top amateur athlete in the United States. It was a storied finish to a great amateur career and an excitement for Orange County knowing he was headed their way.

Jim showed up for spring training that next February in Palm Springs with a lot of excitement, curiosity, and hope that he would be a key part of our pitching staff soon. I don't think there were many people that thought he would start his professional career in the major leagues, though. He was signed to a Double-A contract and was going to start the year in Midland, our Double-A affiliate, but everyone wanted to get a look at him in spring training.

We were looking for a big and strong left-hander and everyone was intrigued by what this kid had accomplished as an amateur. A stellar college career. Winning a gold medal in the Olympics. He brought as much frenzy as anybody. Jim had the excitement of the whole country. People wanted to see him and see him succeed. It didn't matter if they hated the Angels, this was an exciting thing to observe.

Tim Mead, who was the Angels PR director, and his staff had a lot on their plate with all the media attention Jim attracted. They did a tremendous job handling all the requests and allowing Jim the space he needed to become a major league pitcher. It still amazes me that Jim and Tim were able to accomplish all the things they did from a media standpoint. It was not only great for Jim and the Angels, but for the game of baseball.

"I'm convinced we had 50 people for his B-game in Yuma," Mead recalled. "Jim Abbott was as in demand on a national basis as anybody. It wasn't just sports media. It was *Life Magazine,* who spent three days following him around. It was *Good Morning America.* It was Jim Lampley. Everybody wanted him. It was news. Our goal was to accommodate everyone we could, reserve his time and Jim was always open to it. Always."

From his initial bullpen session to his first outing of spring, he opened a lot of eyes. The good outings continued, and he showed many doubters that he could handle fielding his position with ease. Suddenly, people weren't talking about Midland.

Every time he went out on the mound he was getting better. He was getting stronger, and everything was going in the right direction to where the team had to make a hard decision about what they would ultimately do.

Doug Rader was the manager of the Angels, a former scout who understood young players. Doug had a lot of confidence in Jim and had similar traits. They were both great competitors and the two seemed to mesh perfectly.

On Doug's coaching staff was Marcel Lachemann, who served as the pitching coach. He handled situations extremely well with pitchers. He kept things very even and when you're a young pitcher like Jim was, that's especially important. The two put in tireless efforts to get Jim ready for whatever decision they would make, whether it be Midland or Anaheim.

Bill, Mike, and Marcel would call me with regular updates. It was good outing after good outing, and he was holding his own.

Jim showed the ability to set up hitters, pitch inside and adjust during situations when you have men on base and have to try to limit the opposing offense to as little damage as possible. All the intangibles that statistics may not show. Jim showed truly little emotion, even against the best batters in the middle of any lineup. Those intangibles are usually what you send a player to the minor leagues to work on, but Jim already had it.

Near the end of spring, close to decision time, I was listening to the radio while traveling from Arizona to California. Jim was pitching against the Padres in Palm Springs, and found himself in a tight situation facing Tony Gwynn, who was in his prime.

Jim worked him in with fastballs and got an early two-strike count. This didn't bother Tony much. He had plenty of hits with two strikes over his career. Jim fired off a cutter that Tony swung-and-missed on, striking him out.

As I was driving, I thought, "Tony doesn't strike out a lot. Actually, Tony *never* strikes out."

It was then that I thought, "Oh my gosh, this kid has a chance."

I didn't care if it was spring training or not, Tony *never* strikes out.

Not long after, Doug announced that Jim had made the major league roster.

Jim made his first start April 8, 1989, our fifth game of the season. It was a Saturday night with Seattle in town for the middle of a three-game series.

Among the sold-out crowd, I took my three kids and got seats behind home plate. We sat 15 rows back watching a young man who I had seen just over a year prior pitching as an amateur on a cold night in Texas. It was one of the most exciting and nerve-wracking games I've been to see a player we signed make his major league debut.

I'm nervous about anyone we sign for their first game, but this one in particular was different. We had a big crowd, and they were there to see Jim pitch. Nowadays with all the prospect rankings, you may see a crowd gather for the debut of a premier prospect. But in the late 80's, that wasn't the case.

There was plenty of media hype—around 200 media members according to Tim—and there were more people focused on what he was doing than it would have been with anyone else. You still have your doubters, and you have those who want success more than anything.

He had a shaky first inning, allowing back-to-back singles to lead off the game and allowed both runners to get into scoring position on a wild pitch. Both baserunners came home on groundouts, but Jim got out of the inning with just the two runs allowed.

He went on to retire nine of the next 12 before running into trouble in the fourth where six of the next seven batters would reach base. That was the end of his debut. Four and two-third innings with three runs allowed.

After he came out of the game, I said to myself, "He's going to be able to compete here and he knows it. He learned a few things, but he did okay."

We didn't win that game, but he kept us in it. We went on to win six of the next eight games Jim pitched in, including his first major league win against Baltimore two weeks later.

Things began to fall into place that first year, highlighted by a shutout of the Boston Red Sox at Fenway Park where he allowed just four hits.

Jim finished the year with a 12-12 record, 3.92 ERA and finished fifth in American League Rookie of the Year voting. When you complete the year with a .500 record and win over 10 games as a rookie, you've had a decent year, especially when he was our fifth starter.

Sometime during that year, someone wrote an article calling Jim, "America's Rookie." When I saw that, it made me feel that much better that not only did we get the right player, but we got the right player the country wanted.

Our team finished with 91 wins and Jim was a solid part of that turnaround after losing 87 games both of the two years prior.

He continued to have a solid 10-year Major League career with an 18-win season in 1991 and a no-hitter against Cleveland as a member of the New York Yankees in 1993.

In 1995, we re-acquired Jim from the White Sox and ended up tied for the division lead, giving us a one game playoff with Seattle with the winner making the playoffs. Near the end of the season in September, we had two nine-game losing streaks, which is un-friggin-believable. Jim stopped both of those losing streaks. It may not sound like a big deal, but without those wins, we don't get to compete for a playoff spot.

Jim did everything you could hope for from a pitcher. He had success, provided inspiration, leadership and an obvious love for the game that is too often taken for granted. When people think of Jim, they don't look at his pitching career enough. They too often look at him as being a one-handed pitcher.

How many major league pitchers would like to say their career was his career? He pitched for a decade, threw a no-hitter, and inspired a whole darned nation. He brought a good feeling towards the Angels, but more importantly, to the game of baseball.

On one occasion, I took my son, Jimmy, down to the clubhouse because he wanted to meet some players and one in particular, Jim.

When you grow up around the game, you're around a lot of players and baseball people and you lose that awe-factor at seeing a major leaguer up close at times. When I took Jimmy down to the clubhouse that day, I had never seen him so nervous or excited to be around a player.

Jimmy looked at Jim like he was an inspiration. Jim was an inspiration to those, not only that had a physical disability, but those who didn't. I believe young kids learned from Jim and were inspired by Jim. If you really want something you can get it no matter what you may be told and whatever obstacles are in your way with no excuses. Even to the point of pitching as a major leaguer with one hand. My son still remembers that day meeting Jim and my kids loved him as a player. My son applied that approach to his own career, and I have often thought that Jim's example helped him understand that.

Jimmy wanted to be a photographer when he moved to New York. He lived in a building that was condemned. He worked all night as an intern to learn the craft and learned how to be a photographer without schooling and did it from the ground up.

When you look at people like Jim and see what he did to become a major league player, you can't help but think he helped people like my son to think that way. I'm not going to say that was the only reason my son found success in his career, but it certainly let him know you could do what you wanted to do. My son is now a top-flight photographer.

Jim made time for everybody. Baseball might have a lot of great people in the game, but they will not have anyone better than Jim. They may have someone as good or close to as good, but they'll never have someone better in my mind.

Jim always said he didn't want to be an example for people, but he was an example by trying not to be.

"As a young person, I ran away from my difference," Jim told Fox Sports in 2017. "I wanted to be like other people, but I realize now that I'm older that it shaped me, and it molded me and it's who I am. I think the danger is to deny that because I wouldn't have gone to the places I went to without it.

"There is freedom and liberty in knowing that you can go after anything in this world that you want to do. You can pitch on a mound with one hand and you can play with the best players in the world. You can play in Yankee Stadium. You can pitch a no-hitter in Yankee Stadium. Then, what's not possible?"

Every scout has an opportunity to sign or be involved with the signing of a player that is special to the game. These times don't come often, but when they do, you know it and it makes you feel special about baseball.

Jim may not have been the best player I've been involved with, but for me, Jim was the most special and made me feel good about the game. Not only was he a successful major league pitcher, but a leader, a quality individual, and an inspiration to so many.

Jim Abbott made you feel good about the game of baseball.

"Jim Abbott"

CALIFORNIA YEARS
– RUSSIA

"I was in Berlin last fall and met a guy. He looked at me and said, 'Bob, when those guys signed and they made their baseball card, that made me think that I could do this.' That reverberation went throughout Russia and Europe. It's like a small town where nobody has ever made it. When one guy makes it, other people think they can too. They should have thought that before, but they didn't. It set a precedent that Major League Baseball is looking for the best talent worldwide, regardless of what country or what language they speak or what they look like. Bobby Fontaine started something, and it's going to produce a big leaguer from Russia. I don't think the way it's all happened would have ever happened unless he decided to get on a plane to Moscow one day." – Bob Protexter, Moscow Red Devils coach (1990-1991) and Angels scout (1992-1996)

When the Russians started playing baseball in the late 1980's, they didn't receive much notice. Many nations, including the Union of Soviet Socialist Republics (USSR), were showing interest in developing the sport when the Olympics had baseball as a demonstration sport, and everyone figured it would become a medal sport.

One thing I remembered, because I'm older, is how Russia did in basketball and hockey. When they put their mind to it, there wasn't anybody in the world better at hockey than the Russians. With basketball, they could compete with the college kids in the United States and were relatively equal with them. The Russians never wanted to concede a sport in the Olympics, and you knew that when they put their mind to it, they would develop faster than other people.

They brought in baseball and track and field instructors from Cuba because the Soviet Union was the main ally for Cuba. Along with the Cubans, they had a lot of Japanese influence. Their biggest issue was trying to manufacture equipment and finding suitable ballplayers.

They began taking athletes from sports that might have some compatibility with baseball. Sports such as tennis and rowing to turn into hitters, track and field for baserunners, and javelin throwers for pitchers, with most of the athletes being in their late-teens and twenties. You began taking notice of some of the youth leagues and started saying those would be the kids in the next group who hopefully would be better because they played at a younger age.

They started to play internationally with a team that came over to play Johns Hopkins in a series of games. Obviously, they didn't do well and were beaten rather soundly. However, the next year, they played much better and had shown some progress, winning a game or two. I started to think, "I know it's only Johns Hopkins, but that's pretty good."

Their commitment to learning our game was in motion.

In 1990, the Soviets sent a national team to the Goodwill Games in Seattle and Tacoma, Washington, to compete against the best amateur teams in the world. That was when the USA team was your top college players, and it was an honor to play for the club. You asked them to be on the team and they were on it, and they were the best college players in the nation without a doubt.

Most of the Soviet kids had only a handful of years playing the game and the coaches, in many cases only knew what they read about the game with some help from the Cuban coaches. This would be the first look at where they stacked up on the international stage, and we wanted to be there to see them.

Bill Bavasi and I had discussed the Russians and what would happen if they approached baseball the same way they did with basketball and hockey. This might be a good avenue in the event the Soviet Union ever let the players come over and play in the United States.

It was decided I would go with one goal in mind.

Everybody was heading to Washington because the Goodwill Games would be played at Chaney Stadium in Tacoma. When I arrived, I told everybody I was there to see the USA players like everyone else, but I had no reason to see the USA team. I'd seen them enough. Just like today, how many times do you have to see them? I went up there with one purpose and one purpose alone; to see the Russians and see where they were developmentally as baseball players.

Obviously, they were outclassed. They played in Seattle and were beaten 17-0 by the USA team. But you know, there's a difference between being embarrassed and holding your own and they weren't embarrassed, and even with the lopsided scores, I was impressed. You didn't sit there and ask, "Why are they here?"

They went up against teams with the best amateur players in the world who have played the game their whole lives and played with enthusiasm, never discouraged by the scores of the game. These kids were having fun and were there to learn.

That is where I saw two of their youngest players, Yevgeny Puchkov and Ilya Bogatyrev, who showed instincts for baseball and had better fundamentals, both offensively and defensively, than I expected. They got some hits, turned a double play, and did some little things that made you say, "That's not easy when you start off."

Puchkov, the team's third baseman, had the best fundamentals on the team. He had a good swing, good hands, and good arm action. He only ran fair, but he only began playing at about 18 years old, and you started thinking if he would have played at eight, he might be ok.

Bogatyrev wasn't a bad shortstop but was much more mechanical. He played hard and liked to compete, and that was why the two kids stood out to me. Both were the ripe age of 21.

They knew they weren't going to win games, but they were never intimidated and didn't embarrass themselves and, in my mind, I thought that was exciting.

It was a fact-finding mission and we needed to follow their development closely over the next few years. When I left Seattle to return to Anaheim, I told Bill, "We have to keep tabs on this."

Little did I know that the Soviet Union would fall in just over a year.

In December 1991, the USSR dissolved and became the Commonwealth of Independent States. Their economy had fallen and basically all the countries that were part of the Soviet Union put together this new government that lasted a few years.

After these developments, Bill and I thought this could be an ideal time to establish ourselves in Russia and see if we could tap into the country's vast number of athletes and try to establish a stream of baseball players. I started to plan a trip to Moscow to see if it would be possible to work out some players and set a foundation.

We didn't have a big international budget, around $40,000, and we were regularly signing kids for $1,500. Russia could be an outlet to find some talent without going up against the big bidders. Our only concern was the Los Angeles Dodgers, who had some influence in the region. Peter O'Malley had been over there, they had a bird dog scout in the country, and we knew they would be the most interested club.

We encountered one problem, a big problem, right from the beginning. No person was allowed into the Commonwealth without permission and an invitation. No individual, no sports team, no nothing without an invite.

Relations between Russia and the United States were better at the time because Mikhail Gorbachev, Ronald Reagan and George H.W. Bush had decent relationships. Even though Gorbachev was out by this time, Boris Yeltsin came in as President and was probably a lot easier compared to Nikita Khrushchev and other former Russian leaders. Relations were never good, but they were not as bad because Russia had too many domestic problems to worry about. Regardless, we still needed an invitation.

Luckily, Bill's sister-in-law, Judy (the wife of Peter Bavasi), was teaching at Moscow State University. Judy was over there half the year as somewhat of an exchange teacher who taught English.

Bill talked with Peter to see if Judy could obtain an invitation for me through the University. Judy was able to obtain one through the athletic department so that I could get a visa and make reservations to go. I was on my way by March 1992.

Before leaving Anaheim, I got Bill's approval that if there were one or two players worth signing to go ahead and do it. I had already seen two players of interest at the Goodwill Games, Puchkov and Bogatyrev, so there was already a starting point.

The plan was to get two or three players to come over and play a couple years, and then they would go back and become instructors with more knowledge of the game. More importantly, they were going to become scouts for the Angels, and that was how we felt we could develop the country. If you sent back players who had been taught at a higher level of the game, they would become premier coaches. Bill and I hoped that would happen, not knowing what would occur once I got there. But when I left, I had contracts ready.

Bill had talked to Sy Berger with Topps, the chewing gum and baseball card company, and gave me baseball card contracts for players we may sign. Sy was the best and he was the king of baseball cards with Topps. Sy thought it might help any kid we signed because they could make some money with the card and autographs. Every player that signed a contract with Topps would get a $5 check, and that gave Topps the rights to produce a card when you became a big leaguer. Every minor league player got one, signed it, and sent it back. Although it seemed unlikely I could get anyone signed on this trip, I was prepared if it did happen.

I flew to John F. Kennedy Airport in New York where I got a Delta ticket. There were some Americans traveling to Moscow on the flight, including one gentleman sitting across from me who was a reporter for the Wall Street Journal. We spent the nine-hour flight in conversation about my upcoming responsibilities while he informed me about Moscow.

He was surprised when I told him I was going to Moscow to look at potential baseball players. He was going there for work and little did I know, he was going to write a story later about my adventures. I was naive enough to think the Wall Street Journal was only about business, and yet, this story would make their front page.

When I got to Moscow, Judy met me at the terminal and had a guide with her to help as an interpreter while I was there. The kid's name was Sasha, and he was able to help direct me where I needed to be. He spoke English very well.

The first day I checked into the Moscow Radisson, and then Judy and Sasha took me to get a monthly subway pass (it cost 50 rubles, which was about 50 cents). They told me everything I needed to know and then drove me around to Red Square and to Pizza Hut for dinner, which was a big new thing there.

McDonald's was already present in Moscow, but Pizza Hut was brand new. When we arrived, there were two doors to the restaurant. One door had a line that went a block long for those that were paying with rubles. The second door was for those paying with dollars and had no line, allowing us to be seated immediately. It was easily the most expensive Pizza Hut I had ever been to. It's tough to imagine waiting in line a block long for pizza.

Over the next few days, I spent a lot of my time alone and was on my own on the subways and busses. For me, the Russian language looked like an eye chart and was a real challenge. I saw Judy and Sasha a few times when I needed help, but mostly, I went all over that town by myself. I would read the eye chart and look for a certain number or letter backwards and have a basic concept of where Reds Square was, where the University was and how to get to Moscow Circus (which was one of my main goals). But I did it on my own and it was cool.

On the second day of my adventure, Judy introduced me to the baseball coach at Moscow State, Valery Varinsky, and he was a great help to me. Valery didn't speak much English and had one of the players help with translation, but what a true gentleman he was.

Valery's team had been working out and he allowed me to put them through a tryout and evaluate his players. The workout I ran by myself was a regular professional tryout which was quite foreign to the players, but they seemed to thoroughly enjoy the attention of someone from American baseball being there.

A major league or professional tryout is something you'll commonly see across the baseball landscape. It begins with players running a 60-yard dash and follows with them going through defensive drills and throwing from either the outfield or shortstop. Players go through batting practice so you can get a basic concept of their offensive skill set and pitchers throw from the mound or the bullpen.

The stadium at Moscow State was the nicest, and probably the *only*, one in Russia. It was built by the Japanese with AstroTurf that was still in decent shape, with nice stands and an office underneath. As you looked over the stands and beyond the outfield wall, they had Stalin-era buildings, with one of the University buildings having a big red star on top with trees surrounding the park. It was the pride of their baseball facilities.

"L: Valery Varinsky and I; R: Moscow State University baseball field with red hammer and sickle on building"

I had brought some equipment with me – mostly gloves, baseballs, and wooden bats – and baseball items to give to people at appropriate times. Equipment at that time of any quality was very scarce and hard to come by. They had some Japanese and Cuban equipment, but they were trying to make equipment that was incredibly low quality.

At the conclusion of the workout, after spending a few days with this team, I went to say goodbye to all the players and staff. The team lined up on the third base line and I handed out all the items I brought along with me to each player. By the end, I left with not a single item remaining.

The standout was the team's catcher. I had brought a catcher's mitt and when I gave it the young man, he got emotional and was overcome nearly to tears, just to get a good glove. It was a good feeling to give him that glove and to see how appreciative he was to receive it.

After I was done, the players said they wanted to present me with some items of appreciation. They handed me a certificate that by coincidence, had a hammer and sickle on it with a picture of

Lenin and a couple of athletic medallions. At the end, the captain presented me with the flag of the USSR. They weren't able yet to get a new Russian flag, but they wanted to present what they could. It was a gesture I won't ever forget.

"Certificate given by Moscow State baseball team including picture of Vladimir Lenin"

There I was, an American, holding a bright red flag of the USSR with the hammer and sickle. This was wild for a guy who grew up during the Cold War.

The leaders of the Soviet Union did not have a glorified past when it came to American culture. Joseph Stalin was a brutal dictator, and I remember Khrushchev and the others that came afterward - all who had threatened the United States.

I had made a point to watch the Russian Red Army hockey team when they were in the U.S. and they intrigued me as the most disciplined athletes I'd ever seen. As far as the people, I didn't have any kind of expectations because I didn't know any Russians and I didn't know what to expect, but there were reservations based on the past political leaders and the highly disciplined athletes as the only Russians I'd ever known.

After the team presented me with so many fine items, Yevgeny told me they would like to invite me to a special workout the next day. I happily accepted and asked what time it would start and when he wanted me there.

"1:00," he replied.

"Great," I said. "1:00 in the afternoon works well. Would you like me there at noon?"

"*Nyet.* 1:00 in the morning and we leave at 11:30. I'll have the assistant coach come pick you up at the hotel."

One in the morning? Are you kidding me? Welcome to Russian baseball.

I agreed despite the surprise, and it gave me time to explore Moscow the following day.

That next morning, I woke up and took in the streets and wonders of Moscow.

With the ruble being worth about a penny, a dollar went a long way. Of course, I wanted to bring things back for people, so Sasha took me to Arbat Street, which is a big street that had a lot of artists, arts and crafts, flea markets and souvenir stands.

I started buying a lot of Russian Army hats and badges from former soldiers for two dollars each because I thought they were cool. I would end up going back multiple times over my trip and after the third time I went back people would see me and call me, "*Shlyape Chelovek*,", or in English, "The Hat Man."

Continuing on with my day, I went to Red Square and got within three feet, if that, of the soldiers who were guarding Lenin's Tomb, who goose stepped in perfect unison and changed every hour on the dot. It was amazing because these were things I grew up with and never thought I'd see.

You look to your right and see the Kremlin. Look left and see St. Basil's Cathedral. Directly behind you was GUM Department store, which was wild because you might see an appliance store and right next to it, chickens hanging from the ceiling.

The highlight though was attending the Moscow Circus. My whole life I wanted to be in the circus and honestly would have rather had a career in the circus than baseball, but I didn't have the ability outside of selling popcorn and cleaning up after the elephants. I've always loved baseball, but I always wanted to be in the circus, and I'd go to the circus as often as I could.

"St. Basil's Cathedral, Kremlin, Red Army soldiers"

Above everything else for my extracurricular activities on the trip was to see the Moscow Circus and their world-famous bears. I went to the box office, paid 10 cents for my ticket, and went in to see the bears I'd wanted to see my entire life. They performed flawlessly, and a lifetime goal had been met. It was unbelievable.

That day, and the ones prior with the team, was when I really began to grasp the people of Russia as a whole.

The people would ask me all kinds of questions, like, "How many families live in your house?" or "Why don't you like Russians?"

It would break my heart to tell them that just my family lived in my house and they couldn't believe that only one family was in a single house or apartment and not just one bedroom or living room. They would have two or three families living in a single apartment. When I look back at things like this and things I've seen in the world, it makes me wish every kid in the country could see these things and hear these questions and stories to gain a better appreciation of what they have. Others don't in a lot of places on Earth.

In downtown, there was an Irish pub and there would be women during lunch hour lined up in business attire holding up clothes, makeup, shoes or anything else they could try to sell to make ends meet while on lunch break from work.

There were some things you expected because you'd always hear about shortages and rationings, but you could look in a store and although there would be some items behind the glass in the front of the store, the shelves inside would be nearly barren. This was noticeable in some of the grocery stores that I saw as well.

You know how you look at Russia and think Russians don't like Americans because of the government? They felt the same way about Americans. They didn't know about the people just like I didn't know about them. They were hard-working people who didn't have the luxuries of those living the American lifestyle yet were great people and just like us without as much in the way of material items.

That evening at 11:30 pm, the assistant coach of the baseball team, who spoke no English, picked me up at the hotel with four players sitting in the back of an old Ford sedan from the 1930's.

These four kids hassled him non-stop throughout the car ride about the car and he was getting upset. He didn't speak a word of English and I knew about a dozen words in Russian, with seven of them being, "May I have a cold beer please?", but I wanted to tell these kids that they didn't know how valuable the car actually was and that they should be jealous.

We traveled about an hour through the streets of Moscow and to this day, I still have no idea where we were and could have been halfway to Siberia for all I know. We would pass statues of Stalin and Lenin and the players would make remarks in clear English, "Thanks for a great life you son of a bitch."

It was an eye-opener. After I heard them say that, I realized those kids and the younger generations would never give up this freedom that Communism denied them.

When we finally arrived at the gym for the workout in who knows where Russia, we had to wait a half hour for the women's soccer team to finish before getting the floor. Baseball was last in priority, but they were simply happy to get the time.

Precisely at 1 a.m., they blew a whistle, and the soccer team left the floor with the baseball players running right on.

They stood in position and as soon as the coach blew his whistle, all hell broke loose.

Baseballs began whizzing past my head and flying everywhere. They were bouncing off the hardwood floor and walls from throws and ground balls. I had no idea what was going on and it felt like I was in a human pinball machine. This lasted for about an hour and they blew the whistle to cease, and everyone did and proceeded to leave. I learned *absolutely* nothing. As we headed back to the car, I was thinking this was unreal.

We drove off and the players continued to hassle the coach about the car, and I continued to think about its value. He dropped each kid off and when it was me and him, he looked at me like, "What am I going to do with this guy?"

After about 20 minutes of driving in silence and the pitch black of night, he pulled the car up to the front of my hotel. I thanked him and thought to myself how baseball can bring people together despite being from different countries with a language barrier. Baseball is a bond that can make people feel comfortable real fast.

On the Sunday I was in Moscow and I was almost out of rubles, so I walked into town from my hotel to the only currency exchange I could find that was open. It was near the White House and when I got there all I had was a $100 US bill. When I gave it to the clerk, she looked at me in awe, as that was a lot of money for them. One ruble was about the worth of a penny and they only had one-ruble and five-ruble bills, and five-ruble bills was all she could give me. I had no choice and said it was ok.

Suddenly, there were stacks of wrapped five-ruble bills being placed on the counter. Next thing you know, the clerk went and got a paper bag and started putting the stacks in. It looked like I was robbing the joint.

By this time, I had looked over and saw that three large, thug-looking, men were watching me closely during the transaction. This was $100 which was a lot of money at the time and as I left, they began to follow me. I started telling myself, "These ain't cab drivers."

I never could run well but was in pretty decent shape and after watching these men follow me out the door and down the street, I broke into a dead sprint, running as fast as I could thinking I was about to be robbed.

I ran down the street, turned right, ran across the bridge and in front of the White House, past the government buildings, into a residential area, turned left through the Kiev Train Station, and saw daylight with the Radisson Hotel directly ahead.

I lost the three men somewhere near the bridge but continued running all the way up to my room where I opened the paper bag and poured all the money on the bed.

I sat there looking at the stack of bills and began laughing hysterically. Looking at the money I realized that a five-ruble bill was the equivalent to five cents. You had to have cash because there were no debit cards and most places didn't take your credit card, but as I looked at the cash I thought, "What am I going to do with this?"

It looked like I had just robbed a bank, yet here I was with $100 in rubles. It was hysterical.

The next day I met Judy, some staff, the baseball coach, and Sasha, for lunch at Moscow State University. We were to meet at a restaurant at the college and I remember walking through the school on our way there.

It was dark and quiet in the hallways. Not pitch dark or silent, but kind of gloomy, and how you would visualize a Communist college in your own mind. It was something I noticed in the subways and at other places in town - how quiet and aware of the surroundings the people were.

People often didn't talk out loud and whispered a lot. They were accustomed to people listening to report them to the government and didn't want to say anything that could cause them or their families problems. Younger people would converse more than the adults, which I'm sure was a common thing from the days in a Communist environment.

When we got the restaurant, I was told that the lunch menu was set and it would be five courses, but unlike at home, five courses added up to about one. It began with a funky small appetizer, a small salad, borscht soup (which I won't touch with a 10-foot pole), meatballs and potatoes, and a small cup of pudding. It was bland tasting but considered an important and special meal.

We all sat and talked for a while going over what I had been able to see and what I needed to still do. Judy wanted to make sure everything I needed was translated to them. Her time was taken up teaching and this kind of opportunity was not going to happen again.

At the end of the meal and conversation, I asked for the check, as this was my treat. The server brought me a piece of paper that had R250 on it (which is $2.50 US). I was amazed and asked what type of tip I should leave and was told no tips were necessary. Our waitress had worked her butt off, and I wouldn't have felt right not leaving some form of gratuity, so I asked if R25 (25 cents) was alright. The reply was more than enough.

I paid the check and gave our waitress 25 rubles. She looked at it and asked, "What is this?"

I replied that it was a tip, and she began to cry. She was so appreciative and couldn't believe what she had received. It turned out she may have only made a couple hundred rubles a month and this was probably a day or twos equivalent salary.

When I found this out, I felt horrible. If I would have known it would have that kind of impact, I would have left her $20. I was following what everyone told me, but she was so thankful for those 25 rubles which is basically a quarter.

As my trip started ending, I had accomplished quite a bit. I had a better knowledge of the setup of Russian baseball at the youth levels, as well as with the older players. I had the opportunity to observe some 10 to 14-year-old kids and could see that they would be much further along when they reached their late teens and early 20's than those of that age today. They would have a better opportunity to play more often and hopefully obtain better instruction.

Of the players I saw play at Moscow State, there was one of interest to me, Rudy Razhigaev. A tall left-handed pitcher, who had the making of a good delivery and a loose, free arm. He did many things naturally that meant he could get better.

He was 21 years old and had only played a short time, so baseball was incredibly new to him. The other kids knew more because they played internationally and had more knowledge of the game. Rudy threw a mid-80's fastball and would try to throw a curveball, but it didn't improve until he came stateside.

A former paratrooper in the Red Army, Rudy had become a distance runner when one day, the baseball coach asked him to throw a baseball. When he did, the coach recognized there was something there and added him to the team.

"Rudy was jumping out of perfectly good airplanes in Siberia somewhere," Joe Maddon recalled. "You would think the ninth inning wouldn't bother the guy, right?"

I had hoped to run down Puchkov and Bogatyrev while I was there to try and sign them, but they were at spring training with the Moscow Red Devils (the Russian equivalent to the New York Yankees) down in Odessa, by the Black Sea.

I was fortunate to be able to get in contact with Rick Spooner, an American businessman who was prominent in baseball in Russia. He was even considered the "Johnny Appleseed" of Russian baseball.

Rick had connections in the region and spoke Russian fluently, so I contacted him and told him about my interest in signing Russian players, and my hope to start development for potential professional prospects. He was exceedingly kind in helping get me in contact with Yevgeny and Ilya and helped get them to agree to a contract. Without Rick, things would have been much more difficult. Those were the two that we had hoped to get, and we decided to try and sign Rudy, so that we could have a pitcher to go with the two infielders.

I planned to meet with Rudy at the hotel, but when he arrived, he wasn't granted access. They wouldn't let him in because the only citizens who had access to the hotel were Russian officials on official business. I raced down to the lobby to meet him, where we explained the situation, and he was finally allowed entrance.

Rudy was dressed nicely and was amazed at the hotel when he entered and saw the lobby. We went to an area just outside the lobby where there were tables and chairs and began discussing what we wanted to offer him.

Even though his English was reasonably good, I had to work hard at explaining what the opportunity was and what the contract meant. This wouldn't mean he would be joining the Angels major league ballclub, but instead, would be going to our Arizona Rookie Ball affiliate, where most first-year players begin their career. Luckily, I met an American at the hotel who could interpret when necessary, and Rudy didn't seem to mind or care where he went.

As I started to explain what we hoped to do and what the contract was all about, Rudy just beamed, and said, "I can't believe it."

When I made him the bonus offer of $1,500, and the monthly salary for the season, he just smiled. I asked him if he wanted to discuss it with his wife, and he replied as his eyes began to water up, "She wants me to have the opportunity to go to the United States, to play baseball. I can now buy things for my little girl."

I later learned that the bonus we offered at this time was worth a few years of salary.

After Rudy signed the contract, I loaded him up with Angels souvenirs, and then proceeded to tell him I had a contract for him from Topps Baseball for the rights for his picture on a baseball card.

"What's that?" he asked.

I tried to explain, but finally told him to sign it and you will be glad you did. He signed it and I gave him the standard $5.00 check that comes with it. He looked at it with no idea what it was.

Ilya and Yevgeny had baseball cards printed because they played for the Red Devils, and they had cards for the players that were used to raise money for the team. They had a little more knowledge about this, but for Rudy, it was all brand new.

When I told him to cash it at the bank, I could tell he didn't know what to do with it, so I handed him a $5.00 bill and he stared at it with a smile and repeated again how he was going to buy his little girl some diapers with the money.

"Rudy Razhigaev signing professional contract with Angels"

When we left the hotel, he was about as happy as any kid I had ever signed. As he left, he looked at me and said, "I can't wait to get to America where you play perfect baseball."

"Pal, you didn't see us play last year," I said through a laugh. "It wasn't perfect."

We had finished in last place.

With everything concluded, I headed back to California after a week in Russia. Without the help of Judy, Rick, Sasha, and the coaches at Moscow State, this trip never could have been a success. I made Judy an associate scout when I left. She became our Commonwealth of Independent States Associate Scout and would let us know if she heard of any good players in the region.

I was heading home with a lot more items than I came with, as I loaded up with souvenirs from Arbat Street. Mostly military hats and badges, pins, artistic items, and other neat things you didn't see at home.

The morning I left, I was told there would be a driver that would pick me up at the hotel and take me to the airport. To this day, I don't know who set it up, but afterwards when I found out, I knew exactly why.

The driver started at a quick pace and was speeding the entire way. It wasn't long before we were stopped by the police and I thought we were in trouble. The driver showed the officer some credentials, and the officer apologized and quickly walked away. We sped off once again and made it to the airport in about half the time. I thanked the driver, and off he sped.

I later found out the car had been supplied by the Kremlin, and I have no idea who arranged it for me. But I did get to the airport quickly, just in time to start the next adventure of the trip.

I had about three hours before the flight and thought I would get through security and customs quickly and be able to relax before the plane left for New York. As I was getting close to the front of the line, the guy in front of me had a box opened by the guards, and inside were Russian stamps. The next thing I knew, a big, strong, husky woman guard began yelling at him with two armed guards with big guns taking him to a side room.

"*Nyet! Nyet!*" she yelled at me, and pointed to the other line, which by now was about a block long.

I began to worry about making my flight as I was down to two hours before departure and if I missed it, I was in trouble. There were no commuter flights on the hour from Moscow to New York.

Luckily, a couple from Denmark saw what occurred and said I could get in front of them in line. After thanking them and informing them that my flight left soon, I asked if they knew why the man was taken away?

They said that you are not allowed to take out of the country anything of historical or military nature.

I began to panic. Almost everything I had in my bag was of that nature, and I thought if they take that guy to a side room for a few stamps, they are going to hang me with all the stuff I have.

I was sweating bullets when I got to the front of the line. There was a cute, young female guard, and I smiled thinking I may get away with it, and she just waved me through, smiling back.

I couldn't believe my luck, and when I got through customs, I headed to the bar and downed some strong Russian vodka to calm me down. As I boarded the plane and realized I wouldn't be arrested, I relaxed, while the vodka helped me sleep for most of the long plane ride.

When I woke up, I found out the Mayor of Moscow was on the flight. I wanted to talk with him, but I didn't during the flight because he had a lot of people around him.

As we were getting off the plane, I went up and introduced myself and talked to him for a minute. He listened and was a very nice gentleman, as the focus of my conversation was that I had a plan that if signing these Russian ballplayers worked, I would try to get a hold of George H.W. Bush, who was friends with Yeltsin, to see if he could open up Russia for the Angels.

When I finally returned to California, I found out that the reporter I had met from the Wall Street Journal on the plane to Moscow had written an article about our signing of the players and my trip there. He had attended and helped me with the tryout with the Moscow State team.

The article was titled, *Here's Real News: Baseball Player Asks, "What's A Contract?"* and was on the front page of the paper.

I now started to understand how big of a deal this was, as I got interview requests from network morning and news shows, as well as from newspapers and publications from around the country. It seems the experiment Bill and I were starting was of interest, and when you think that we were just four months out of the Cold War with the USSR, it made some sense.

Signing these three kids from Russia made you realize how special our game was and how even people from places that didn't have the opportunity like kids from our country appreciated it. The appreciation and excitement these kids displayed when they were in the United States made almost all around them appreciate it a little more as well.

"When you're going to practice and you're going to the game and you play in the game, that's a dream come true for me," Rudy said in an interview with MLB.com in 2016. "I never expected in my life that I would have such a great experience."

Ilya, Rudy, and Yevgeny arrived in the U.S. before the start of the Rookie Ball season in Mesa, Arizona. They came to Anaheim where we introduced them to the press, and they could spend some time with our major league coaches.

We added Bob Protexter, a former college player and junior college coach who had spent time in Russia as a coach, to help us with translation and the extra work that the players needed when they reported. He would spend the whole summer with the players, interpreting and coaching.

After a few days, they all left for Mesa for their first taste of professional baseball.

Bill Lachemann was the manager there, with Joe Maddon as our minor league coordinator. Those two, along with Bavasi, gave these kids the comfortable environment that they needed to get started and get the most out of the experience.

This brand-new experience could have brought brand new problems. These kids didn't speak much of the language, were in a new environment, were a long way from home, and wouldn't be going home for a while.

Lachemann did a great job of incorporating them into playing in games, and Joe was so positive with them that these kids felt comfortable in a hurry. That atmosphere helped them with their teammates, and they meshed in like kids from anywhere.

In an interview with MLB.com in 2016, Yevgeny shared an experience he had with an American teammate and friend, Rob Tucker.

"One evening (Rob) came to our room, about 10 days after we arrived. We drank some vodka and whiskey and then beer. At 6 a.m., we went swimming. Walking back, we were hugging. Lachemann saw us but didn't say a word. The next game, I went 4-for-4, Tucker was 3-for-4 and good behind the plate. After the game, Lachemann asked us, 'What were you drinking?' I answered, 'Russian vodka.' Bill said, 'Do the same thing tonight!'"

It brought a new experience to the team and to their opponents. Ilya and Yevgeny would yell at each other in Russian in the infield, and other teams would look and say, "What in the world is happening?"

Ilya, Rudy, and Yevgeny were amazed by the fields in Mesa and looked at the ones that weren't being used during the game. They'd be sitting on the bench and not playing in a game, wondering why they aren't using the empty fields for practice.

Going to their first game in Mesa, as someone that grew up during the Cold War, it was unbelievable to me. Who would have thought 10 years back, we went from countries that were enemies, to watching players from Russia playing catch with American teammates on a team called the Angels? It made me emotional and was a moment I will never forget.

During that spring, I got a phone call when one of our veteran instructors was working with Yevgeny in the batting cage and there was a misunderstanding.

When a hitter tends to lean forward and hit off his front side, it is referred to as "rushing". Well, Yevgeny was getting out front and our instructor, Bob Clear, yelled, "No! No! You're f***ing rushing! You're f***ing rushing!"

Yevgeny stopped in his tracks and stared at him in disbelief, as he thought he had called him a "F***ing Russian."

Yevgeny dropped his bat and was ready to go to war. They calmed him down and Protexter explained what had happened, and everyone had a good laugh.

During the season, they all played a fair amount of games, with Yevgeny playing the most and having the most success. What they learned with the opportunity to be on a professional baseball team helped expedite their development.

They were accepted very well and were a great example to their American teammates for their work ethic and appreciation for what they were given. The next year, regardless of their statistics, they were better players and just like any other member of the team.

The three of them played for two seasons, with Yevgeny playing as high as the Midwest League at the Low Single-A level. If he had played as a youngster, he might have been a prospect. He had a good line-drive swing, good actions in the field, and a decent throwing arm.

Ilya repeated the next season in Mesa with drastic changes. He raised his batting average 78 points, and I believe when the three were separated, he improved the most with more confidence.

Rudy went to our Northwest League affiliate Boise and pitched a handful of innings, again showing progress and becoming a member of the Northwest League championship team.

All three were released at the end of the 1993 season, but they all learned a lot and went back to Russia as better players and teachers of the game. Our plan all along was to have the players, after they were done playing in the United States, go back to Russia and coach, as well as scout for the Angels.

Topps Baseball did come through for the three kids, like Sy Berger said it would, and they produced a card of the three of them together. In Russian, it was titled, "Russian Prospects," and it generated a few thousand dollars for them from. Most importantly, it left a lifetime evidence of what these three players did.

"Signed photo of signed Russian players; L-R: Yevgeny
Puchkov, Rudy Razhigaev, Ilya Bogatryev"

Protexter, after his first year with the players at Mesa, went to
Russia to scout for us. He signed three more players, Nikoloz
Bezhuashvili, Alexander Nizov, and Denis Grishkin, and our
experiment continued until 1997.

We had made a proposal to ownership to start an academy in
Moscow where we would own a Russian team and sign 25 players.
We would teach them the way we teach players in our system, play
games, have them attend classes, and help with their immediate
families. When a player appeared ready to come to the U.S., we
would sign him to a minor league contract and thus start the
steady flow of players from Russia to the United States.

The whole plan would cost around $50,000 a year. Unfortunately,
ownership turned us down and our Russian coverage ended.

I had even contacted George H.W. Bush, who loved baseball and
played at Yale, to inquire about his help. He was the president at

the time, and getting a hold of him would be challenging, but I was able to get through to him through George W. Bush, who was president of the Texas Rangers. I sent a letter and asked if he would send it to his father for me, and he did.

I told President Bush about what we had done in signing Russian players and what our goal was. I told him that the efforts of President Ronald Reagan and himself had made this possible with all the great changes that they helped to bring about in the world.

I asked if he could help me with Yeltsin. When he responded back, he didn't say anything about that. Oh well, it was a shot in the dark. If he had, I was going to offer him a bird dog scouting job.

LETTER FROM GEORGE H.W. BUSH, Dated April 7, 1993:

Dear Bob,

Son, George, passed along your thoughtful letter of March 24. I loved hearing about the newest members of the California Angels. Your words about my contributions during my presidency are very generous, but credit and congratulations go to the Angels organization for moving forward in a most positive way on the dramatic changes that have taken place in our world during the past four years. I wish you great success in your future plans.

The photograph you sent is wonderful. My thanks for that, and my best wishes to you and to all the members of your team.

Sincerely,
(Signed, George H.W. Bush)

Mr. Bob Fontaine, Jr.
Director of Scouting
California Angels

2000 Gene Autry Way
Anaheim, California 92806

I still feel to this day, with no doubt in my mind, that had we started that academy, there would have been a major league player today from Russia. Their athleticism, strength, size, and work ethic are tremendous.

I do believe that when we left the market there, that the government could no longer subsidize baseball like they did in hockey and basketball, and development of the sport slowed to a snail's pace.

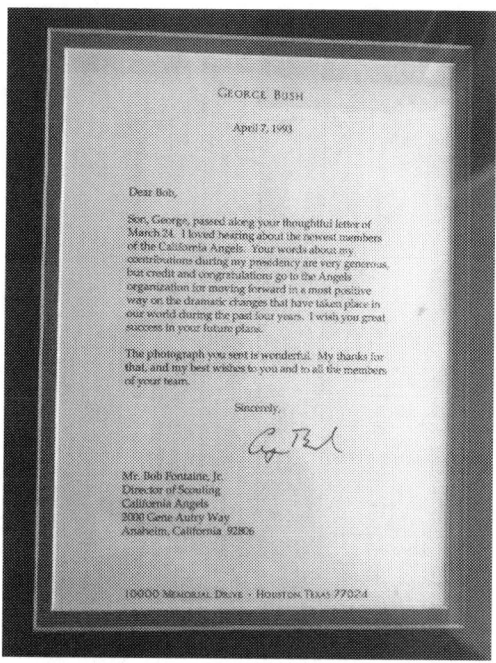

"Letter from George Bush"

CALIFORNIA YEARS – REPLACEMENT BASEBALL

On August 12, 1994, Major League Baseball halted to a stop. Players began to strike over a proposed salary cap, collusion in free agency, and mistrust between the players and owners. It was the eighth work stoppage in baseball history. In mid-September, the World Series was canceled for the first time, and the season came to an official end.

Over the following winter, little progress was made for resolving the strike. As the offseason went on, nobody really felt it would get to the point of teams having replacement players.

Replacement rosters consisted of former major leaguer players who had either been released or retired and wanted one last opportunity to be in the big leagues; as well as minor leaguers who felt it may be their chance (and maybe only chance) at reaching the major league level and getting that experience.

There was talk of replacement players, but we didn't think much of it and we also thought we would be able to use our minor league players that weren't on the 40-man roster. It turned out we should have taken a more serious approach. Most of the minor league players wouldn't play.

Sometime around the first part of December, Bill Bavasi asked me, "How's it coming with our replacement roster?"

I was kind of surprised as I still didn't think we would get to that point, so I replied, "Haven't done much, because we can put together a team from our non-40-man roster."

It turns out there was a lot of pressure being put on minor league players, especially young prospects, by their agents and the Major League Baseball Players Association to not agree to play or cross the picket line, as it could affect them later on. When you find out you couldn't use most of your top minor leaguers, you realize you may have a problem.

"We can't put pressure on our kids," Bill said. "Unless they are veterans towards the end of their careers and would like to be in a big-league atmosphere while this lasts. You guys better get going."

We immediately started after that, and for the next five weeks and over Christmas, Tim Mead (assistant GM), Ken Forsch (minor league farm director), Jeff Parker (assistant minor league farm director and scouting director), Bill and I worked every day, trying to locate as many players as we could, with the focus on those we thought could help us.

The process of putting together a replacement team proved to be more of a challenge than I could have ever imagined. We started putting together a list of our former players that we knew, and then rated them by overall ability, age, and when they last played professionally. We went through the computer and made a list of possible candidates, split them up amongst ourselves and started calling.

Players who thought their career was over were now becoming the focus of major league clubs all over again.

It was amazing talking to players who hadn't played in years, and when I would ask if they were interested in playing for us, the reply was usually: "Yes, but I have to see if I can get off work, and I have another six offers on the table."

It was so comical that money was thrown around like Monopoly money. If a player said he was offered $6,000 a month, I would come back and say we'll give you $7,000 a month.

The feeling was that the season wouldn't start with a replacement team, so whatever it took was fine. Most players were offered a lot more than our present minor league players were making, but we had to get a team together.

I remember after we had signed a player, one club called us and said that he had a good arm and not to worry, "He was acquitted."

"Acquitted of what?" I thought.

This was just the start of things to come.

After we did as much as we could to sign former pros and veteran minor league players from our system that were towards the end of their careers and wanted to taste that big league life before they retired or got released, we started to run tryout camps. We ran a handful across the country and signed a few more players, but we were still about 20 players short and decided to have a local tryout at Cal State Fullerton. We knew being the local team would help attract more players than in other areas, but we had no idea what was about to happen.

In January, we set up an evening tryout in Fullerton, followed by an afternoon workout the following day. The first day was for amateur players, and the second day would be for former pros.

Our headquarters were set up at the Fullerton Marriott, located on campus. Tom Davis was the staff leader on the field, and we had Rick Ingalls, Jack Uhey, Steve Gruwell, Tim Kelly, and others to run the tryout. These were veteran scouts who knew how to run a camp and we figured we would have a couple hundred kids show up.

The campus gave us four hours to run the camp at their ballpark, so we would run each player in the 60-yard dash and have the position players throw from their best position, while the pitchers would throw 10 pitches in the bullpen. The best pitchers would be asked to stay and throw to the best position players, who were asked to stay and hit.

Bill, Tim, Ken, Jeff, and I were not allowed on the field, as there was a directive for front office personnel not to be a part of any tryout activities. No big deal for me, as I always watch from the side or behind a fence or light pole. I would just park myself by the left field corner behind a fence, so I didn't miss a thing.

When we left the hotel to go to the ballpark, I told everyone we would meet right after it finished to go over what we have. The camp was set to run from 6 p.m.-10 p.m., so I figured we would meet back around 10:30 p.m.

We got to the field, and the masses had already beaten us to the park. There were television crews, newspaper writers, and every player seemed to have a group of five or six people with them. The signup totaled over 960 players.

I have never been involved with anything even close to that, and neither had any of our scouts. We had four hours to get this done and I've never seen so much organized chaos in my life. Players were running everywhere you looked, and balls were being thrown in every which direction, and somehow, we got it done in the four hours that the college allotted to us. It was one of the most comical and heartwarming days I've ever experienced in baseball.

Players gave it everything they had for a chance at a professional contract and the dream of a lifetime. None of these nearly 1,000 players had ever played professional baseball, and this was their chance. The worst thing they would get out of it was a chance to tell their friends and family they had a tryout with the California Angels.

We had two injuries from kids in their mid-to-late 20's that I had never seen before, or again. One was an outfielder who was throwing from right field when his knee gave out and he fell to the ground. He couldn't stand up, and yet, fought being taken from the field as he said this was his chance and he wasn't leaving. The other was in the bullpen when a kid was throwing his 10 pitches off the mound and his arm broke after a few throws.

As sad as it was to see, you had to admire these two, and all the others that gave it their all to try and achieve their dream.

Tom, who oversaw the tryout, was on television interviews most of the night. The guys got on him about how his back was to the field most of the night, and the staff gave him the nickname "Hollywood Tom" because of all the interviews. All kidding aside, he did a fantastic job directing the camp and the staff in an unbelievable situation.

We got a few kids out of this evening, but the laughs and memories will always be there. If we would have sold concessions and souvenirs that night, we would have made a mint.

We got to the hotel room around midnight, and everyone was numb from the evening's events, so we went over the possible few names we got out of it, set a time to meet the next morning, and broke for a quick night's sleep. We knew the second day would be all former professionals, and have less players, but after what happened that evening, we didn't know what to expect and our original plan for the second day felt like it could be tossed out the window.

After our morning meeting at the hotel, we went over to Cal State Fullerton where we had a meager 250-plus players on hand for the second day of tryouts. We had ex-pros who were now FBI agents, firemen, teachers, cops, stockbrokers, as well as many other occupations.

After watching the amateur players the day before, these guys, even as out of shape as many were, looked like big league players in comparison. The group had many former upper-level minor leaguers, as well as a handful of former major leaguers. The day ran smoothly from start to finish, and we were even able to play a simulated game with the best players there.

The day finished and we were able to see players we had interest in and make enough offers to give us a roster to start with in spring training. "Hollywood" Tom was able to complete the interview demands, and we went back to the hotel to finish what we had accomplished for the two days and drink some well-earned beer.

As I look back at the overall event, I can't help but smile at what had happened. Most of all, the enjoyment that it gave to so many players who can now say they had a tryout with the Angels, even in this replacement year. Players and families had the look of pride and accomplishment, even though very few received a contract.

It was great, but I don't think any one of us would ever want to do it again.

Once we had enough players, everything seemed to quiet down as we prepared for spring training. The strike was still going on, and we all got to Tempe a few days before the players, where Bill and our manager, Marcel Lachemann, held meetings. Everything seemed fine until the day the players arrived, and we had a mix up with one of the players.

When we signed a player, we gave his name to our traveling secretary who would handle the player's travel arrangements. He would look up the name on the computer, get the players information, and then set up his ticket.

It just so happened that one of the players we signed had a name that was shared by someone else, and our traveling secretary made arrangements for the wrong guy. When he called the incorrect player and told him he'd been signed, the guy was surprised, but said sure and that he would love to come.

He came.

When the player arrived, he needed to be told about the mix up. Since we had heard he was a large and physical guy, we voted Ken to tell him since he was by far the largest man in our group. Ken told him, and he obviously wasn't pleased but went home, and we ended up getting the right guy to camp.

Between signing a player who had been "acquitted", a tryout camp with nearly one 1,000 players (including one each with a broken arm and knee), and signing the wrong player with the right name, this had already been quite an experience, and we hadn't even seen the players on the field yet.

As the players arrived and took the field, they looked enthusiastic and worked hard. Then the sore and pulled muscles started, and the training room became an exceedingly popular place. The daily grind hit them hard and early in camp. Not to mention, we had the police show up at one of our workouts to take a player to jail for unpaid child support while he lived in Arizona. There was never a dull moment.

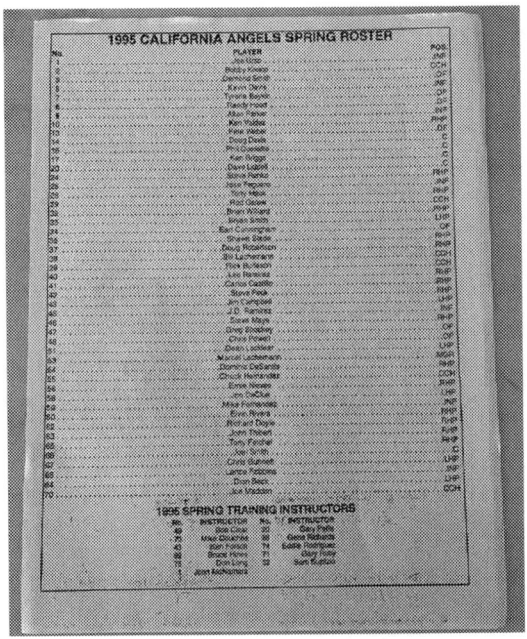

"1995 California Angels Spring Training roster"

Our first game was March 1 against Arizona State in a charity game at Tempe Diablo Stadium. It was the first replacement game played in over 80 years, and the next day would start the spring season for the other clubs, so all eyes were on us.

Arizona State was ranked in the top 15 of college baseball and people (mostly college coaches) had said for years that college baseball was equivalent to Double-A professional baseball, leaving most thinking we would get hammered.

There were numerous members of the media there, with most hoping we would fall on our face and show that replacement baseball wouldn't work. It was said that we had put our team together in the parking lot of a 7-Eleven, and we wouldn't hold up.

There were over 2,000 fans that showed up, which was a decent crowd in those days for an early spring training game. TV shots were showing the empty seats and not the ones that had fans, and it became obvious that most were rooting against us.

We got calls throughout the day from colleagues from other teams saying they were watching us and pulling for us to do well. That was when it hit us that all the clubs were depending on us, if we were going to go forward with any respectability with replacement baseball.

I sat in one of our offices down the first base line, nervously thinking that this had to go well. I don't think I have ever been so nervous before a game than I was that night.

The first inning was tough to watch, but we got through it. The first batter hit a ground ball to our shortstop, who overthrew the first baseman. When the runner tried to go to second base, he was thrown out by our first baseman who had the ball bounce back to him after it hit the railing of the dugout behind him.

After a couple scorching line drives, it was like we settled down and took charge. Our guys were confident after that first inning and played well.

We went on to hammer them, 13-5, and it wasn't really *that* close.

The media packed their bags after they realized what was going to happen, and most left early. I wish I could have waved them goodbye.

After the game, some observers said that no one was going to watch us. That it was Single-A ball and going to ruin the game. Well, so much then for college baseball being the equivalent to Double-A baseball.

Marcel doesn't get mad often, but when he was told of those comments, he said it could have been worse because he called off the offense to let the non-regulars play so it wouldn't be worse. He handled it great and with class.

Our staff, and baseball, took a big sigh of relief after that game.

The regular spring training season started like you would expect, with a lot of enthusiasm on the field, but very erratic and sloppy play at times. As the spring proceeded, everyone expected there would be a settlement between the players and owners soon, and the strike would end.

With about two weeks to go in spring training, things started to change. There was a breakdown in the negotiations, and for the first time, it looked as though the season might actually start with the replacement teams. We were playing against the Cubs at Hohokam Stadium in Mesa. It was like a light flipped, and suddenly, the players and staff alike got a little more serious and the play picked up a notch. Over the next two weeks, our club improved and played much better baseball.

When the team broke camp to go to Southern California to play the Dodgers for two games in the exhibition Freeway Series, we had a good replacement ballclub. Marcel and his coaching staff did a great job in preparing this team, while Bill made sure that the players were to be treated like major leaguers and the overall feeling was positive.

However, by the time the club arrived in Southern California, a deal was struck, and the season would start with the striking major league players in a few weeks after a shortened spring training.

The decision was made to play one game in Anaheim against the Dodgers, and another game the day before at Dodger Stadium, and then replacement baseball would be over.

What happened at that game was a moving experience. Both teams played a hard, well-executed game, and gave the large crowd a good show. At the end of the game, the players were given a standing ovation and came out of the dugout to acknowledge the fans. The people in attendance appreciated the effort and sacrifice these men gave to keep the season going.

We worked hard to put together a team in a situation that none of us wanted to be in. Bill and those of us that worked to sign players - as well as our major league and minor league coaching staffs - made this the best of a bad situation. Our team kept getting better and showed how special it is to play and be a part of this game, even if it is for a brief time.

I think back to 1981, when the players went on strike during the season, and we went about two months in the summer with no baseball. I was the scouting director with the Padres, and we had an open tryout camp at Jack Murphy Stadium to try and keep the game in sight. There was a great turnout, and we even had a sportscaster wired up and had him go through the tryout to show people what it was like.

On July 3 and 4, we had our Single-A affiliate, the Reno Silver Sox, play against the Angels Single-A affiliate, the Redwood Pioneers, with the games to be played the first night in Anaheim, and then the next in San Diego.

The first game in Anaheim drew a good crowd, around 20,000, and both clubs played a solid game after some obvious nerves. For most of the players, it would be their only opportunity to play in a major league stadium.

The next night, we played in San Diego to a full crowd. It was a better played, one-run game than the night before, and the fans all enjoyed a Fourth of July Celebration at the ballpark. Those fans were also appreciative of the effort of the young players and gave them a great ovation. It was a special two days for baseball.

Since that strike in 1994-95, there has been relative peace in Major League Baseball. I think if you look at what took place, you realize baseball is something that can affect anyone. It is one of the few sports that has a place for everyone to play in an organized league: Men, women, boys, girls, seniors, and those with disabilities.

Baseball means the start of a new year and hope for successful things. I learned that during the 1994/1995 strike that the game itself is more important than any individual player or owner.

CHICAGO WHITE SOX, PART II (2000 – 2003)

"2002, Chicago White Sox Dominican Academy"

My second tour with the White Sox came in 1999 after I resigned from my position as scouting director with the Angels after 13 years. I was brought over as a special assignment scout to work under Duane Shaffer and do some work for Kenny Williams. It was a good place to be after the way things ended in Anaheim, even though I took a huge pay cut. I was working with baseball people, starting with the owner, Jerry Reinsdorf, and general manager, Ron Schueler.

The White Sox had a strong pitching philosophy and Duane and his staff had done a great job of signing pitchers that got to the Majors. They had such talented scouts as George Bradley, Dave Yoakum, Ed Pebley, Gary Pellant, and so many others that it was a privilege to join this staff.

The first week I was there, Jerry called me and said they were going to give me the negotiation for their second-round pick from the draft that they were having trouble signing. I was delighted to get the opportunity. I asked where the figure stood and how much more I had to work with. Jerry told me the figure, and said there is no more, and to call him in a few days to let him know how it was going.

I was shocked but moved forward. The player was Bobby Hill, and the agent was Scott Boras.

Scott and I had a good relationship from past negotiations. He was tough, but we got more things done than not in the past. This, however, was tougher than normal, and I tried everything I could think of and even went to meet with him in his office, but to no avail. I called Jerry and said I tried, but I couldn't make any headway.

Jerry was good about it and I think he probably figured it doesn't hurt to try with the new guy to see if he can do anything with it. Hill ended up signing with the Cubs the next year.

As I got to know him better, I enjoyed working for Jerry and appreciated his loyalty to his employees and scouts. Jerry, who grew up a Brooklyn Dodgers fan and loved baseball, always spent time with the scouts and the minor league staff. He would take us out for dinners or have sessions during organizational meetings out at the pool just to talk with the guys. We had meetings in Las Vegas, which of course, was a big hit with the staff.

Jerry is one of the funniest people I have ever been around, and I laugh every time I see him. He could have been a standup comedian. He has a great delivery and always has a cigar in his hand. He is hysterical.

The 2000 season was a fun year going around the country seeing players. It was a good group of experienced scouts that Duane had put together, and along with Doug Laumann, who was the national crosschecker, it became a good setup.

Our 2000 draft saw our first three picks all get to the big leagues. Joe Borchard, an outfielder from Stanford, was our first pick. He was a classy kid who was a great athlete. He played quarterback on the Stanford football team and had all the tools as a baseball player. Good speed, arm, defensive ability, and a quick swing with well above-average power from both sides of the plate. Even though he didn't play as long in the majors as we thought he would, this was the type of athlete and player you would take every time. He wanted to be so good that I believe he couldn't handle the failures that come with being a good player.

In the third round we got Michael Morse, a high school shortstop from Nova High School in southern Florida. This kid had such good raw ability and played with a lot of enthusiasm. He had potential with the bat, especially with power, and although a big kid, he had a chance to reach the majors as a shortstop. Not only did he make it to the majors, but he made it as a shortstop before moving to other positions. He absolutely loved the game and became a clubhouse leader on the 2014 World Series-winning San Francisco Giants team before finishing a 13-year career in 2017.

At the end of the 2000 season, Ron Schueler resigned as general manager and Kenny Williams was promoted to replace him. Kenny promoted Duane to senior director, Doug to scouting director, and offered me the minor league farm director position.

I was kind of surprised because even though I was involved with minor league player decisions in the past, I never ran a system. After I thought about it, I looked at it as a good challenge and looked forward to moving to Chicago.

Right from the start, I realized that it was a 24-hour job. Agents calling all the time, signing players, managing seven rosters, and dealing with problems, many of which I never would have thought of in a million years. Kenny would look at me when I was getting overwhelmed and laugh, saying, "After being a farm director with all those rosters, being a general manager and only worrying about one roster is great."

I understood, but we both knew that the roster he had to worry about was the one we all depended on.

As farm director, I worked with Grace Zwit, the director of minor league administration, and Brian Porter, who was my assistant. Two great people who saved me many times over from making a bad move or handling a situation wrong. Grace is the most knowledgeable minor league administrator I have ever been around and so many times, she would say to me, "Bobby, you can't do that!"

Brian had such a great disposition that players and agents alike loved about him. A bright kid who had knowledge of the departments but who always wanted to continue learning.

I finally let him handle a majority of the items that required talking to agents. When we would release a player in spring training, I would have Brian in the room with me when I talked to the player. At the end of the meeting, the player would be mad at me, and hug Brian. They really liked and respected him.

I looked forward to budget time every year, when we would meet with Jerry to go over the upcoming season's budget, because of Grace and Brian. Grace, Brian, and Kathy Potowski (Grace's assistant) were masterful in putting the numbers together. I would tell Grace what things I really wanted, but other than that I got out of her way, as she is the best at player development budget. The proposed budget that was given to Jerry every year was so thick that it looked like a phone book.

When we would go to meet with Jerry, he would tell you that you better get what you need now because he didn't want you coming back later asking for more money. That said, you better have a good reason for what you were asking for.

We would sit at a table and he would have several Post-it Notes in the budget and would start to ask questions. You never knew what he might ask. Why are you budgeting for more food in the clubhouse? Why more spring training costs?

I was usually getting into trouble for moving players from affiliate to affiliate too often between our teams, which could add up to big dollars. He was right on that and by my last year we had that under control.

My last year with the White Sox, we changed our hitting philosophy in the minor leagues. We were bad at run production, walks, home runs and getting deep into the opposition's bullpens because we swung at too many first-pitch fastballs whether they were strikes or not. One night in a Class-A game, I saw our team get beat in a nine-inning game with 90 some pitches thrown against us. Almost impossible these days to have that happen.

I got approval from everyone, including Jerry, to change our philosophy and our numbers improved dramatically the next year. I wish I could take some credit, but it was a philosophy stolen from many clubs and good hitting coaches that made a difference along the way.

With the philosophy changed going into the season, Jerry looked at me at the budget meeting and said, "You have a $10,000 increase in bats for next year. Why?"

It was a good question, but I had the answer.

"Jerry," I replied, "We have a new hitting philosophy and because we are planning on a lot more contact this year, we will break more bats."

He thought for a minute, chewing on his cigar, and then finally said, "Ok."

Jerry could be tough, but if you made sense and believed what you were saying he worked with you. I really enjoyed those meetings.

That first offseason as a farm director was busy signing six-year minor league free agents and filling in some spots on our staff. When we finally got to spring training, I was going to have to address the entire minor league staff who was surprised, confused and for some, a bit ticked off, that a scout was hired to be the minor league farm director.

Our first day, I addressed the staff in a meeting to explain what I envisioned for the staff and for any items or complaints they wanted to express. It was a lengthy meeting, but I wanted everything on the table because I thought we were a good fit. I explained to them that they are the teachers, and I am the evaluator. When it came to instruction, I would tell them what I think we needed to get out a player, but it was up to them to do it as I'm not an instructor. I would make the final evaluation with their input, as that was my strength. They are the teachers, and I would not tell them how to get the instruction that the players need because that is their strength.

They would always have a say, but on player moves, mine would be the last. It is hard to be impartial on a player when you get to know them well. If you have them for a season, you probably end up either liking or disliking a player. That is human nature. That is why it is tough for a manager or coach, and why I tried to never know a player well, as I wanted to keep as much impartiality as I could when it came to decision time.

I understood how this may be received, but I looked forward to it as I honestly believed it would work out well. It was an open conversation, as I like to think every staff I ever had was able to say what was on their minds. I think we complimented each other well.

Although they never said much about it, I believe they liked the approach, and it took some pressure off them to do what they do best. On my end, I really liked this staff, as they were professional, dedicated, and they liked to have a good time. We talked baseball all the time and I learned a lot from them.

When I moved back to scouting later, I thought I wouldn't miss the job. Even though I didn't miss the nonsense that comes with the position, I did miss the staff and the players. I also missed the nickname the players had for me, "The Mustache".

When I got the position, everything was pretty much in place with procedure and personnel. Jim Snyder, a long-time baseball man, was the field coordinator. Don Cooper, the present White Sox pitching coach, was the pitching coordinator. Mike Lum was the hitting coordinator, Daryl Boston was the outfield coordinator, and Tommy Thompson was the catching coordinator. I brought over John Orton from the Angels to be a manager and we added Wally Bachman as a manager, and Mark Haley and Ken Dominguez as hitting coaches.

The pitching instruction in the White Sox system was particularly good, as it was consistent throughout the organization. Pitchers were never exposed to unexpected things as everyone was involved with what went on. It was similar for the hitters, but so much of the success of the White Sox was their pitching. Part of their philosophy was to make guys throw 10 percent changeups every game. They had kids learning how to throw some rather good changeups, and when you learn to throw a changeup well, every other pitch gets accelerated a notch.

Kirk Champion, Curt Hasler, Juan Nieves, and J.R. Perdew were already among our pitching staff. In time, we were able to add Richard Dotson who has been a tremendous asset to the system.

With managers like John, Wally, Nick Leyva (a former major league manager), Nick Capra (who would later become the farm director and major league coach), Jerry Hairston, and later, Chris Cron, Harold Baines, and Greg Walker, we had solid baseball men throughout the system.

We had spring training in Tucson, Arizona, and shared a complex with the Arizona Diamondbacks. It was a good setup and real nice facility on the south side of town. Tucson was a good place for spring training, but one of the biggest problems was that our minor league teams could only play the Diamondbacks and Colorado Rockies because they were the only other teams in Tucson. The other clubs didn't want to travel down from the Phoenix area. That got to be old for everyone and by the time we were ready to break camp, everyone was anxious.

I always drove to Tucson from Chicago, and the time driving gave me a lot of quiet time to think about things waiting for me when I arrived.

Spring training days are long. Waking up at 4 a.m. and falling asleep around 7:30 p.m. becomes the norm for most of the six weeks there. After a while, as the saying goes, "it's like Groundhog Day".

I spent three spring trainings as a minor league farm director, and each year it got easier and easier. Jim used to have early meetings in the morning and start early work on the field around 6:30 am. The first year, I tried to make all the meetings, but by the second year, I said to heck with it. I would show up at 7:30 am and get filled in. Besides, player evaluation meetings were always in the afternoon anyways, and in what league do they play baseball at 6:30 in the morning?

The toughest part of spring training, and the job period, is releasing players. As hard as it is to let someone go from a job, this in some ways is even more difficult. For most of these players, this has been their only job, their passion, and their lifelong dream. When you release a player, you are killing their dream.

I used to release each player myself, but after a year I had Brian sit in with me so there was no confusion on what was said.

When I did release players, I would release them all in one day. We would usually release around 15-18 players yearly. We didn't take a lot of players to camp since it was not only a waste of many players' time, but also cost more money.

This approach made things easier. When you release a player, for me, it is just as tough to release one as it is 18. It also kept players off guard on when it was going to take place, and everyone kept playing instead of going on the disabled list to try and buy time. We would do it in about three hours and then it was done.

I wouldn't sleep the night before and I left right afterwards for the day. It was the toughest thing I ever had to do in baseball.

Over the three years I was here, our goal as a system was to play .500, win a couple of league titles, make an environment to experience winning as well as adversity, all while putting development and what is best for the player first. Development came first, but having a target of .500 meant some teams would win and some wouldn't, helping the players experience both winning and losing because when you reach the majors, you will experience both. For the most part, I believe we accomplished that.

The system included Triple-A Charlotte, Double-A Birmingham, High-A Winston-Salem, Low-A Kannapolis, Rookie League Great Falls, Rookie League Bristol, and our Dominican Summer League affiliate. Jerry and Kenny worked hard to get the clubs close together to make for easier travel as well as a financially good setup. They accomplished this, with five of our affiliates being within seven hours of each other.

My first two years, our low Rookie League affiliate was in Phoenix as part of the Arizona Summer Rookie League. We played at Phoenix Municipal Stadium, which was the Oakland A's spring training stadium. It's a great facility, but it was so hot in the summer and had no fans in the stands with some of the instruction starting at 6 a.m.

The environment and lack of enthusiasm is not professional baseball for me. If I did anything right in my three years there, it was getting us out of Arizona in the summer.

After Grace found that the costs were the same if we stayed in Arizona or the Pioneer League, Jerry said go for it. I visited the ballparks and met with ownership groups in the three available cities in the Pioneer League.

Great Falls was by far the best of the available cities and I went and made my pitch. I found out right away that the other clubs that had been there before me told them they would get a winning team. I couldn't in good conscience do that. I told them we would do the best we could and would probably send most of our older players there but couldn't guarantee them anything but our best effort.

I told them of the good experiences with my father when I was a kid, going through Great Falls and the Pioneer League, and what a great city and league it is. I meant every word of it and must have come across sincere, but when I left the meeting, I thought there was no way they would pick us. They were great people, but I didn't see it happening and thought we would end up elsewhere.

About a week later, I got a call from the people in Great Falls, and they said they wanted to go with us. They appreciated that we would do our best but couldn't guarantee anything more, and they liked my experiences in their city and league and thought that was good.

Although I was only with the White Sox two more years, I really enjoyed those trips into Great Falls. Through 2020, the White Sox still had an affiliate in Great Falls.

By moving to Great Falls, we were able to move the Phoenix affiliate to Bristol, Virginia, and what a difference it made. Even though fans in the Appalachian League are usually 500-1,000 nightly, the kids who otherwise would have been in Arizona playing in front of no one played with extra enthusiasm and effort.

They played at night in front of people and acted like they were in Yankee Stadium. That young group played .500 ball that summer, going 33-33, but their improvement for me exceeded what they would have gotten in Arizona, even if they had won. I still think this was a solid move and am so happy we could do it.

During my time as farm director, I had the privilege of working with Roland Hemond. Roland was a special assistant who did things for Jerry, Kenny, and anyone who needed his assistance. I must admit, I used his services more than my share, but to be around him and learn so much was great. He helped me through some tough situations.

I once got a call from one of our affiliate owners who was irate with me.

"Do you know that we have lost 11 in a row here? What are you going to do about it?"

"Yes, I am aware," I calmly replied.

I guess he thought I never read the game reports and followed the clubs.

"When are you coming here?" he asked. "We need to talk."

"Be there soon," I replied.

That's when it hit me. ROLAND!

I decided to ask Roland if he wanted to go in my place.

"So, Roland, how would you like to go visit one of our clubs? They have had some trouble lately and I think they would love to see you."

Roland of course said yes and went to visit the club for about a week.

A few days after he got back to Chicago, I received a call from that club's owner. I figured he was going to air me out again because they still weren't winning much, but instead, all he could talk about was Roland's visit and what it meant to them. I was back in good graces, thanks to Roland.

I told Roland about it later and he just smiled and said how much he enjoyed the visit and that we had a good setup.

We went regularly to our affiliates and not only could he give great advice to our affiliate staffs, he was a great ambassador for the White Sox and baseball. Those were great times working with and learning from Roland.

One of my fondest memories during this time came in Kannapolis.

In November 2000, months before I was named farm director, the famed NASCAR driver Dale Earnhardt purchased the Kannapolis minor league baseball team just north of Charlotte. It was our Low-A affiliate in the South Atlantic League.

Tragically, he died after crashing on the final lap of the Daytona 500 in February 2001, and never saw our team play in Kannapolis.

I met his partners and son, Kerry, who also raced, at the Winter Meetings that following winter. Genuinely nice people and they wanted to keep the club. The team was appropriately named, "Intimidators," a nickname bestowed on Dale for his driving style.

Early in the season before a game they had a ceremony honoring him. The park was packed and there were many local dignitaries there, including his wife, Teresa. I sat next to Cal Ripken Jr. and was there to represent the White Sox.

I must admit, I am not a racing fan, but that day I couldn't help but feel like part of the community. Dale was born and raised in Kannapolis and beyond his fame, he was a local who farmed, shopped and walked with his fellow Kannapolis natives. Everyone there felt they knew Dale and that he was one of them. By the end of the day, I felt the same way. He must have been quite a person.

It was nice to be able to converse with Cal, as he wasn't just a great player but is involved so much in professional and amateur baseball.

After I gave my talk and presented Teresa with a White Sox jersey with his name on the back, I had a whole new outlook on racing. I'm still not much of a racing fan, but I sure do like the people.

During the winter of 2003, Roland and I were visiting Hermosillo of the Mexican Winter League (Roland is big in other countries as well as here) where we had some players getting work in. While in Mexico, Bill Bavasi was named general manager of the Seattle Mariners.

When we got back to Chicago, Kenny told me Bill had called and asked permission to talk with me about their scouting director position. Because it is an equivalent move from minor league farm director to scouting director, the White Sox had every right to decline. When the Mariners added the Vice President title to the job, I was granted permission. Kenny told me I had a day to consider because he didn't want this to linger, and he had someone in mind for the job if I left.

The last year some tension began in the front office that started to make me uncomfortable, and my obvious desire to return to scouting made the decision that much easier.

Kenny let me run the department the way I wanted, and I appreciated that, but we were starting to differ on the evaluations of our players. A general manager must have someone in that role who thinks like him and for the first couple of years, we did, but he needed someone more on his page. I made the decision to go to Seattle and I was really looking forward to working with Bill again.

My time with the White Sox was overall a great time and experience. I still consider them and the Angels as my two baseball homes.

Working in Chicago with Jerry, Duane, Grace, Doug, Brian, Kenny, Rick Hahn (who would later become the general manager and who spent time with me getting a feel for our minor league system), the scouting and minors league staffs was great.

I left to join Seattle in early December and was excited to head up a scouting staff again. Seattle is a beautiful city that I enjoyed living in as much as anywhere I have lived. It is a good sports city with a nice stadium and a run of good seasons at the major league level. The start of that run basically came when I was with the Angels and they beat us in the 1995 AL West division title tiebreaker game.

I was glad to be joining Bill, and sorry to be leaving the White Sox. Of course, the White Sox won the World Series two years later.

My three years there had many of the future 2005 World Series championship team in the minor leagues, as well as many players who would go on to solid big-league careers. Players like Jon Garland, Joe Crede, Danny Wright, Aaron Roward, Michael Morse,

Willie Harris, Miguel Olivo, Jon Rauch, Brandon McCarthy, Chris Young, Jeremy Reed, and Aaron Miles, among others. It was a good group of kids that were acquired either by draft, trade, or free agency, and that were developed by the minor league system.

When I talked with Jerry before I left, he told me that you know you are leaving a home.

"Jerry," I said, "I know, but I really want to scout again. Working for you is like working for Gene Autry. The two best owners in baseball and I had a privilege to work for you both."

I meant every word.

SEATTLE MARINERS

"Credit: Seattle Mariners PR"

In November 2003, Bill Bavasi was named the new general manager of the Seattle Mariners. Soon after he got the job, he called the White Sox and asked for permission to speak with me about the scouting director position.

I had a good job with the White Sox, as the minor league farm director, but the desire to work with Bill, scout, and head up a scouting staff again was something I couldn't pass up.

I always liked Seattle, and they were coming off a rather good year. Many people thought they had solid prospects and that good years were still possible now and in the future.

One of the first things I did in Seattle was buy a townhouse on Bainbridge Island. Karen and the kids were going to move back to Orange County, California, after we sold our house in Chicago, so this would be a great place for her and me to have when it was just us.

Bainbridge Island was across Elliott Bay from Seattle and had a Scandinavian vibe to it, with pine trees surrounding the island from the bordering Olympic National Park. It had fine dining, beautiful bayside vistas, and a relaxing nature away from the city.

It was a ferry ride of close to an hour each way from Seattle and became a two hour commute each day to and from the ballpark, despite only driving two miles daily. It sure was rough sitting on the boat and going to work reading a paper, having a cup of coffee, and going home drinking a beer. I still miss that.

Seattle had a checkered history with the draft, having signed two of the greatest players in the game with Ken Griffey Jr. and Álex Rodríguez, and some exceptionally good players such as Adam Jones and Jason Varitek. They also had some swings and misses on quite a few high picks.

I only knew a handful of the scouts they had, as well as assistant general manager Lee Pelekoudas, so I needed to familiarize myself with a lot of new people.

Roger Jongewaard had been the scouting director for many years and someone I had a lot of respect for. He was now assistant to the general manager. Ironically, when Dick Balderson was general manager in Seattle, he wanted Roger to leave the New York Mets and become his scouting director. At some point, Roger didn't want the job and didn't want to leave the Mets, so Dick called me, and I thought I had a good chance at getting the job. I guess Roger had a change of heart and got the job because he was who Dick wanted from the get-go.

Benny Looper was the minor league farm director but would now be overseeing both scouting and the minor leagues. He had played in the St. Louis Cardinals organization as a minor leaguer for half a decade and had climbed the scout and executive ladder with the Mariners after his playing days.

Frank Mattox had been the scouting director and was now moving to be the minor league farm director. Frank spent seven years in the Milwaukee Brewers farm system in the late 80's and had worked with Roger and Benny with the Mariners for quite some time. He was a wonderful guy.

Bob Harrison, who I had worked with in Anaheim and who is a great evaluator, had become an assistant to the general manager.

Knowing these four gave me a start, and I looked forward to it.

One of the toughest items I had to address when I arrived was an uncomfortable item with the scouting approach. They had more of a high-risk, high-ceiling approach, which means usually taking high school players who are crude, but that you think may be very good in the future.

I had the approach that ability is ability, regardless of the age. If everything is even, I would go with the player closest to the majors, and never felt that age was a benefit if the ability wasn't just as good. I also think the high-risk draft comes with the older kids, because people expect them to be in the majors quicker and tend to watch them closer with more criticism.

The good thing in baseball is that any approach can work. I just happen to feel more comfortable with the way I mentioned.

There was a lot of resistance from the start, which is expected to a point, but it was more prevalent here. Eventually, we all were headed in the same direction, whether it was their personal preference or not.

As I look at the five years of drafts I oversaw in Seattle, it wasn't a great run, but was far from bad.

I had hoped we would stock up with position players, particularly left-handed hitters with power. There's a tendency, whether it's mental or fact, that right-handed hitters are hitting into the Grand Canyon in Seattle. If a hitter can go the other way, Seattle is a good place to hit, but what happens is right-handed hitters tend to pull the ball, and it takes quite a bit to hit it out to left field and left-center field. Left-handed hitters, the ball just jumps and can clear the short porch in right field.

Although that plan fell short, we did have success with pitching, and had the best individual pitching draft I have ever been a part of.

I didn't make any changes to the staff but added two scouts to help make the transition easier, as well as provide solid evaluations to the process. Tom Davis came over the first year, and Rick Ingalls the second year. Those two were able to help the scouts understand where we were coming from and what I expected. Tom spent a lot of time with our young scouts, helping them with their development, and I thought it was turning into a staff that could work together.

In the office, Hallie Larson and Jim Fitzgerald gave us great support administratively, which I always needed.

Hallie was a long-time scouting administrator who was with their Mariners not long after their inception and had been through multiple owners and executives. She was a delight and was great to the scouts, and the scouts loved her. She had as fine a personality as you ever want to meet, and she sure bailed me out of a lot of jams.

From day one, I was told that Jim would basically be my assistant, which I was fine with. He was a wonderful kid who later became the assistant athletic director at the University of Eastern Washington.

The staff had some scouts that I learned to utilize and rely heavily on. Ken Madeja, Steve Jongewaard, Ron Tostenson, Rob Mummau, Stacey Pettis, Craig Bell, Kyle Van Hook, and Greg Whitworth, among others, worked hard at what was asked of them.

Tom, Rick, Steve, and Ron were our national crosscheckers over the years and were a very solid and thorough group that was tireless in its efforts.

Because the major league team had come off a good year even though they missed the playoffs, the team was older than we thought and the prospects that were supposed to step in didn't quite fill the open spots. Most of the veterans were near the end of their careers and either didn't have much trade value or retired. Because of this, we signed quite a few free agents, which limited us to only two picks in the first three rounds over a two-year period.

The first year, in 2004, we didn't get our first draft pick until the third round. With 92 picks in front of us, it was tough to have a good idea of what players would be available, so we looked at some other options like players expected to be difficult to sign or multi-sport athletes.

We hoped to have a chance to get Hunter Pence, but in early May, we realized that wasn't likely to happen. Pence was an interesting player out of the University of Texas-Arlington, who looked unorthodox in baseball aspects most of the time but was a great athlete with a great attitude. He had an aggressive approach with the bat, made solid contact and had some power potential. He could run and was aggressive with his speed, with his biggest drawback being his arm from the outfield, which in time, became accurate and enabled him to play right field. We worked him out and he was a great kid who was well liked by his teammates, and later became a leader on some World Series-winning clubs.

That same year, one of the top high school quarterbacks on the West Coast was at Woodinville High School, just 20 miles northwest of Seattle. This young man also played shortstop on the baseball team.

Matt Tuiasosopo, the son of former National Football League defensive lineman Manu, was a fine athlete who everyone thought would attend the University of Washington to play football.

This is usually the type of player that you would compete for in the first round, if at all. Obviously, the opportunity to play at the local university that plays a top schedule, and is often a national power, makes it difficult to pry away to play baseball. Matt had a family history at the university as well, with both his brothers, Marques and Zach, playing football at Washington and later in the NFL, and his sister Leslie being a premier volleyball player and now coach for the program. His father was also a local legend, enjoying five years with the Seahawks.

This was a great family, with a closeness that showed in the support they had for each other.

When I first saw Matt play, I expected to see a football player who is a great athlete trying to play baseball. As I watched, he came across to me as a good baseball player that could play football.

He had great first step quickness and instincts. He showed good hands and a strong, average arm that could get better and keep him in the infield. He was a good runner underway but didn't get out of the box well because of the length of his swing. He showed good balance at the plate, with a quick, level swing and power potential.

He was a first-round type talent that we felt most clubs would shy away from because of signability, and it turns out, we were right. All our scouts were on board if we took him, so Benny and I visited with Matt and his family before the draft to see if we had a chance.

Benny and I asked if there would be any interest in signing with the Mariners. They were quite interested, but only for first-round money. Being that we didn't have a first-round pick, we had the money, but because he would be drafted in the third round, the bonus would be well above the recommended slot amount.

Seattle was one of the few clubs that followed what the recommended slot was, but Matt could be an exception, because of his situation as a football player. Bill Bavasi and Chuck Armstrong were on board, and Chuck notified Major League Baseball of what we wanted to do.

The slotting system then was different than it is now, and because we followed it, we lost some players along the way. We drafted J.P. Arencibia in 2004 and Lance Lynn in 2005 and had the money to sign them, but couldn't because it would be over the recommended slot amount.

I told the upper management that I hope when they judged us, they would remember the players we lost that we could have signed. They didn't.

We selected Matt in the third round of 2004 and signed him. It caused somewhat of an uproar in town with all the Washington fans, as we took their quarterback of the future.

I loved it, as we got a first-round talent in the third round.

Matt is a great kid who played in the major leagues for a few years, even if it wasn't as long as I thought he would. With a father and brothers who played in the NFL, Matt added a major league player to the family.

In that 2004 draft, we selected three other players that reached the majors. Rob Johnson was our fourth-round pick and served as a backup catcher in the majors for seven seasons. Mark Lowe, our fifth-round pick, was a hard-throwing reliever who pitched for 11 years, including twice in the World Series with Texas. Michael Saunders, our 11th-round selection, was a talented outfielder with good tools and a sweet left-handed swing that helped lead to a nine-year career and a 2016 all-star appearance with Toronto.

The following year we had the third pick in the first round and were leaning towards a position player with power potential. There were some good players to consider with Jeff Clement, Alex Gordon, Troy Tulowitzki, and Justin Upton.

We followed all four closely, and soon realized Upton would be selected before us and hoped that Gordon would slide to us.

Gordon, a third baseman from Nebraska, reminded me so much of Darin Erstad in his approach to the game. He had good offensive potential and the versatility to play a prime defensive position. We realized a few days before the draft he wouldn't get to us, so we shifted our thoughts.

It turned out to be a solid draft all the way through, especially in the first round where Upton went first overall, and Gordon went second. Tulowitzki, a shortstop from Long Beach State, and Clement, a catcher at USC, were the next two for consideration for us and we liked both.

I really liked Tulowitzki's attitude and ability, but we had Yuniesky Betancourt at shortstop on the major league club and he was a fine defensive player who was young, so I made the decision to go with the catcher, a position of need in our system.

Clement was a three-year standout with the Trojans, who had solid offensive potential. He had quickness to his bat and could make hard contact. What I really liked was the left-handed power he had that would fit nicely in Safeco Field. He was an average defender with an average arm that would play easily if he could hit.

He looked like he was going to hit and with power. We selected him with the third overall pick in the 2005 draft. He was a great kid from a baseball family, and I really felt we were in good shape with our catching for the future.

Clement got to the major leagues relatively quick, but he started to have injury issues which hindered him throughout his career and prevented him from becoming the player I believed he would be. He spent parts of four seasons in the majors before his career ended.

With the success of quite a few players that were drafted that year in the first round, I received some criticism. I accept all responsibility for every player I ever approved selecting, but I still believe that if Jeff had stayed healthy that he could have had a solid major league career and that he was deserving to be a high selection.

We selected two additional players in this draft that played in the majors, with one being Anthony Varvaro, a right-handed pitcher out of St. John's University.

Varvaro was regarded as a first-round pick, but in May, he hurt his arm and required surgery. We decided that if he slid in the draft because of the injury that we would draft him and try to work out a deal that would be good for both sides. This kid had a fine arm with an above-average fastball and hard curve that was tough to hit if thrown for a strike. He was an aggressive competitor that had good potential.

We selected Varvaro in the 12th round and worked out a deal for about half of a first-round pick. It was a good deal for him and a good gamble for us, even with the uncertainty that we both faced. We explained to him that who better to rehab him as a pitcher than a major league organization? He agreed and went on to a good six-year career in the majors as a relief pitcher, mostly with Atlanta.

The following season would prove to be the best of the five years in Seattle, and also the year I received the most criticism that I would get, which also put pressure on Bill.

We were looking to try and acquire as much pitching as we could from this draft to stock our system. This draft had pitching depth, and we drafted fifth in each round. The draft had good arms such as Luke Hochevar, Ian Kennedy, Clayton Kershaw, Tim Lincecum,

Andrew Miller, Brandon Morrow, Max Scherzer, and Chris Tillman, among others. We were fortunate to get two of them.

We were looking to get someone that we thought could get to the majors quickly, and with all the college arms we thought we were in a good spot.

I saw Brandon Morrow with the University of California early in the season against UC Irvine, and he was impressive. He had a smooth delivery with a quick and free arm that repeated well and had a good downward angle to the plate. There was power to his fastball with late life, a quick breaking ball and a hard splitter. He had the build and everything you look for in the delivery and arm. From that point on, he was one of the definite candidates for our first pick.

Chris Tillman from Fountain Valley High School in Southern California was a kid that clubs knew about for years, and like Morrow, had a sound delivery with a quick arm, an above-average fastball, and a power curve that was one of the best from a high school pitcher I have seen. He was having a fair season and we heard he was slipping, but we didn't think we could take him in the first round and we didn't see him getting out of that first round.

We knew early on that Hochevar, Greg Reynolds of Stanford, and Brad Lincoln of Houston were going to go in front of us. We narrowed down our possibilities to Morrow, Miller, Lincecum and the hard-throwing Daniel Bard from North Carolina. As the draft got closer, the opinions among our staff started to differ. Everyone liked all of these arms, but there was no consensus on anyone.

As the amateur season was ending, Lincecum was finishing strong right in our backyard at the University of Washington. Since he was local, there was some building pressure to take him.

He wasn't a real big kid and threw with some effort but had a big-time arm. He had an above-average fastball that didn't have great movement, but he had a curveball that was big and quick and was very tough to hit, making his fastball look that much faster. He was a tough competitor who I thought would go to the big leagues quickly mostly because of his curveball, but probably in relief.

When draft day came, I felt that Morrow would be the guy. It is hard to pass on the type of pitcher who can throw 100 mph and projects to be a frontline starter or a closer.

Even though our scouts made cases for the others, I still feel you take that kind of arm every time and you will be right more often than you are wrong. I have always thought there were times you could go with an exception, but there is a reason there is a rule and exception to the rule. If the rule fits the type of player you like, you go for it.

After we drafted Morrow, some local writer wrote an article that he was hurt and there was panic in the organization. We knew it wasn't true and the writer admitted it was a joke, but with Morrow already known to have diabetes, there were people that thought I made a big mistake.

Brandon signed at the end of the summer, and after a few innings of minor league experience he went to spring training the next year and broke camp with our major league club. He started to dominate major league hitters, and although the plan was to have him start, a need in the bullpen caused us to pitch him in relief. Moving him between starting and relieving didn't help his development, but it did show that he could do both like we thought.

After taking Brandon in the first round, we immediately started to focus on our second pick. As I have always said to get your share of players plus some of other clubs' shares, you must approach every round as if it is the most important round of the draft.

As we got down to the lower part of the first round, both Tillman and Bard were still available. I expected Tillman to go as each pick came up and felt we may have an outside shot at getting Bard.

Boston took Bard at the end of the first round, and as we headed into the compensation round, Tillman was still available.

I kept telling our people not to get excited because he won't be there, while deep down inside, I was getting excited that he might be.

The time it took to go through the compensation picks and the picks in front of us in the second round seemed to take forever. I continued telling our staff, "Don't even think about it."

"Don't think about it," I continued as we got closer and closer. "It's going to break your heart. He ain't gonna be there."

We got to the second round, four selections ahead of us, and now I really told them not to think about it.

"The closer the pick gets; you're going to die if you think about it."

When it got to our pick, the room was ecstatic. We got Chris Tillman.

I believe this was a case where people saw a lot of him, and maybe his performance wasn't everything they wanted, and his abilities got overlooked. That's why performance shouldn't interfere if a player is healthy and is still doing the things that you like fundamentally and physically. It was like we got two first-round picks.

In the fifth and seventh rounds we selected Nate Adcock and Doug Fister, respectively. Adcock was a right-handed prep arm from

Kentucky, who went on to pitch parts of four seasons in the majors. Fister, a right-handed pitcher from Fresno State, pitched 10 years in the majors - three for us in Seattle - and started 226 games up until his retirement in 2019.

These two pitchers, along with Morrow and Tillman, worked as starters in the major leagues. To get four pitchers who started in the majors out of your first seven draft picks is the best draft I have been involved with when it comes to pitching, and a credit to our staff.

In between Adcock and Fister, we selected Adam Moore in the sixth round out of the University of Texas-Arlington. There weren't many players scouts were following that year at Arlington, so after we saw him and knew we had interest, I instructed all our crosscheckers that if they go to see him play, not to go into the park, but rather watch from outside through the fence or from a place where you couldn't be seen. I didn't want to let clubs know that we had interest in this kid.

For me, he was a blue-collar, hard-nosed player who could catch, throw, and make good contact. Even though we would have taken him as high as the fourth round, we got him int he sixth, as we didn't tip our hand and Mark Lummus stayed on top of it by knowing the competition.

Moore played parts of nine years in the majors, mostly as a backup catcher, but had he not been plagued by injuries, I am sure he would have had more opportunities.

Five players out of our first seven picks reached the major leagues, yet I got a lot of criticism because we didn't take Lincecum. It ended up causing me, and I am sorry to say, Bill Bavasi, something negative to deal with.

Nevertheless, we got seven players to the majors. Morrow pitched 12 seasons in the majors, including a few as a successful starter before finishing his career as a dominant reliever. He pitched in the 2017 World Series with the Dodgers once struck out 17 batters in a game. Tillman and Fister enjoyed many good seasons with successful teams. This draft was an example of why you need to wait to evaluate a team's draft rather than try to make an immediate evaluation. Unfortunately, we didn't get that time.

As we entered the 2007 season, the big-league team was improving every year even though we were under .500. That year, the club started to break out. With Mike Hargrove as manager, we got to 20 games over .500 in late August and were in good position for the wild card spot in the playoffs.

Unfortunately, Mike resigned on July 1, and we faltered some to finish with an 88-74 record, six games short of a playoff spot. We finished second in the division, but the outlook with our mix of veterans and young players gave reason for optimism for future years.

In the 2007 draft, we selected 11th in each round. This draft did not have as much quality or depth that the previous year had. David Price of Vanderbilt went first overall and was probably No. 1 on most clubs' lists, if not all of them. His control was an issue in college, but he overcame that in pro ball to become an ace. We were open to players at any position, whether they were in high school or college.

Early in the spring, the Canadian Junior National Team was in Florida and they usually played an exhibition game against the Toronto Blue Jays every spring training. They had players that were high school juniors and seniors, and to see them against superior talent was a big asset for scouts.

It was my first look at a tall, 6-foot-7, strong right-handed pitcher by the name of Phillippe Aumont. This kid had an intimidating delivery, especially against right-handed hitters, with a quick arm and one of the best hard sinkers I have seen from a high school pitcher. He complimented this with a hard-sweeping slider that was extremely difficult for right-handed hitters. Being tall, he was able to throw from a lower angle that could eat up a hitter. His control was a little erratic, but he had so much potential. Our scouts really liked this kid and he immediately became one of our potential players to select.

The Canadian team traveled to the Dominican Republic later in the spring. As when they played in Florida, it was against superior competition, which helps to accelerate the development of their players.

Greg Hamilton - who was then manager and is now the general manager on Team Canada - and his staff do a great job in Canada developing their players. On this team, Jason Dickson, who pitched for us in Anaheim, was the pitching coach. Jason was able to help Phillippe and gave me good information about him.

I made the trip down there and was surprised there weren't more scouts from the United States to see these players. Aumont did just what he did in Florida and overmatched the hitters. You could see not only the present ability, which was above average, but you could see so much room for improvement.

Even though I have never been a fan of taking high school pitchers first, this kid fit. With most of our staff on board, we took him with our first pick.

After a month or so, he signed. When he came to Seattle to finish the paperwork, Benny Looper and I took Phillippe and his agent out to dinner. He was an interesting kid who had only spoken English for a few years. He was from Quebec and spoke French most of his life. He had a difficult upbringing and went through some difficult times. His agent said he bought a used car with his bonus, and later we heard that he spent the money on his mom. A great kid.

Aumont was involved in a trade in 2009 that sent him to the Philadelphia Phillies in exchange for Cliff Lee. He spent parts of four seasons with the Phillies, but his lack of control limited his success. When he controlled the strike zone, he was tough. He continued to pitch through 2019 in the Toronto Blue Jays, Chicago White Sox and Detroit Tigers minor league systems and the independent leagues.

We got two other players to the majors from the 2007 draft. Our second pick, Matt Mangini, a third baseman from Oklahoma State, got 11 games with Seattle in 2010. Shawn Kelley, a right-handed reliever from Austin Peay State, was our 13th-round selection. Kelley was signed by Alvin Rittman and was a great late round signing. Kelley made it to the majors in 2009 and spent 11 seasons as a solid reliever.

These are the kind of selections that make any draft better, and why you need to take every round seriously.

The 2008 season was a year that we had high hopes for. With the additions to the team to go with the main core from 2007, we felt that we had a strong chance to contend. About two weeks into the season, things started to go south. It had the feeling of 1999 in Anaheim, when a good team got hit with numerous injuries and down years from players expected to produce.

You could feel the pressure building, and we felt it in the draft. When the chairman of the team and one of the owners came into the draft room the first day, holding a national publication's Top 100 prospects ranking, I knew I was under scrutiny. Turns out I was right.

We were aiming for a starting pitcher that could get to the majors quickly. We were drafting 20th in the first round, and knew it was going to be difficult.

As the season went on, we thought we had a good shot at taking Andrew Cashner, a right-handed pitcher from Texas Christian. We thought that we knew he had a good chance to get to us, but the one club we couldn't get an idea from was the Chicago Cubs, who drafted in front of us at 19. When it got to a couple picks in front of us, we thought we were going to get him. Then, the Cubs called his name.

Luckily, I've learned to always be prepared for anything, and we had a plan B that we were confident could achieve what we were hoping to accomplish. We felt if all the starting pitching was gone we could go to a reliever that had the potential to quickly become a setup man or a closer.

Going that route would free up Morrow from the bullpen to join the starting rotation, which would probably be even better down the road. So, when Cashner was selected right in front of us, we selected Josh Fields, a right-handed reliever out of Georgia.

Fields wasn't a tall kid, but he had a quick arm with a plus fastball and power breaking ball. He profiled as a setup man or closer and would be quick to the majors.

After the first round was over, I met with the press for a few minutes between rounds. Most of them were surprised we had taken a reliever and didn't seem impressed at all by what we had done.

We couldn't tell them that we wanted to move Morrow to the rotation, so I didn't say anything about it. One writer did ask me, "Is this something that you think could lead to options that may improve the rotation?"

Bingo.

I can't remember who she was, but she was the only one that had figured it out. The others didn't catch on, so the overall reaction of the press wasn't great.

Our initial thought was that Fields could be in the big leagues by September and Morrow would be in the rotation the next year. It was a good plan, but it never came to fruition.

First, Fields held out and didn't sign, even though he was a college senior, until the next spring. Second, Bill Bavasi was fired during the summer as we struggled through an injury-filled season. I got fired at the end of the year by Jack Zduriencik, the new general manager.

When Zduriencik got to Seattle after he was hired, we were scheduled to meet. I had known him for probably 25 years and had gotten along with him. When we met, our meeting was basically, "Hello, I'm making a change."

We didn't talk about the staff, our preparation for the next year, or if there was some role I could fill for the final year of my contract for 2009.

I was disappointed, not because of what had happened to me because I understand that comes with the job, but because I wanted to tell him about our staff and what they could do to help him.

I know it is the option of a general manager or scouting director to have the people he wants, but if given a chance, many people can show they deserve to stay. Several of our people didn't survive the shift.

When Fields finally signed with Seattle, they traded him to the Boston Red Sox after two minor league seasons. He broke into the majors with the Houston Astros and later established himself as a solid reliever with the Los Angeles Dodgers.

We also drafted three other pitchers in 2008 that reached the Majors, including Brandon Maurer, a hard-throwing right-hander. We took him in the 23rd-round because his signability was questionable. Our scout, Timmy Reynolds, did a good job getting to know him and he was able to sign him because the kid really wanted to play.

Bobby LaFromboise, a crafty southpaw reliever from New Mexico, was our eighth-round pick, and reached the majors with Seattle and Pittsburgh. Andrew Kittredge, a slider-heavy reliever from Ferris High School in Spokane who we took in the 45th round, is currently having success out of the bullpen with the Tampa Bay Rays and made the 2021 All-Star Game.

Our five years in Seattle produced a major leaguer from every first-round selection, and although we had one All-Star position player drafted, it was our pitching that proved to be a strength. We drafted some quality starters, middle and setup relievers, as well as a closer. If all the pitching could have stayed in Seattle, it would have provided the foundation of a particularly good staff.

From the start, I loved the city of Seattle and so many of the people in the organization. But I never felt completely comfortable or accepted as a part of things there. I think when Bill and I arrived, there was some resentment from some people, and it never felt like everybody worked completely together.

It was still another great experience, and I was appreciative of the chance.

I have continued to scout for many years, but as a director, orchestrating a draft. As the trend started to change towards analytics, statistics, video, and other things, I was not a person that would be sought for my experience any longer.

INTERNATIONAL EXPERIENCES

One of the most exciting things you get to do when you are in the scouting profession is travel to other countries and experience their culture. I have been fortunate to travel to many countries around the world, including North America, South America, Europe, Asia, and Africa, as well as Latin America, Central America, and the Far East. It was a priceless adventure that didn't cost me a dime.

I was supposed to travel to Australia for work a handful of times but have never gone. One of my goals is to go for at least one day and jump on a ship to Antarctica so I can say I have been to all seven continents. I plan on doing this with my son, Jimmy.

The years I was scouting director with San Diego, Anaheim and Seattle, and minor league Director with the White Sox, I was able to experience many different things internationally.

The way that clubs scout internationally today has changed drastically. Players are observed more in tournaments than ever before, with clubs having more international scouts. Agents are involved with players in many parts of the world, with some representing players younger than the eligible minimum signing age of 16.

My first trips to the Dominican Republic, Venezuela, and Puerto Rico in the early years were much different than today. Baseball was played everywhere. You didn't see an empty field or vacant lot not being used to play ball. Kids wanted to play badly and to sign a contract to play in the United States. You would see kids playing with a stick for a bat, a sock taped up for a baseball, and gloves made from cardboard. They would play barefoot if they didn't have shoes and would play from first light to sundown.

Baseball in these countries has evolved from what I described, and signing for bonus money of very little, to today where they are trained by agents and sign for money well above what they would get in the United States. You pass by empty fields all the time now and don't see the desire for those pickup games that were played everywhere.

I had international budgets that were less than $30,000 for the year and we could sign 8-10 players a year easily. Teams now have multiple millions to spend on the international market and more and more players sign every year for over $1 million.

There needed to be an increase in what the players got in those countries, but like we have seen in the United States, it never seems to find a suitable middle ground that is good for everyone. The players in many of those countries get more bonus money now than a player of even or superior talent in the United States.

If money were spent on players in the draft and internationally like it is today when I was scouting director, I would have been fired with the failure rate there is for the money spent. It is accepted today, and in some cases rewarded. Some things do change.

PRESTON GÓMEZ AND CUBA

When I worked with the Angels, I had the privilege of working with Preston Gómez, who was our special assistant to the general manager. He had been a major league player, manager, and coach, and was respected as royalty all over Latin America. If you were with Preston, you had an in.

He had been with Buzzie Bavasi for many years with the Dodgers and Padres and came over to the Angels when Buzzie did. He helped all of us with our dealings in international countries and made life a lot easier.

Preston used to go to Cuba every Christmas to do clinics. He knew Fidel Castro, and with Castro's love for baseball, he would allow Preston to do these clinics. It also allowed Preston to help his family who was still in Cuba and try and get his brother out of prison.

Preston would meet with Castro when he would go to Cuba and talk baseball and bring supplies every time he went down. He tried to help family the best he could and in time, he was able to get them out of Cuba, but Preston continued to help the people and his friends there seeking refuge.

When the Cuban National Team would come to play the United States team, Preston and I would go and meet with their officials and try to learn as much as we could in the event signing Cuban players became possible.

In 1987, Cuba played the United States in Richmond, Virginia with Jim Abbott pitching a great game against them. At this time, the Cuban National team was the best amateur team in the world. In actuality, they were professionals from Cuba's major league, Serie Nacional, with some players spending nearly a decade together.

They trained year-round together and their living expenses, as well as their families, were taken care of by the Cuban government. They played in their late 20's and 30's against our team of college players. There were some great games played between the two countries.

One of the best players of his age I have seen was Omar Linares, their third baseman. He was so good that the talent he played against didn't challenge him. He had all the tools, and I believe at 21 years old, he could have played in the majors. He never got that chance, but did play in Japan in the late 1990's.

When the Cuban National team played the Baltimore Orioles at Camden Yards in a two-game series in 1999, I attended the game with Preston. Before the game, we met with dignitaries from Cuba, and I had the opportunity to meet Teófilo Stevenson, the Olympic boxing champion who won three gold medals and fought in the Muhammed Ali era. Like Linares in baseball, Stevenson would have most likely been the heavyweight champion of the world had he left Cuba. Stevenson signed the back of my ticket stub.

That night in Baltimore was my first opportunity to see José Contreras pitch, and even though it wasn't a great outing he displayed outstanding stuff, and not long after went on to have a successful 11-year career in the majors. Linares had four hits that night and showed he belonged at that level, even though it would never happen.

Preston tried three times to get me to Cuba to give me an opportunity to understand baseball in the country and to meet people both in sports and in the government. Since no one with a major league club could go to Cuba without permission, I was denied twice by Major League Baseball. I believe teams that had employees of Canadian citizenship were able to get in, even though baseball didn't want them to.

One time, Preston helped me get a six-month visa to Cuba, and I was going to get there through Mexico City. Somehow, the State Department found out and I was denied for the third time.

I really wanted to go. Preston said we would have had the opportunity to meet with Fidel Castro and talk baseball. The country still isn't open for players to leave, but time and money have made it easier for players to leave and the Cuban National team is nothing like it used to be.

DOMINICAN REPUBLIC

In my early years with the Angels, we started to explore the possibility of putting an academy in the Dominican Republic. In the mid-1980's, it was starting to become the way clubs operated in the country and has continued to this day.

Our first venture with an academy was in 1987 in San Cristóbal. Most academies at that time were at available fields and kids were housed in hotels. It was not like today where teams build a spring training-type facility with players rooming in dormitories, high-end training rooms, cafeterias with dietary training, and English classes before games.

The facilities in the 80's left something to be desired. We crammed as many bunk beds as we could in a room, but in the hotel, we could house 25-30 players. It was still clean and safe, and we found a restaurant down the street that fed the players well, and in a lot of cases, more food than they were used to.

One day in town, Eddie Rodriguez and I were sitting at a street cafe having something cold to drink after spending the day checking everything out. There was a lot of traffic and not much good driving taking place. As we were sitting there, right in front of us, a car hit a guy on a motorcycle and threw him from it. The guy got out of the car, helped the motorcyclist get up, brushed him off, retrieved his motorcycle, brought it back to the rider, and then they both headed on their way. It brought back that line from *The Wizard of Oz,* "I don't think we're in Kansas anymore."

We were only based in San Cristóbal for one year. The following year with Preston's help, we landed the jewel of the island, La Romana. We secured a working relationship with the La Romana team of the Dominican Winter League and with that, we got a field to have our academy.

Our players lived in a hotel downtown, but the staff got to stay at Casa de Campo, which is one of the top resorts in the Caribbean, sitting right on the water with one of the top golf courses in the region. A beautiful place with lovely homes in the area, and a spot on the top of the mountain, Altos de Chavón, with great restaurants, shops, and a large outdoor amphitheater where Frank Sinatra once performed. The view looking down at the river at night paints a picture that almost doesn't look real.

La Romana was a great setup for us the few years that we were there, but one thing about being in a beautiful tourist town like that with modern hotels, home, and restaurants is it doesn't take much to bring you back to reality.

Eddie and I were at the field one day and some young kids were hanging around the ballpark and kept following us, wanting to talk and ask questions about the United States. As we turned to the hose to water the field, one asked, "How many hours a day do you have water and electricity in the United States?"

These daily luxuries we have weren't available to these young kids or the people of the region, and he asked because he didn't know and wanted to know. Such nice kids, and it brought back how lucky and fortunate we are and how soon we forget that.

We ran our Dominican operation on a shoestring budget for most of the years I was with the Angels, but even with spending little money and cutting corners, we signed Ramón Ortiz, who pitched 12 years in the majors and helped us win the 2002 World Series.

Ramón is a great kid who loved to be at the ballpark. He had such a loose arm that you could project more growth to come. That signing alone made everything we tried to do at that time worth it.

The stories and people from the Dominican are so vivid and memorable in my mind, including the time I got 64 mosquito bites in one day on my two ankles while looking for sites to build our academy. I know because I counted all of them.

I was with the Padres in the early 1980's on my first or second trip to the Dominican and we had a young infielder that lived out towards Haiti on the ocean. We went to his village to spend time with him, which made him look good among his friends and family.

We were heading out from San Cristóbal to see him, driving for about an hour before getting off the main highway and on a dirt road all the way to the ocean.

When we arrived at the little village, we saw the kid and little else. There were maybe four or five houses that had electricity and running water, with the kid being one of them due to his signing bonus. We were introduced to the town constable who wore a cutoff and tank top with a pistol hanging out of his pants.

We walked down to the river and were soon told we needed to leave because the locals were coming to bathe and wash their clothes. We walked a way out to the ocean where men were fishing with a net from the beach. I had never seen anything like that.

When we got back into town, the kid asked us if we would work out a few kids from town. We replied that we'd be happy to.

The ball field was a small rectangle, where cows and burros grazed, with houses surrounding the field. In one corner, they had a wooden home plate and wooden pitching rubber, with three patches for the bases. I got out there and thought, "This'll be great!"

As soon as we started the workout, the whole village arrived. The *whole* friggin' village.

I began hitting ground balls to a local young man who played shortstop. On the first one, he went to his right and as he went to plant his foot, he stepped in cow poop. He began sliding and couldn't make a throw. I began biting my lip because I couldn't believe what I just saw, but not one person in town said a thing. It was no big deal because that was their field.

The next kid was a pitcher, and as he got on the mound, the villagers lined up four to dive deep on each side from the pitcher's mound to home plate. Every time the kid would throw between the lines, the onlookers would go "Oooh," and as the catcher would throw back, they would continue with, "Ahhh". The young man was throwing his fastball about 68 miles per hour.

I stood there thinking that I watched a guy slip in cow crap at short, and a guy throwing 68 mph who people think is Nolan Ryan, the constable has a pistol hanging from his pants, and I don't know where the hell I am. How are we going to get out of here?

I couldn't tell them the truth, so I basically did my best and said to the kids that they had potential, to keep up with this, keep doing that, and patted them on the back. I then turned and looked at Eddie and said, "Let's get the hell out of here."

The Chicago White Sox used to have their Dominican Republic Academy in a small town, south of Santiago, about 30 minutes away in the Cibao region. The Cibao portion of the country is primarily agriculture and industry. While there we would stay in Santiago, which is a major city but doesn't have much of a tourism industry, and thus doesn't have many upscale hotels. In Santiago, they serve the coldest beer in the world, *Presidente*. There is no better beer in the world. Not even close to it.

The ballpark we used for our academy was an older city park with bleachers that held about 300 people. The field was in good shape because we maintained it, but the structure of the stadium was run down and needed a lot of maintenance.

Our players were housed under the bleachers in a dormitory-style setting with an eating area for them. We had full-time food staff, maintenance staff, and security. For many of the kids, this was the best diet and food they had eaten.

The academy was run by former major league player Danny Gonzalez, his staff and Miquel Ibarra, our Latin America supervisor. It operated more like the modern-day facilities with player housing, eating areas with full-time support staff. Players received excellent instruction, English lessons, and baseball knowledge. It was a fun atmosphere, and I enjoyed going there very much.

In the summer, we played in the Northern Division of the Dominican Summer League. Because we worked with a limited budget, we never were able to sign the higher-priced players and our facility was not as good as most of the other clubs.

As farm director, they always made sure I had what I needed. One of those things was a constant supply of tostones, which are fried plantains. I love those, and I could eat them with every meal. I would get a chair outside the dugout to watch field activities, and one of the staff members would bring me a plate of tostones. They got a kick out of this American eating so many fried plantains that they awarded me the nickname, "Señor Tostones".

Every day, people from this small town would come and watch our practices and games. The stands held around 200-300 people, and it wasn't uncommon to have a hundred plus fans at most games. Most people were killing time and talking with each other, but it did create a better atmosphere for our kids.

One day, one of our coaches told me as the day was starting to watch out for the *Wheelbarrow Man*.

"Who's that?" I asked.

"Wait and see."

About a half hour later, this skinny elderly man showed up in the stands and started to shout at our players. Nothing bad, but certainly noticeable.

After a few innings, I heard the people in the stands start to holler and laugh. I looked over and this man was holding a paper bag and soon produced a bottle of rum. He opened the bottle and proceeded to chug the entire thing without stopping.

All I could think was, "Oh sh*t, he is going to kill himself!"

That was when the show started.

Over the next 15 minutes he was at full running speed in the stands from the first base side to the third base side, yelling at the top of his lungs at our players. Onlookers kept yelling and encouraging him as he went faster and faster, eventually trying to climb the screen between the stands and field.

Not long after, he was standing behind the home plate screen, still yelling at our kids on the field, when I suddenly saw his legs start to shake and wobble. At that point, one of the fans in attendance went outside the stadium and came back instantly with a wheelbarrow and placed it right behind him.

Moments later, he passed out and fell back into the wheelbarrow and was wheeled out of the ballpark while receiving a loud standing ovation from the people in the stands.

I was told this was a regular event and I did see it on many occasions.

Thus, the *Wheelbarrow Man.*

VENEZUELA

Venezuela has been a great country for baseball. When I first started going there for San Diego, it was a thriving country that had a lot of money. Caracas was a booming metropolitan city. It was a great place to visit and watch baseball.

We had success in Venezuela with the Padres, and the Angels as well when I joined their organization. We sent many players to play winter ball and were active in signing players from the country. As the years went on, it was sad to see how the country changed.

I would walk all over Caracas and other cities by myself with no worries. After a few years I began being followed, on occasion by multiple men. You had to be aware of your surroundings so you didn't get in a situation that could be dangerous. Luckily, I stayed in crowded areas until I could get to the hotel. It got to a point where you didn't leave the hotel except to go to the ballpark or out to eat with a group.

One day in Caracas, our scout came to meet with me, Ken Forsch, and Jeff Parker. He met us in the lobby of our hotel and had with him a briefcase. We found a table in the lobby and I figured he was going to give us some reports on players that he had in his briefcase. He opened the case, turned it over, and three guns fell to the table. He wanted to know if we wanted to pack heat. My Spanish came out clearly, *"Gracias, NO!"*

What a shame to see it get to that.

My last trip to Venezuela in 2007 nearly ended in disaster. There were about 12 of us from Seattle on the tip to watch our players in the winter league, including Brandon Morrow. By this time, the country was going through many changes under a dictatorship.

Food was in short supply, people were leaving the country, and unrest was popping up. Our trip was to last until the day before the election, where all authority would be handed over to Hugo Chávez.

Bob Engle, who was an extremely successful international director for Seattle that signed Félix Hernández, set up the trip so we could see all the players in about a week. After five days, we split into two groups. One headed back to Caracas, and our group was to head to Maracaibo and then leave for home from there.

You could feel the tension in the stands about the upcoming election during the last few games we attended. There was a larger military presence and a lot of chanting and fights.

When we arrived in Maracaibo we stayed at a nice hotel, but you could hear things happening in the streets, with gunshots ringing throughout the night. One of our guys slept on the floor all night worrying about stray bullets hitting his room. I wasn't smart enough to think of that.

The final morning, I showed up in the lobby about 20 minutes before we were to meet to go to the airport, thinking I would be the first one. I was last. Everyone wanted to go home.

We got to the airport around 6 a.m. and it was already packed with people. We got our tickets, went through initial inspection, and headed for customs.

I was last of our group in line and when the agent got to me, he took a long time looking at my passport and then at me. He gazed at his computer for a while and then said to me in Spanish, "You aren't in the computer and your passport isn't stamped. Please get out of line."

Luckily, Eddie Rodriguez and Pedro Grifol stayed with me and began speaking to this guy in Spanish so fast that my high school Spanish was lost after the first few words. I could see on Eddie and Pedro's faces that there was a big problem.

When I had entered the country, airport customs took our entire group's passports, stamped them, and entered them into the computer before giving them back to us. Mine was neither stamped nor entered. I was technically an American illegal alien in a country whose government doesn't like Americans a day before an election to give all power to a dictator. Great.

The customs agent said he would have his supervisor come over when he could, but that he couldn't do anything else. Eddie and Pedro kept talking to this guy and finally, I heard the magic words.

"Cuánto dinero?"

I knew we were making some progress.

"Do you have $200?" Eddie asked me.

I had learned a long time ago to always travel with bribe money, and quite frankly was relieved it was only $200.

"Yes," I replied.

The deal was made, and my passport was stamped. To the gate we went.

It was a good thing Eddie and Pedro were there, or else I might still be in Venezuela.

I found out later that this was common practice when groups came into the country, locals would "accidentally" not stamp a book or two depending on the size of the group.

I was still uneasy when we got into the boarding area, but as time went on, I started to feel better. I went to the duty-free store to get rid of my bolívars (Venezuelan currency) which you can't exchange at home.

I began to relax as I sat down on the plane when suddenly, the flight attendant called my name to come to the front of the plane. All I could think of was that son-of-a-bitch agent who took my money and turned me in. My friends had looks of fear on their faces like there was a big problem ahead.

I got up to the front expecting the worst when I was handed my duty-free bag of junk I had purchased.

I don't usually drink in the morning, but this was an exception. I was never so happy at the takeoff of any plane I had ever been on.

That was my last trip to Venezuela. Wonderful people and country, but what a shame to see the changes and current state.

"EL DUQUE"

In 1997, Orlando Hernández defected from Cuba and was stranded in the Bahamas. "El Duque", as they called him, had been a highly successful pitcher in Cuba and on the international stage. He had been seen by clubs for years and was attracting a lot of attention with his power sinker, curveball, and athleticism.

There was some question about his age. We had rosters that showed a different date of birth than what we were getting from his group. Our scouts felt he was the older age and is still listed by both dates depending where you look it up. Regardless, he could still pitch, and it didn't matter because he wouldn't be spending time developing in the minors. He was going to make an immediate impact.

The United States decided to offer him special admission, but he and his agent accepted an offer of asylum in Costa Rica instead. It was a financial benefit because if he had come to the U.S. directly, he would have gone through the draft and most likely would have received a much smaller signing bonus. By going to Costa Rica, he could sign with anyone he wanted to and for as much money as he could get.

The Angels decided to get involved when he was working out for teams in San José, Costa Rica. I went down there with George Lauzerique and Rich Schlenker to watch El Duque and four other Cuban defectors work out.

When we got to the ballpark in San José, there were a ton of scouts everywhere from almost all the clubs. Even *60 Minutes* was there to do a special. The CBS people went around talking with all the scouting directors to set up interviews, but when they got to me, I told them thanks, but no thanks.

Disney had recently taken over the club and had a policy that we weren't allowed to speak with the press without first clearing it through PR. It was a good policy, but CBS didn't like my answer.

I thought I was in the clear but during the workout I felt a tap on my shoulder and when I turned around there was a camera pointed at me and Morley Safer put a microphone in front of my face. He asked me what I thought of Hernández and the players there. I answered with double talk and said, "It's great to be here and to see these players on such a fine afternoon. Too soon to come up with an opinion but it is good to be here in this beautiful country."

Morley got upset and they turned off the camera. They thought if they surprised me, I would get flustered and talk. That didn't happen. Speaking in double talk is something I am proud of when I need it. I wasn't going to get in trouble over this and I felt great beating them at this game.

Turns out they aired it on television and ripped me for my response. It was great.

Hernández didn't have a great day, but he was naturally not in the best of shape yet and that could be expected. He had been in hibernation for a few months. He really could pitch though. When you're going to see a guy like this, you're going to see their health and how easily they do things. You're not there for performance, and if you're there for performance, you're wasting your time.

We were a player in the negotiations and Bill Bavasi took it quite far before we got outbid by the Yankees.

Hernández went on to enjoy nine years in the majors, including five World Series appearances and four championships.

It was an interesting process and really the start of many more players from Cuba defecting to play in the majors.

MEXICO

When you work for teams in Southern California there is obvious interest in any major league player that comes from Mexico. I made my first trips to Mexico when I was with the Padres in the 70's.

I got an assignment in 1976 to go to Puerto Vallarta to see an outfielder on the minor league team there. When you get to Puerto Vallarta and see what a beautiful resort city it is on the ocean, you only imagine they would have a nice ballpark. Not so nice.

I took a cab to the park about five miles out of town where it was surrounded by a big brick wall and broken glass cemented onto the top to act as barbed wire. Very interesting structure.

The manager of the club was a nice man who let me see the player I was there to see do what he could do in a workout. I was going to see him a couple of days later in a game, but this practice really helped, and I had a feeling, which turned out right, that I wouldn't have any interest.

After the workout I went to the main road to look for a taxi, but there weren't any. I hooked a ride on an old worn-out bus that was packed with no air conditioning and even some live animals on board. People were nice, and it got me to town, but for me it was a new experience, and I would never complain about a Greyhound bus again.

On that trip, I found two non-baseball items that remain fresh on my mind. The first was the introduction to 15 cent margaritas and how many you could drink on a warm day. The second was "Montezuma's Revenge".

When I got back to the U.S., I got so sick that I never felt anything like it before or since. I didn't want to be further than seven feet from the bathroom for a week, and it was a tough way to lose the weight that I needed to lose. It was horrible, but I learned for the future that when young players come to the United States, they can get sick too, as bacteria is different in a lot of places and can cause temporary issues. Man, I was sick, but knock-on wood I would never get sick internationally again.

My years with the Angels had a lot of travel to Mexico and many adventures to go with it. We tried hard to establish ourselves in Mexico like the Dodgers had for so many years. It was a lot harder than we could have imagined.

Most players signed out of Mexico are purchased from teams in the Mexican League. The cost is usually quite high, but because of a gentlemen's agreement there was no team from the United States allowed to sign a player from Mexico unless through a purchase from a team there. We took the approach that we would get an agreement with a Mexican League team, scout the country for young players, and we would have first choice of those signed.

This was a good deal for a team in Mexico. We would sign players for them and the ones we brought to play for us would still be their property, so when they were done playing in the U.S., they would come back to Mexico a much better developed player regardless of if they played in the majors or minors.

Our first association was with the Unión Laguna team. They were great people to work with, but the association was expensive and didn't show much of a return. We loaned them some players that had Double-A and Triple-A levels of ability. For them, it was a good setup.

We held tryout camps in different parts of the country, mostly on the western side. We would take four to six scouts, and along with two from Unión Laguna, and go to towns and have open tryout camps.

Reception in the towns was rather good and we would usually get strong media coverage. Some of the fields were rough and not ideal for a good look at a player. Most of the kids knew how to play, as baseball is still popular in Mexico, but we didn't see much speed or power. When we did see a kid of some interest, they were usually already under contract with a Mexican League team. We didn't see a lot of kids with average fastballs, but many had good secondary pitches because those are emphasized in the Mexican League.

Lin Garrett, Jesse Flores Jr., and Bobby Myrick drove a van and had camps in little towns from San Luis to Mazatlán. I flew down to meet them and then worked our way back north to Nogales, but we weren't able to sign many players of any ability.

We had camps in Mazatlán, Culiacán, Los Mochis, Navojoa, Obregón, and Hermosillo. We stayed at a resort in Mazatlán, a nice motel in Culiacán, old motels in Los Mochis and Obregón, and a nice hotel in Hermosillo. Lodging could be an adventure, but the food in every city was outstanding with steak, chicken, fish, beans, and tortillas with every meal.

We had good turnouts in these places, especially Los Mochis. We signed a few kids for Unión Laguna not knowing yet if we wanted any of them to play for us.

When we had our camp in Los Mochis, we had such a good turnout that we held two that day instead of one. We saw a couple of infielders that could field and throw and that kept our interest. When we finished, we got about a two-hour late start.

One thing we were told before we started on this trip was to not travel to Hermosillo at night on the expressway, especially near Guaymas. But there was a restaurant in Hermosillo that I really wanted to eat at, and I talked the other guys into going. It turned out we should have stayed in Los Mochis that night and made a potentially awful move.

By the time we got to the Guaymas cutoff to take the Hermosillo expressway, it was dark. As we started down the road there was a guardhouse and stop signal on the road and we were flagged over. We had been told that people were flagged over at times and had drugs planted when the car was inspected, then put in jail and held for a large bail.

We started to sweat as we were pulled over. A guard dressed in regular clothes with a badge staggered over to our car, very much intoxicated. He looked at us and asked who we were. Luckily, Jesse spoke Spanish. I guess what we had to say wasn't enough though, and he ordered us to empty out the van.

We began offering the guard hats, decals, and equipment, but to no avail. We thought we were in big trouble when the guard slurred out that he knew someone that scouted for the Pirates.

"Do you mean Angel Figueroa?" we asked.

"*Si mi amigo!*" he replied, perking up.

That was all it took.

He told us to put everything in the car and we could go on our way, and we went from thinking we were going to jail, instead, to going to a great dinner in Hermosillo.

When we later told Angel about the story he just laughed and said, "I told you I was a big man in Mexico."

He was right, right when and where we needed him.

In the 1990's, the Mexican League ran an academy where all clubs would participate. Young players were sent to Pastejé, an agricultural community a few hours from Mexico City. They would instruct players over a period of time and then hold a draft. It was a good structure, and I attended a few times.

We would stay in Mexico City and commute to the academy each day. We hoped to see some kids that we would have interest in and then have the team we had an agreement with draft them and send them to us. Problem was that the players we had interest in were usually drafted before the team we worked with could make the selection.

It was a good facility and location that provided few distractions for a young kid to keep him from concentrating totally on baseball. It was a good time to see many of the better young players that were headed to the Mexican League soon, and even if you couldn't get them there, you would follow them when they started to play in the league.

One of the owners in the Mexican League owned a mansion in the Pastejé area where George Bradley and I were invited for lunch. It was a huge home with a large area of land around it, like something you would see in a James Bond film. There were several old cars in front, like a Rolls Royce, Mercedes, Jaguar, and many other exotic cars that were worth a fortune. They looked as though they hadn't been driven for years and all I could think of was I would like to have just one of them.

I asked our host, "How often does this owner of the house come here?"

"Maybe once a year," he replied.

On this trip, George and I were walking around in the area near the hotel in Mexico City and George got taken in to have his tennis shoes shined. As we walked, I began looking behind me to see George trying to talk this guy out of shining his tennis shoes, but it wasn't working. George told me this policeman was telling him he was a tourist policeman who could help tourists. While talking to him, the guy started shining George's shoes. It cost him $10.

On another trip to Pastejé when I was joined by Duane Shaffer, we stopped for lunch and I dined on cabrito (goat) for the first time in a little restaurant in a tiny village. It was outstanding, and I became a goat eater after that. Mexico has great food, and I always seemed to gain weight when I went there.

On a separate trip with Duane, we decided to ride the subway after dinner in Mexico City and see how far it would take us. For a few cents, we went all over. At one stop, we got off and went upstairs to an area that had no paved roads, with the next stop having a neighborhood with a carnival ride in the middle.

We decided that the Tilt-a-Whirl was worth at least a ride before we got back on the subway and headed back to the hotel. Big mistake.

We bought tickets and got on the ride. We were the only two on, and each had our own whirl as it started. It is a good ride, and everything was fine until about 10 minutes and it was still going. I started looking around for the operator and couldn't find him. After another 10 minutes, we began getting woozy, and I finally spotted the operator across the street having a beer. I yelled over to Duane to look over where he was sitting, and we started screaming at the guy to come over and stop the ride.

After another 10 minutes, he finished his beer and came over to stop the ride. We staggered to the subway and headed towards the hotel. The Mexican Tilt-a-Whirl experience was over, but a memory we'll never forget.

We were fortunate with the Angels to have Mario Mendoza, who scouted for us in Mexico when he wasn't managing in our minor league system in the summer. He was a great player from Mexico who was extremely popular in the country and a solid baseball man. I cannot imagine how we would have done so many of the things we did without him. He opened a lot of doors for us.

In the mid 1990's, we had an agreement with the Oaxaca team. It was a great setup as it didn't cost us hardly anything, and in return, we signed players for them and signed a couple decent players for ourselves.

We got this arrangement for truly little because we challenged the unofficial agreement that said we couldn't sign players without going through a Mexican League team. It made them nervous, so this was set up easily.

One spring training, we lost a preseason exhibition game against the Dodgers that was supposed to be played right before the season at Anaheim Stadium. Bill began looking for an opponent to play against us and brought the Oaxaca team to play the game. It turned out to be a big success.

With bad weather, we still had a large crowd. Before the game, I went into the Oaxaca clubhouse to say hello and the players were extremely excited. Many were in their 30's and had played in the Mexican League for many years, but that evening was their chance to play in a big-league ballpark against major league players. It was a well-played two-run game.

One year during this agreement with Oaxaca, we decided to do a hard press on covering the country with tryout camps. We took almost our entire amateur staff down there and separated them into two groups.

The eastern group, led by Tony LaCava, started in Yucatán, and the western group started in Guadalajara, led by Darrell Miller. Each group would work their way up the coast until they got to the United States border. We had two buses and each group had about 10 scouts together. It took two weeks to complete, and we signed quite a few players, most of whom ended up playing in the Oaxaca system.

I started with Tony's group in Yucatán and stayed with them for about three days. I would then join the other group for three or four days and then back again, staying with each group twice. It was a chance to really see and understand the country. We saw a few tourist spots during the process, but most were villages, towns, and cities that were geared more towards agriculture and industry.

The first stop was a small village two hours from Yucatán. We had a workout at the ballpark that had large grandstands that were gutted and looked as though they were bombed. There was a strong turnout and after the workout we stopped in town to get lunch and have a cold beverage because it was extremely hot and humid.

"Bombed stadium in Mexico, circa 1997"

We found a cantina downtown and had fun talking with the locals. Tony and I participated in a basketball game in the park across the street, and Jeff Parker, our farm director, borrowed someone's burro to take a spin around town. The people were great and we had a lot of fun. I still don't know where we were to this day.

When I joined the other group in Mazatlán, we didn't have a large turnout and there were few players with talent, but we did stay at a nice resort on the water. The first night, four of us went down to the beach and found a couple guys renting horses to ride on the waterfront in the waves. Darrell, Juan Wayne Burden, Tommy Burns and I rented four horses to hit the waves. After a few beers, we thought we were the experienced horsemen to handle this.

We got on the horses and started down the beach. It was like what you would see in the movies or on *Bonanza* when the four Cartwrights ride up at the start of the show.

We were having a great time when suddenly, we realized Tommy wasn't with us. We turned around and saw the horse he was riding heading back to his stable. Tommy was trying to get control but to no avail. We rode back in a gallop, retrieved Tommy, and the four us headed again down the beach.

It was a blast riding in the waves, and I wouldn't know where to go to experience that again. The experiences you enjoy in baseball just never seem to stop and make the travel so much fun.

As the trip continued from both sides of the country, we worked out kids on all kinds of fields. Every now and then one would be well groomed, but it was mostly poorly maintained fields with high grass that hadn't been mowed. Some that didn't even have grass and were full dirt lots. It was tough, but we did the best we could.

On one occasion on the west side, we encountered a military blockade that stopped our bus and made us empty everything out. There were quite a few soldiers with big guns, with most of the soldiers looking as if they were 16 years old. After an hour or so, they let us load everything back on the bus and sent us on our way. I'm still not sure what they were looking for, but whatever it was I'm glad they didn't find it.

There was a night spent in Culiacán, the capital of Sinaloa where drug cartels thrive, where we heard gunshots ring through the night. Nothing came of that luckily.

When we were finished with the trip, we had learned a lot about scouting young players in every part of the country and realized that even though it was the right approach, the money spent wouldn't reap a good return.

We saw some interesting kids and signed quite a few, mostly infielders and pitchers. The reception was good, and it gave all our staff a better understanding of the country. There are players in Mexico, but under the present system, it is awfully hard to get a young player unless you pay a team and scout with them for the talent.

JAPAN

Japan is an interesting place to scout players. They play a different style than others in the world, show great discipline, and have a true appreciation and passion for baseball.

Japan has a major league of their own. Scouting in a professional league is fun with the atmosphere inside the ballparks. Fans wave flags, blow trumpets and horns, and chant throughout the game's entirety. It creates a loud and exciting environment to watch a ballgame.

Watching players do their pregame activities can be quite interesting. They have two batting cages on the field pregame so two hitters can hit at one time, with all other players doing other baseball activities.

My first time in the Tokyo Dome, I saw guys my size hitting balls out regularly and then realized there were no dimension numbers on the outfield walls. The next day I measured it off myself, walking from home plate to the wall. They were much shorter distances than in the U.S. That is a practice I used when I would go to see a power hitter and questioned the numbers.

They play an aggressive brand of baseball and even though they play more, pitchers throw more. Players have been able to come to the United States and not only compete, but in some cases become stars like Ichiro Suzuki, Hideki Matsui, Hideo Nomo, as well as current day talents like Shohei Ohtani, Masahiro Tanaka, and Yu Darvish.

One of the most exciting and different high school game experiences I ever had was when I went to Osaka to see Yu Darvish pitch in the National High School Baseball Invitational.

I was with Seattle at the time. Bob Engle, our international scouting director, and Ted Heid, our Pacific Rim supervisor, along with many others in our international department, felt we had a chance to sign Darvish out of high school. I went to give them another opinion. In most cases, you wouldn't expect to spend a week in advance to see a pitcher, but you did in Japan.

When I arrived in Osaka, I was met by two of our young scouts from the region and they were going to take me around while I was there. The first day, we went and watched the team workout and saw Darvish throw a bullpen session. Right away you could see this was a special arm.

It was a long practice, like they all would end up being. When we got to the hotel, I was so hungry that I told the two guys we were going across the street to eat at Outback Steakhouse.

I could tell they were a little nervous when they looked at the prices on the menu. Things can be expensive in Japan, especially for travelers. I asked them if they wanted a beer, and they just looked at me. I then asked if they wanted appetizers, and again, they just stared. Finally, I said, "I'm ordering. Bring us a beer each and three appetizers and then we will order."

They ordered, and even though the meal was expensive, it broke the ice. We had a wonderful time, and they taught me much about the customs of Japan.

There were nights we ate the local cuisine and I think I provided more entertainment for them and the staff of the restaurants than anything else. Watching me try to eat with chopsticks certainly provided more food on the walls and ceiling than I got into my mouth. I did try, at least.

They were both very respectful young men, and I appreciated their approach, but when I took them back a week later, they didn't hesitate. This time they ordered beverages, appetizers, and a meal.

We watched Darvish's team practice every day for six days at six different sites, and he threw off the mound each of those days, a practice you never see in the United States. The practices were as interesting as they were intense, and the coaches were tough. At one point in the practice, players would stop, and bow to the coach.

Since we weren't supposed to be at these practices and because I stood out, we had to stay hidden, which I loved. One practice while hiding behind a tree in the outfield, a ball was hit to the fielder closest to me and he just butchered it. The ball rolled out by where I was standing behind the tree, and as the player got near, I yelled to him, "You have to make that play, Meat!"

Our two scouts freaked and said I couldn't do that, and we had to move places. I couldn't help it. The kid needed to make the play.

The last day in Osaka was the day Darvish was going to pitch in the tournament. Our game was in the afternoon at Hanshin Koshien Stadium. It is like their version of Fenway Park. It is an old stadium with a dirt infield, and with horrible weather and a lot of rain that day, the field staff worked hard to keep it playable.

This tournament is a huge event that is televised nationally and played in front of big crowds. The day we were there, they had bad weather. About 35,000 people were in the stadium, which holds 55,000. It's a very impressive and competitive venue.

We got to our seats down the third base side right near the high school cheering section. They had a huge group all waving flags and dressed alike with a horn section. It was entertaining for a while, but their theme song was the music from *Popeye the Sailor Man*. The drummers and horns never stopped with all supporters chanting and yelling the theme song. It's a wonder how they watch the game. After nine innings of that, I could scream.

Darvish didn't disappoint. He had such a fluid delivery with a loose, free, and quick arm. He threw five pitches from different angles and could throw strikes from each angle. It gave him what looked like 15 pitches, as well as the ability to change speeds on each pitch. The ball was live out of his hand with a great finish to his pitches.

He ended up throwing about eight innings and probably well over 125 pitches before they took him out of the game. His team lost, but he was very impressive.

I turned in a report saying that if he were in the amateur draft in the United States, he would be in the top part of the first round. He was probably as polished and confident as any high school pitcher I have ever seen. He was so good and did so many things other kids cannot do at that age. It was unbelievable.

I was disappointed when we couldn't sign him, but it didn't take many years before he was pitching in MLB. He has pitched nine seasons through 2021 and is recognized as one of the best Japanese-born pitchers in major league history.

Scouting internationally outside of North America and Latin America for me had become the most fun areas to work. The players are not sidetracked by stats and money like the other places, and only care about winning. They play because they genuinely love the game and are very appreciative when you take the time to see them play and help with their understanding and development as a player.

Europe, Africa, and China remind me very much of what it was like when I first started scouting. The thing that matters is your opinion and instinct, as there is little outside information to use to aid in recommending a player. They are areas that an evaluator can really use their ability.

Baseball is truly a worldwide game.

FAMILY

In a baseball life, there are many things that affect family life, both good and bad. A job in scouting requires much time away from home during the season, and even though you are around more in the offseason, the things you miss in your family's life can be substantial.

The sacrifices that they make in your absence are numerous. The baseball games, soccer games, basketball games, lacrosse games, school events, conferences, birthday parties, and other important events in their lives that you miss are unfortunately common. But the life in baseball can bring many good things to all family members that others outside would never have.

I not only grew up in a baseball family that taught me what the game offers, but also one that had lived the working baseball life. It can be a very tough situation for a wife and many times a disappointing time for a child. I tried to treat my kids to the same experiences I had, and even though I am sure I would never be a "Husband of the Year" candidate, I tried. A partner's independence is a necessity, and a lack of it is understandable in this industry.

The wife of a baseball scout is the key to any type of family life. I have been married three times and the two failures are my fault, with the successful one being hers.

I was married young for a couple years when we both knew we shouldn't, but we did. Joni didn't want this life and she found what she wanted. Teri, my second wife, tried hard and we lasted 17 years before we parted. Karen and I were married for 23 years before she passed away.

Karen and I have five kids between us, with only nine years between the oldest and the youngest. I had three kids and she had two when we got married. A great group of kids that we are extremely proud of.

I had been married for 17 years to a very nice woman and a great mother. Teri and I eventually split as our lifestyles and goals for the future changed. The baseball life can create this, and I take the blame for it. She and I remained friends because we always put our kids first, even though we went different directions.

When Karen and I got married, I knew she would be a great baseball wife. We had met when she worked on and off for the Angels over the years. She absolutely loved baseball and if the truth be known, she loved baseball a whole lot more than I do.

She understood the lifestyle and could handle the time apart. She had the independence while still knowing what I needed to be involved with when I would be on the road. She was great to my kids from the start, and we were able to have a family of five kids that were close and appreciated being together. They basically grew up together and now that they are older, they enjoy when the rare occasion comes when we are all together.

The oldest child is Jim, who was around the ballpark for most of his formative years. He liked baseball and played some, but he had other interests.

He told me once, "Dad I want to have a life like yours, but not in baseball."

Turns out he did. He is the photographer for Atlantic Records in New York City and does many freelance assignments. His rise as a photographer was a lot like a baseball player. He started at the bottom, living in a condemned building, working as an intern during the day and scrapping tile at night to make ends meet. He now lives in Greenwich Village and has a studio on Broadway.

He has become a top photographer in his field, and has found my lifestyle, but not in baseball. His girlfriend of many years, Monique, works at a boutique hotel in Soho, and they have become real New Yorkers.

Josanna, our second child, is the happiest kid you ever saw, and has found her niche as a dental assistant. She has the personality to deal with people and make things pleasant. Her husband, Luke, is a beer meister, and they are a happy couple living in Fallbrook, California.

She likes baseball and being in a baseball family even though she isn't an avid fan. She moved back to Chicago for a year to live with Karen and me, to be with us and experience life in the Midwest. Her and our younger daughter, Caitlin, tried their best to mix in to Midwestern life, and looking back, appreciated it a lot more now.

Joey is our middle son. He is a special needs kid who has been challenged with more obstacles than anyone should have. He has traveled with me for much of his life and loves the ballpark, even though he will be the first to tell you that he doesn't like baseball. He loves being around the scouts, staffs, and players. Of all the people I know he has the most right to complain and say he is having a bad day, and yet he never has. He truly is our family's ambassador.

Joey loves the baseball atmosphere, but not the game itself. I remember one day I had him at Anaheim Stadium with me when I was with the Angels. It was in the morning before we left for a game in the afternoon. I used to put him in the war room where we would discuss trades and other club business to watch television while I did my work before we left.

One day I went to check on him and he was gone. I started looking for him in public relations, and then in the rest of the baseball section, and couldn't find him. I started to panic and walked over to the business side where all the Disney executives worked. I walked by Tony Tavares' office, the president of the club, and saw Joey wheeled up to the front of his desk and chatting with him.

Even though Tony and I did not see evaluation of players the same way, he was good with Joey, and I think appreciated that Joey didn't care who anyone was. By the time I had reached the office, Tony saw me at the door and had started laughing. Joey had already said what he wanted to say.

"Joey just told me I was full of beans!" Tony shouted.

That's Joey.

When Tony Reagins worked with me, Joey would always tell him that he was fired. Tony still laughs about that. Joey just loves people and to be happy.

Our younger daughter, Caitlin, is a huge Angels fan. Although all the kids enjoyed the Angels experience, Caitlin became one of their biggest fans, win or lose. Although she enjoyed hanging around Comiskey Park in Chicago, she was hooked by the Angels. Her and Karen, I believe, like baseball more than the rest of us.

Caitlin has become a remarkably successful hair stylist after spending time employed by Disneyland. Her and her husband, Steve – who is an auto parts manager – have two children as of this writing: Ryan and Reece.

Matt is the youngest and has followed a career in baseball. He played in high school and in junior college before following into the scouting profession. He spent time doing video work for Cincinnati and administrative and scouting work for San Diego before moving on to work for one of the top agencies in baseball.

During his scouting years, he worked in the Midwest, and although for just a couple of years, he did get a low draft pick that he signed that has made it to the majors (Kyle McGrath, 36th round, 2014). Good scouting. It was also living in the Midwest that he met his wife, Jordan, who is a buyer for a major shoe company. They now have a baby daughter, Finley.

All our kids were impacted differently from being around baseball. It was tough for them at times and enjoyable at other times. They got to travel and be around baseball parks around the country, often taking for granted the experience that so many others would like to have.

Through it all we are extremely proud of them all for taking responsibility, working hard, not looking for an entitlement, and just becoming good people.

Looking back, I see how my father's time in baseball affected everyone in my family.

My sister Sandy and her husband, Jim. My niece, Erin, and nephew, Scott. My brother, Rick, and nephew, Jeremy. My stepsisters Carol, Nancy, and Lori. We all have memories and experiences that are different or are shared. It's a different lifestyle and the uncertainty is quite common, but through it all, not many can say they lived a baseball life like members of a family in baseball.

Anything good that I have accomplished in baseball is due to my family and the support and sacrifices that they made for me to be able to work. They never complained, even when I would cancel going to something important in their life.

Baseball gets into your blood, and during the process you feel everyone shares in the enjoyment and satisfaction that you are having, even though they might not. Baseball scouting can be a lonely, frustrating, and gratifying occupation, and the support from home is so important.

I am incredibly grateful for my family and the opportunity that they gave me to survive in the game for almost 50 years.

"Karen and I at Angels Baseball function; Kids,
L-R: Jim, Josanna, Joey, Caitlin, Matt"

EPILOGUE

The Final Draft

Looking back at my 48 years in baseball, it is amazing how minor any changes were until about the last decade or so. I have seen the closeness and loyalty of clubs and employees change from close knit to very distant, with little loyalty from either side. The patience to do a job right has been replaced with a more "do it now" attitude. People work under more stress and micro-managing than I can ever remember.

You better have a lot of money to succeed today with all the new stats, technology, and inventions that cost a great deal of money yet don't give you a competitive edge. It is how I guess you are to survive today.

As I have said before, a number has no desire to win – a person does. To see so many of my former colleagues out of the game because they have been replaced by a formula or model is hard to see when they have so much to contribute no matter what the approach is. There are no additional players getting to the majors, just as many teams losing as winning, no more wins for a pitcher, no higher batting averages, and so on. Oh yes – the team that spends the most money still seems to win the most.

I know that people in the game today will say I'm old school – a dinosaur or out of touch. I just want someone to tell me that the game is better, more productive, and with a more competitive edge than before when it worked for 100-plus years. I think it is just a different way that costs a lot of money. If the new ideas that are productive were truly incorporated with traditional evaluation and the input of experienced baseball men, you would think that things could really be at their best in the game.

I don't like getting older any more than anyone else does, but I wouldn't trade my experiences and work I did to become a scout to operate like they are required to today. I learned how to project which players can get better and which usually don't based on things to look for and not what a number says.

I worked with and against so many fine baseball people that have a true passion and respect for the profession and the game. People that didn't do it for money as much as they did for their love of the game. A special fraternity that I am proud to have been a part of.

I hope this book has shown not just what it has been like for me, but to understand what the veteran, experienced baseball scout life was all about, and appreciate their dedication for the profession and game.

I never received a World Series ring during my career in baseball, even though I had a small part in helping to develop World Series winning teams. Most people look at a ring as a symbol of your success in baseball, and it certainly is important. I would have liked to have better timing in that regard, but I wouldn't trade my share of any success I have enjoyed with so many fine people for a ring. The sense of accomplishment is what matters the most, and I am very comfortable with that.

Baseball has provided me with a fabulous opportunity to see the world and work in an industry that most people envy. I didn't get rich, except in experiences. To meet and work against so many fine people, as well as some great general managers and Owners, has been a privilege.

In the mid 1990's, I worked with Bill Guilfoile of the National Baseball Hall of Fame, assisting him to get the first scout's exhibit in the Hall of Fame: "Ivory Hunters."

Six scouts were recognized for their contributions and success as scouts: Joe Cambria, Wish Egan, Howie Haak, Paul Krichell, Bobby Mattick, and Cy Slapnicka. It was exhibited for a few years, and then in 2013, a new exhibit was unveiled that was so well done through the effort of Roland Hemond, Roberta Mazur, Joe Klein, Pat Gillick, and others. To have been a part of the early effort with Bill was very gratifying and an honor.

I have experienced some difficult times, as well as some great times, as has my family. My family and I have traveled and enjoyed the Major League Baseball life, and we are all aware of how many people would have enjoyed what we had.

I have had the opportunity to work with and against so many great baseball people that went on to big jobs in the game, and to be able to assist a number of young scouts get started in the business. When you see a member of a staff you are a part of get a big job, it is like seeing a player you signed make it to the majors. I learned a lot from the people I worked with and enjoyed facing times of both adversity and success together.

That opportunity to help assist young scouts at the start of their careers is one of the most enjoyable things I have done in baseball. Emphasizing the importance of going on record for what you believe, not being afraid to make mistakes, relying on your gut instinct, and to always be open-minded to learn was a chance to pass on what I learned that was so important to my longevity in the field. The eagerness to learn and the endless amount of energy that they showed reminded me of when I got started and helped to keep my enthusiasm and appreciation for working in baseball.

Thinking back on my years in baseball, I have often wondered how I could summarize what is has meant to me. While thinking about it, I remembered an experience that I had in France.

I was working for the Major League Baseball Scouting Bureau and we were holding a tryout camp for young kids, aged 10-14, in Montpellier, France, an old town near the French Riviera with beautiful old buildings, squares, cafes, and stores. We were at the field of the local team and had a large turnout. For most of the kids, all you could see as they put their helmet on, was their smile. A real fun group to work with.

As with all camps, you have to register all the players and give them a number to put on their back, as well as give them an MLB hat. The process takes about an hour, and then the workout begins. Even though the kids were so young, we put them through a major league tryout process so that they would know what to expect as they got older and attended other camps.

After the last kid was signed up, we left the office where the kids were registered and headed to the field to get started. As we were walking, I brought up the rear and was taking my time when a young mother approached me.

"Mister, my son is out on the field. Can I buy a hat?" she asked.

Well, how could I say no? Except, I didn't know if we had anymore.

"Let me go check," I told her. "Stay right here."

I went back to the office and saw there were no hats left. I asked one of our staff members if we had extras anywhere, and he told me they were all gone.

I returned to where the mother was standing and told her there weren't any left. The disappointment in her face was devastating. As I looked at her, it hit me.

As a good veteran scout, there are always two things you know at all times: where the free food is and where the free merchandise is located.

"Wait here," I told her. "Let me check on something."

I went and got the key to our van and went to it. I remembered our equipment for the next day in Barcelona was in the back of the van, with hats as well. I got a hat and went back to where she was.

"*Voici, une chapeau*" I said, trying to impress her with my broken French. "Here is the hat, and it is free."

I asked her not to tell anyone, as I didn't want other parents asking me for another hat. After I handed her the hat, she stared at me and her eyes started to water up and her lip started to quiver.

At that moment, I went into severe panic. What did I say in French? Did I just start an international incident? I broke into a sweat and her eyes kept watering up.

Finally, she started to speak in that beautiful broken English.

"Mister, I am so proud," she said as she put the hat in her purse and went on her way.

That simple moment let me know how to describe what it has meant to be in a profession with so many fine people and that brings so much joy to so many around the world. That young mother gave me one single response and all I needed to describe my time in baseball.

I am so proud.

ABOUT THE AUTHOR
Written by Taylor Blake Ward

Taylor Blake Ward is a sports journalist who has covered the Los Angeles Angels and Major League Baseball Draft for multiple media outlets since 2013. His career within baseball started in 2012 as the Director of Broadcasting/Media Relations for the High Desert Mavericks. His work has been featured and published by *Baseball America,* the *Riverside Press-Enterprise,* and Fox Sports/Scout.com. He lives in Lake Arrowhead, California, with his wife, Heidi.

Edited by Kyle Glaser

Kyle Glaser is a National Writer for *Baseball America.* He has covered baseball at all levels, from the major leagues to Little League, and is the co-editor of the annual *Baseball America Prospect Handbook.* He previously covered baseball and other sports for the *Associated Press, Riverside Press-Enterprise,* and *Victorville Daily Press.* He currently lives in Riverside, California with his wife and daughter.

Printed in the United States
by Baker & Taylor Publisher Services